Folens

angles on psychology

Sec

for Edexcel AS Level

teacher's support guide

Julia Russell

FD2996

United Kingdom: Folens Publishers, Waterslade House, Thame Rd, Haddenham, Buckinghamshire HP17 8NT.

www.folens.com

Ireland: Folens Publishers, Greenhills Road, Tallaght, Dublin 24.

Email: info@folens.ie

Project development: Rick Jackman (Jackman Publishing Solutions Ltd)

Editing, layout and illustrations: GreenGate Publishing Services

Software architecture and design: Haremi Ltd (www.haremi.co.uk)

Software development: Haremi Ltd

Cover design: N H Design

Cover image: © 2008 Jupiter Images Corporation

First published 2009 by Folens Limited.

Every effort has been made to contact copyright holders of material used in this publication. If any copyright holder has been overlooked, we should be pleased to make any necessary arrangements.

British Library Cataloguing in Publication Data. A catalogue record for this publication is available from the British Library.

ISBN 978-1-85008-299-6

Contents

Chapter 1

Introduction

Chapter 1

How to use the CD-ROM

This guide consists of photocopiable worksheets that are also provided in pdf form on the enclosed CD-ROM.

The guide comprises activities and worksheets designed for teachers to use in class and for homework. It is specifically geared towards supporting the new (2008) Edexcel AS specification. The basic structure and approach will follow that of the *Angles on Psychology*, Third Edition, AS text. As a consequence, the resource is structured into topics as follows:

1. Introduction
2. The Social approach
3. The Cognitive approach
4. The Psychodynamic approach
5. The Biological approach
6. The Learning approach
7. Mock Examinations

This ensures that the chapter numbers and topics exactly match those in the AS *Angles on Psychology* text.

A range of print and digital activities is provided for each topic. To help you to use the resources, a quick reference grid of materials showing exactly what activities and information are available follows this section. Each type of resource can be identified on the grid by its icon and each page clearly indicates the type of activity. The meaning of each icon is listed at the start of the grid.

Some of the activity types will be familiar to users of *Angles on Psychology*, Third Edition, such as the Key Issue and Media Watch tasks although there are many other types too.

The following styles of resources are included:

AT — **AT – Approach Tests**: these are test papers provided for each of the five approaches. A mark scheme is provided for each test.

CA — **Class Activities:** these include games and card-sorting tasks that can be used with groups of students.

CE — **Cloze Exercises:** these are fill-in-the-gaps tasks that can be given to students with or without the word list. To achieve an intermediate level of difficulty, or to encourage members of the class to interact, the words could be printed onto cards for students working in different groups to 'trade' around the class. Answers are provided.

ET — **Extension Tasks**: these provide a range of different activity types designed to stretch and challenge the most able students with interesting and varied styles of work to provide differentiation and maintain interest.

KI — **Key Issue**: these are creative activities based on stimulus material to encourage students to use the knowledge they have acquired about a topic in a real-world context. They aim to provide practice for the key issue in each approach.

LAQ **Long-Answer Questions:** these are questions requiring longer answers based on a brief context.

MW **Media Watch:** these are tasks to explore subject content, such as theories, research methods and key issues. Up-to-date media sources provide stimulus material and this is followed by questions.

QQ **Quick Quiz:** these are sets of snappy questions that can be used for class competitions or as a plenary.

RM **Research Methods:** these include two types of activity: first, stimulus-based questions of graded difficulty to provide examples for students throughout the course. Using topic-relevant examples they will improve understanding and provide examination practice. Second, in each approach one or two sources provide stimulus material to set students thinking about their 'evidence of practice' task. This is followed by step-by-step instructions for conducting and writing up the practical task.

SAQ **Short-Answer Questions:** these are scenario-based questions covering topics such as studies, theories and research methods.

SC **Stretch and Challenge:** additional questions at the end of other activities to provide different and interesting tasks as variety for the most able students.

ST **Starter:** quick activities for the whole class to introduce a new approach or topic. Some of these resources could also be used at the end of a topic to stimulate discussion and application of knowledge.

UT **Unit Tests**: mock test papers provide realistic practice for Units 1 and 2 examinations. A mark scheme is provided for each test.

WM **Word-Matching tasks:** these require students to match up related information, such as terms with examples or definitions. Answers are provided.

Icons also indicate to you what is available or needs to be done in advance.

A **Answers**: a set of answers, such as the correct layout of tables and filled-in cloze activities, is provided.

PP **PowerPoint slideshows:** these are used in a range of different ways such as to provide stimulus material, as simple interactive games and as topic starters. In this context, they offer quick and simple introductions to an approach or concept.

prep **Preparation**: some teacher preparation is required in advance of the lesson.

TN **Teacher Notes**: these are additional information for teachers to support the lesson or activity.

Teacher's Support Guide

Chapter 2

The social approach

Grid of materials

Activity number	Activity title	Activity/file type
The social approach		
2.1	Introduction	ST PP
2.2	Starter: agentic and autonomous states	ST CA TN
2.3	Milgram (1963): studying obedience	CE A
2.4	Agency theory	CE A
2.5	Studying obedience	SAQ SC
2.6	Are criminal justice students more obedient?	SAQ SC
2.7	Colonel 'ordered paratrooper to fire at civilians'	MW
2.8	Starter: prejudice – gangs	ST CA TN prep
2.9	Prejudice	ST CA PP
2.10	Social identity theory	CE A
2.11	Explaining and investigating prejudice	SAQ
2.12	Prejudice and questionnaires	SAQ
2.13	Surveys	CE A
2.14	Ethical guidelines	WM TN prep SC CA A
2.15	Sampling	WM TN prep CA A
2.16	Essays: Questions 1 and 2	LAQ
2.17	Murdered for being different	ET LAQ SC
2.18	Creative activities: 1 and 2	KI
2.19	Evidence of practice: conducting a survey	RM
2.20	Obedience at school	RM
2.21	You've got mail: a survey about prejudice	RM
2.22	The social approach quick quiz	QQ A
2.23	Social test	AT A
2.24	Resources	PP
2.25	References	

Introduction

See PowerPoint 2-1: *Introduction*.

A sequence of slides to stimulate discussion on how people affect each other's behaviour, focusing on prejudice and obedience.

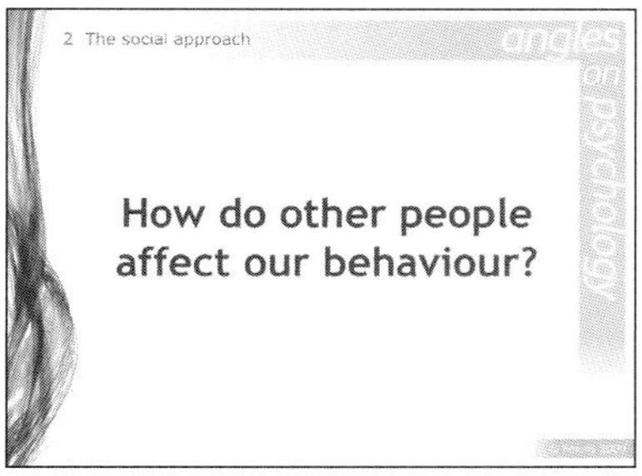

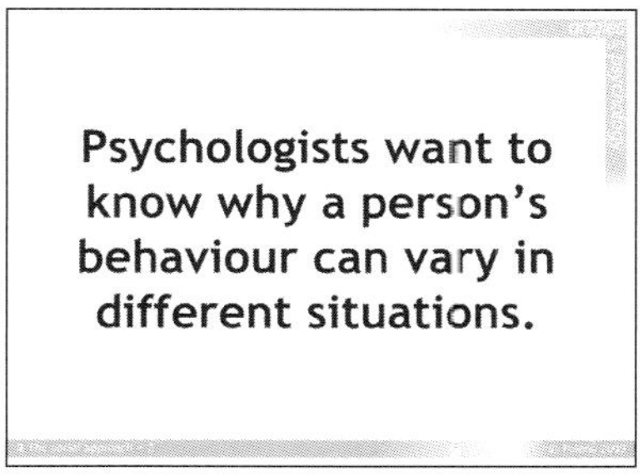

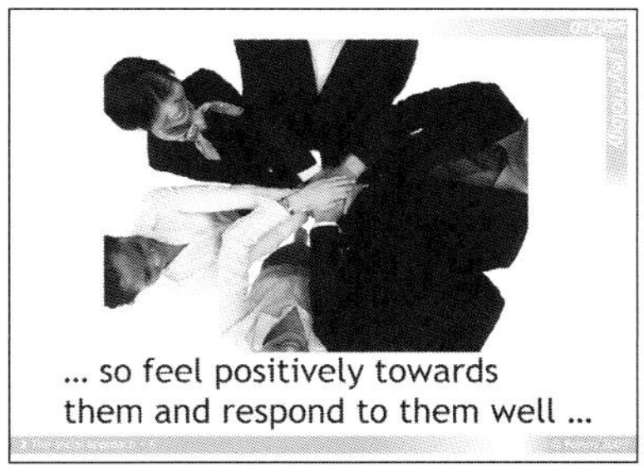

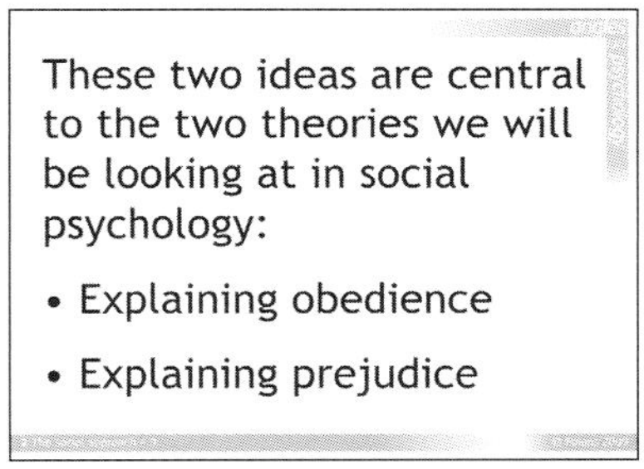

Starter: agentic and autonomous states

Teacher notes

In each of the following situations an individual would respond differently if they were in the agentic or the autonomous state. Present the situations to the class and ask students to record individually what they would do in each case, then pool the responses. Let them discuss which group they might potentially feel allegiance to and why people might choose to act on behalf of that group:

1. You've done your homework but nobody else has. If it's late you might lose marks but if you don't hand it in the teacher might forget until next lesson. What do you do?
2. You have gone to stay for the weekend with your new boy- or girlfriend's family and they take you to church on Sunday. You're not normally a church-goer and his/her mother says you are to make sure you wear a shirt and tie/a skirt that covers your knees. Do you?
3. You've revised for a test and the rest of the class haven't. They want to convince the teacher to do it next week. Do you agree?
4. You are in a rush to catch your bus and a family with a pushchair are in the doorway. You try to get by but they tell you to go and use the next doorway along. Do you push past or walk further on?
5. A phone goes off in a lesson with a teacher who's really strict and you know whose it is. People have silently agreed to deny all knowledge of who it belongs to. What do you do?
6. When you take your books back to the library, you are told that you have to wait to be issued with a new kind of ticket. You consider just leaving the books and coming back for the new ticket another day. Do you?
7. You're in Year 11 and on the way home from school. You see a kid you don't know being beaten up but he/she is in your school uniform. Do you go and help?

Milgram (1963): studying obedience

Milgram aimed to find out why people are obedient to _____________ figures. He advertised for _____________ to participate in a study about the effect of _____________ on learning. These real participants believed they were _____________ allocated to the role of 'teacher' or 'learner' but in fact were always the _____________. They were asked to give electric shocks to another individual, the _____________, who they thought was another participant but was actually a _____________. They had to _____________ the shock level by _____________ volts every time the learner answered a word pair incorrectly. No shocks (apart from one given to the real participant to _____________ them into believing that the machine worked) were actually administered. The learner indicated their distress by complaining, shouting and then going silent but if the participants _____________ to give a shock they were ordered to continue by the experimenter. This authority figure followed a script of _____________. After the experiment, participants were fully debriefed and _____________ a year later.

Milgram found that _____________% of the participants gave shocks up to 300V and _____________% up to 450V. This suggested that obedience is due to the _____________, i.e. perceived authority, not the personality of the participant.

Although Milgram has been criticised, there were many methodological strengths to this study. Considerable effort had been made to control the task and setting, to increase the _____________ of the investigation. For example, participants were _____________ to ensure that they believed the situation was real. They:

- thought that they and the confederate were given their _____________ randomly
- received a test shock from _____________-looking apparatus
- all heard identical verbal prods when they disobeyed, so each person received the same _____________, increasing _____________.
- Also, obedience could be accurately measured as the _____________ reached by each participant.

Milgram is frequently criticised with regard to the _____________ of the study. However, there were again many good points. At the beginning of the study, the participants were told that they could leave if they wanted to and would still receive their _____________, so they were given the right to withdraw. At the end of the study, participants were thoroughly _____________ to ensure that they were not distressed and were introduced to the 'learner' so that they could be sure that he was well. They were subsequently followed up by _____________. _____________% of the participants returned this and _____________% of these were happy to have taken part, so for the majority of participants there were no long-term _____________ effects. Prior to the study, Milgram had asked several colleagues what they thought would happen but none predicted the level of obedience that was found, so he could not have _____________ the trauma the participants would experience. It is important to note that these steps to protect the participants' welfare were taken prior to the publication of any formal ethical guidelines so illustrate Milgram's _____________ in conducting the study.

Milgram (1963): studying obedience *continued*

However, there remain several issues with the investigation, both with Milgram's methodology and ethics. Milgram's participants were all ____________ and were respondents to an advertisement, i.e. they were a ____________. Such groups may be biased so the findings may not ____________ to the wider population. In some respects the measure of obedience ____________ validity as people would not generally expect to give electric shocks to others in a laboratory setting. Ethically, the study raises concerns because the participants:

- were deceived about each person's role and the reality of the ____________
- were put under pressure by the verbal prods and became ____________. This brings Milgram's conduct into question as the experiment could have been ____________ early
- were told that they could leave but this ____________ was contradicted by the verbal prods
- had been invited to a study on memory but it was in fact a test of obedience so they could not give real ____________.

100	ethics	refused
15	followed up	reliability
65	foreseen	right to withdraw
84	generalise	roles
92	increase	situation
authentic	lacked	shocks
authority	learner	stopped
competence	male	teacher
confederate	negative	validity
consent	orders	verbal prods
debriefed	payment	voltage
deceive	punishment	volunteer sample
deceived	questionnaire	volunteers
distressed	randomly	

Milgram (1963): studying obedience

Answers

Milgram aimed to find out why people are obedient to **authority** figures. He advertised for **volunteers** to participate in a study about the effect of **punishment** on learning. These real participants believed they were **randomly** allocated to the role of 'teacher' or 'learner' but in fact were always the **teacher**. They were asked to give electric shocks to another individual, the **learner**, who they thought was another participant but was actually a **confederate**. They had to **increase** the shock level by **15** volts every time the learner answered a word pair incorrectly. No shocks (apart from one given to the real participant to **deceive** them into believing that the machine worked) were actually administered. The learner indicated their distress by complaining, shouting and then going silent but if the participants **refused** to give a shock they were ordered to continue by the experimenter. This authority figure followed a script of **verbal prods**. After the experiment, participants were fully debriefed and **followed up** a year later.

Milgram found that **100**% of the participants gave shocks up to 300V and **65**% up to 450V. This suggested that obedience is due to the **situation**, i.e. perceived authority, not the personality of the participant.

Although Milgram has been criticised, there were many methodological strengths to this study. Considerable effort had been made to control the task and setting, to increase the **validity** of the investigation. For example, participants were **deceived** to ensure that they believed the situation was real. They:

- thought that they and the confederate were given their **roles** randomly
- received a test shock from **authentic**-looking apparatus
- all heard identical verbal prods when they disobeyed, so each person received the same **orders**, increasing **reliability**.
- Also, obedience could be accurately measured as the **voltage** reached by each participant.

Milgram is frequently criticised with regard to the **ethics** of the study. However, there were again many good points. At the beginning of the study, the participants were told that they could leave if they wanted to and would still receive their **payment**, so they were given the right to withdraw. At the end of the study, participants were thoroughly **debriefed** to ensure that they were not distressed and were introduced to the 'learner' so that they could be sure that he was well. They were subsequently followed up by **questionnaire**. **92**% of the participants returned this and **84**% of these were happy to have taken part, so for the majority of participants there were no long-term **negative** effects. Prior to the study, Milgram had asked several colleagues what they thought would happen but none predicted the level of obedience that was found, so he could not have **foreseen** the trauma the participants would experience. It is important to note that these steps to protect the participants' welfare were taken prior to the publication of any formal ethical guidelines so illustrate Milgram's **competence** in conducting the study.

Milgram (1963): studying obedience

Answers *continued*

However, there remain several issues with the investigation, both with Milgram's methodology and ethics. Milgram's participants were all **male** and were respondents to an advertisement, i.e. they were a **volunteer sample**. Such groups may be biased so the findings may not **generalise** to the wider population. In some respects the measure of obedience **lacked** validity as people would not generally expect to give electric shocks to others in a laboratory setting. Ethically, the study raises concerns because the participants:

- were deceived about each person's role and the reality of the **shocks**
- were put under pressure by the verbal prods and became **distressed**. This brings Milgram's conduct into question as the experiment could have been **stopped** early
- were told that they could leave but this **right to withdraw** was contradicted by the verbal prods
- had been invited to a study on memory but it was in fact a test of obedience so they could not give real **consent**.

authority	65	84
volunteers	situation	negative
punishment	validity	foreseen
randomly	deceived	competence
teacher	roles	male
learner	authentic	volunteer sample
confederate	orders	generalise
increase	reliability	lacked
15	voltage	shocks
deceive	ethics	distressed
refused	payment	stopped
verbal prods	debriefed	right to withdraw
followed up	questionnaire	consent
100	92	

Agency theory

Obedience is defined as the tendency to follow ____________ given by an ____________ figure.

Agency theory, proposed by Milgram (1974), suggests that social rules are needed to maintain a stable society and that when we follow them we surrender some of our ____________. He proposed that to do this we have evolved two social states:

- *the autonomous state*: we act as we wish to, according to our own free will or ____________
- *the agentic state*: we give up our free will and act on behalf of the wider ____________.

During childhood, we are ____________ to develop the capacity to enter an agentic state, i.e. to act in the best interests of our ____________, for example by ____________ people in authority. Through this process of learning to accept the authority of others we acquire the ability to act as an ____________ for our society. However, as a result of acting agentically, we may contravene the standards we set for ourselves and, as a result, experience negative emotions such as guilt or remorse. To avoid these, we use ____________. These unconscious 'escape routes' help us to overcome ____________, i.e. the distress caused by acting in an unacceptable way. One of these unconscious responses is ____________. This was apparent in the perpetrators of the Holocaust, who refused to confront what they were doing.

Agency theory is supported by experimental evidence. Milgram (1963) conducted a ____________ experiment which showed how the social situation can put an individual into an ____________ so that they feel they have no choice but to ____________ an authority figure even though they know their behaviour is ____________. In a ____________ experiment, ____________ *et al.* (1966) showed that ____________ to authority figures occurs in real-world situations too. Nurses followed the orders of a doctor even when they knew they could be endangering patients.

____________ (1996) found that ____________ responsibility is attributed to people who are following orders (because it is assigned to the authority figure instead). This suggests that the agentic state does exist. Another strength of agency theory is its usefulness. Knowing the effect that authority figures can have has useful ____________. For example, it can help us to understand how ordinary people can become involved in atrocities such as the Holocaust. It can also explain day-to-day actions, such as why people at work might believe that the needs of their organisation are ____________ important than their own. This can account for people insisting on going to work when they are unwell.

One problem with agency theory is that it cannot explain how ____________ has an effect on obedience. Some people are less likely to follow orders (e.g. some ____________ Milgram). If we are all socialised in a similar way we should be equally likely to enter an agentic state or remain ____________, but we are not. There are also ____________ in people's ability to make others obey them even when they are no different in level of authority – think how likely you are to obey some teachers compared with others! One explanation for this is ____________ which suggests that obedience is partly due to the characteristics of the individual rather than their position of authority. Finally, agency theory cannot explain obedience in the absence of an agentic state or evidence of moral strain – as was seen in Hofling *et al.*'s ____________.

Agency theory *continued*

agent
agentic state
applications
authority
autonomous
Blass
charismatic leadership
conscience
defence mechanisms
denial
disobeyed
field
free will
group
Hofling
individual differences
laboratory
less
moral strain
more
nurses
obedience
obey
obeying
orders
personality
socialised
society
wrong

Agency theory

Answers

Obedience is defined as the tendency to follow **orders** given by an **authority** figure.

Agency theory, proposed by Milgram (1974), suggests that social rules are needed to maintain a stable society and that when we follow them we surrender some of our **free will**. He proposed that to do this we have evolved two social states:

- *the autonomous state*: we act as we wish to, according to our own free will or **conscience**
- the agentic state: we give up our free will and act on behalf of the wider **group**.

During childhood, we are **socialised** to develop the capacity to enter an agentic state, i.e. to act in the best interests of our **society**, for example by **obeying** people in authority. Through this process of learning to accept the authority of others we acquire the ability to act as an **agent** for our society. However, as a result of acting agentically, we may contravene the standards we set for ourselves and, as a result, experience negative emotions such as guilt or remorse. To avoid these, we use **defence mechanisms**. These unconscious 'escape routes' help us to overcome **moral strain**, i.e. the distress caused by acting in an unacceptable way. One of these unconscious responses is **denial**. This was apparent in the perpetrators of the Holocaust, who refused to confront what they were doing.

Agency theory is supported by experimental evidence. Milgram (1963) conducted a **laboratory** experiment which showed how the social situation can put an individual into an **agentic state** so that they feel they have no choice but to **obey** an authority figure even though they know their behaviour is **wrong**. In a **field** experiment, **Hofling** *et al.* (1966) showed that **obedience** to authority figures occurs in real-world situations too. Nurses followed the orders of a doctor even when they knew they could be endangering patients.

Blass (1996) found that **less** responsibility is attributed to people who are following orders (because it is assigned to the authority figure instead). This suggests that the agentic state does exist. Another strength of agency theory is its usefulness. Knowing the effect that authority figures can have has useful **applications**. For example, it can help us to understand how ordinary people can become involved in atrocities such as the Holocaust. It can also explain day-to-day actions, such as why people at work might believe that the needs of their organisation are **more** important than their own. This can account for people insisting on going to work when they are unwell.

One problem with agency theory is that it cannot explain how **personality** has an effect on obedience. Some people are less likely to follow orders (e.g. some **disobeyed** Milgram). If we are all socialised in a similar way we should be equally likely to enter an agentic state or remain **autonomous**, but we are not. There are also **individual differences** in people's ability to make others obey them even when they are no different in level of authority – think how likely you are to obey some teachers compared with others! One explanation for this is **charismatic leadership** which suggests that obedience is partly due to the characteristics of the individual rather than their position of authority. Finally, agency theory cannot explain obedience in the absence of an agentic state or evidence of moral strain – as was seen in Hofling *et al's* **nurses**.

Agency theory

Answers *continued*

orders
authority
free will
conscience
group
socialised
society
obeying
agent
defence mechanisms
moral strain
denial
laboratory
agentic state
obey
wrong
field
Hofling
obedience
Blass
less
applications
more
personality
disobeyed
autonomous
individual differences
charismatic leadership
nurses

Studying obedience

On the way out of their Judo class one Thursday after school, Amita and Shabnam were stopped by a teacher who asked them questions relating to a suspected drug dealing episode on the school grounds. The teacher asked the girls whether they had walked the same route at the same time the previous Thursday. Amita had in fact missed her Judo lesson but hadn't told her parents. Although she didn't want to answer the questions she felt that she had to.

1. Amita obeyed the teacher's request to answer the questions. What is meant by the term obedience? [1 mark]
2. Describe **one** study that attempts to demonstrate obedience. [4 marks]
3. Evaluate the study you have described in Question 2 identifying at least **two** strengths and **two** weaknesses. [4 marks]
4. Explain why Amita was more likely to explain where she really was to a teacher than to a friend. [2 marks]

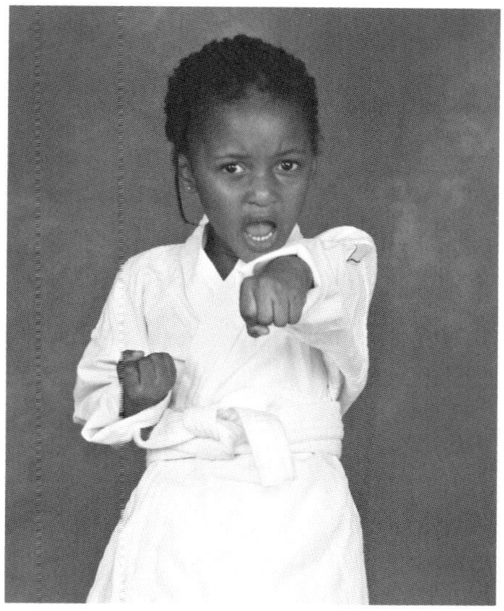

Stretch and challenge

1. Imagine a familiar situation in which obedience occurs such as students obeying teachers or drivers obeying traffic wardens directing traffic.
   a) How does this kind of obedience contribute to a 'stable society', which Milgram believed was a key role for obedience?
   b) Recall Milgram's experiment and the variations he investigated.
      i) Design an (undoubtedly unethical!) study which could measure levels of obedience in a more life-like setting.
      ii) What different realistic variations could be tested and what results would you expect?

Are criminal justice students more obedient?

research now: obedient students

Geher *et al.* (2002)

Aim: to investigate whether participants' academic interests influence perceptions of obedience.

Procedure: this was a theoretical replication of Milgram's obedience experiment in which participants judged whether they, or other individuals, would be more likely to obey. The participants were students with different academic interests (those studying criminal-justice or non-criminal-justice subjects).

Findings: The criminal-justice students' obedience estimates were significantly higher than those of the non-criminal-justice students. The discrepancy between an individual's judgement of their own likelihood to obey compared with the predicted obedience of another person was significantly smaller for criminal justice students than for non-criminal-justice students.

1. What conclusions would you draw from these results? [2 marks]
2. Evaluate this study in terms of **one** strength and **one** weakness. [2 marks]
3. a) Describe one study of obedience **other than** Milgram's. [5 marks]

   b) Evaluate this study in terms of **two** strengths and **two** weaknesses. [4 marks]
4. Geher *et al.* also conducted a study investigating the effect of previous knowledge on perceptions of obedience. One way to test this would be to compare the behaviour of psychology and non-psychology students when given orders, such as if told to exit a room for no apparent reason.

   a) If a study like this were conducted in a college canteen, what research method would be being used? [1 mark]

   b) Identify **one** ethical issue that this research might raise. [1 mark]

   c) Suggest **one** way in which this ethical issue could be resolved. [1 mark]

Stretch and challenge

1. Think about other university courses, or professions, that might be expected to attract people who exhibit greater levels of obedience.
2. How sure can you be that more obedient people have those academic or career interests, rather than become obedient as a result of their training?
3. How would you find out which of these explanations is correct?

Colonel 'ordered paratrooper to fire at civilians'

media watch

Colonel 'ordered paratrooper to fire at civilians'

Richard Norton-Taylor
The Guardian 11 October 2003 p7

A former paratrooper said yesterday his commanding officer, Colonel Derek Wilford, personally ordered him to fire at civilians on Bloody Sunday.

In a day of extraordinary claims at the Saville inquiry he also said he saw Father Daly – the priest whose photograph holding up a white handkerchief as he helped to carry the body of a dead man became a famous image of that day – hiding rifles up his clothes.

The Ministry of Defence has admitted that none of the 13 civil rights marchers killed on January 30 1972 in Derry was armed.

Soldier L told the inquiry that Col Wilford ordered him and other paratroopers to fire if they had a target. He confirmed the contents of a written statement in which he said he fired at a man crawling near him and close to a barricade.

'I fired a round and hit him and he slammed into the wall behind him and bounced back into position on the pavement where he had been crawling. He was still moving,' said soldier L in his statement.

Though he thought he had hit the man under his arm, he continued to crawl and the soldier fired a second shot at the same man and hit him again. He claimed the man was armed.

Soldier L claimed he saw Father Daly pick up two rifles 'and put them up his cassock or coat'.

He also claimed he wished to take Martin McGuinness dead or alive as he had him in his rifle sights during earlier street disturbances in Belfast.

Soldier L said he was waiting for the order to shoot Mr McGuinness dead after seeing him throw bricks and bottles at soldiers. The former para claimed he saw the Sinn Fein leader and former IRA member conducting a running battle with soldiers.

Cathryn McGahey, counsel to the inquiry, asked whether he was sure it was Mr McGuinness.

'Positive, I had him in my rifle sights and I was just waiting for the order to shoot him dead,' he replied.

Soldier L further claimed he saw another paratrooper fire so many shots into a body at point-blank range that when colleagues lifted it to put it into a body bag, it split in two.

Soldier L, who was threatened with contempt of court proceedings for refusing to appear before the inquiry last month, gave evidence from behind a screen.

1. The following of orders, such as described above, is an example of obedience. Define obedience. [2 marks]
2. a) Identify and describe a theory that could account for the behaviour of Colonel Wilford and Soldier L. [5 marks]

   b) Outline **one** strength and **one** weakness of this theory. [4 marks]
3. Why might Soldier L have waited 'for the order to shoot him dead' rather than following his own wish to take McGuinness dead or alive? [1 mark]

Starter: prejudice – gangs

Teacher notes

Risk assessment: consider any dangers associated with building a den out of furniture and omit this if it is unsuitable.

Materials: big sheets of paper, e.g. A2 sugar paper and felt-tip pens

This activity will show students how easily 'in-groups' and 'out-groups' form. Students are generally very willing to get into role especially if enticed with childhood sweets like flying saucers!

Expect to be able to see the social processes of categorisation, identification and comparison in action and to demonstrate in-group formation and prejudice.

Starter: prejudice – gangs

Your role is to behave like a kid (about eight or nine years old).

You will be put into groups. In your group, take a large sheet of paper and space yourself as far as you can from other groups.

Your group is a gang and you can build a den (identify issues in risk assessment if necessary). You have to make up a gang name and password, then write ten 'gang rules' to stick up in your den.

Prejudice

See PowerPoint 2-9:
Targets of prejudice.

This slideshow introduces the components of attitudes and illustrates a range of targets of prejudice.

2 The social approach

Attitudes

The three components of attitudes:

A – Affective component – how you *feel*

B – Behavioural component – what you *do*

C – Cognitive component – what you *think*

Consider all of these questions when you look at each picture:

A - How might people feel about these individuals?

B - How might people behave towards these individuals?

C - What might people think about these individuals?

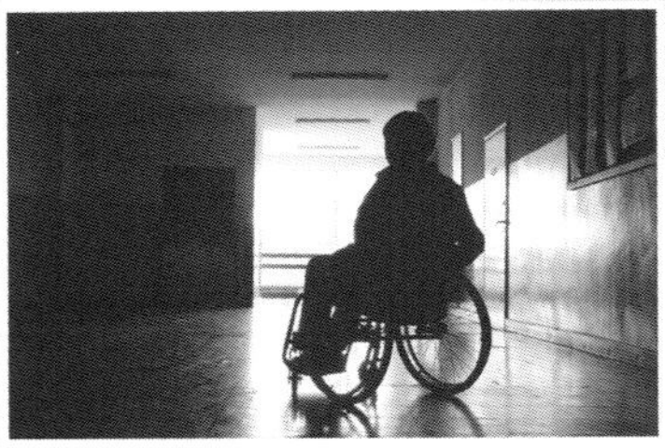

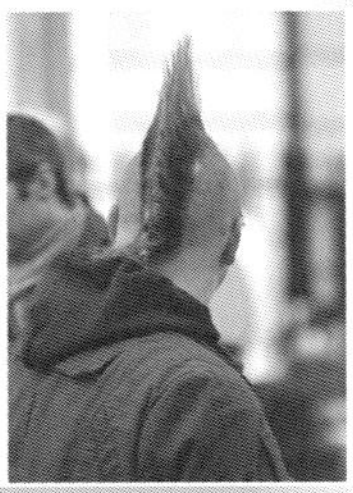

Psychologists try to explain how people's feelings, thoughts and actions in relation to members of different groups arise.

Social identity theory

Social identity theory was proposed by _____________ & _____________ (1979). It has many applications in social psychology, one of which is to explain _____________. This can be defined as an _____________ towards a group which causes the formation of an opinion about a person, based on a _____________, before you have found out about them as an individual.

According to SIT, we use characteristics of ourselves and others to:

- _____________ people as belonging to a range of social groups including classifications like _____________, _____________ and social class.
- _____________ ourselves as belonging to a group, actively adopting the identity of that group, for example by assuming the _____________ or behaviour associated with the group. This identification has emotional significance; for example it is linked to our _____________.
- _____________ members of our own group to other people. We tend to judge our own group to be _____________, thus preserving our self-esteem. As a consequence, members of other groups are _____________.

As a result of social categorisation, identification and comparison, our _____________ towards members of our own and other groups differs, i.e. we show in-group favouritism, which causes _____________. Devaluing the out-group leads to negative behaviours such as _____________. However, because the dominant group has more _____________, the less powerful (_____________) groups can suffer oppression. When the dominant group is seen as inaccessible or _____________ to others, and if the _____________ of the dominant group seems unfair or changeable, the subordinate group is likely to work together against it. This is called _____________. Reicher & Haslam (2002) demonstrated this using an artificial prison situation. The _____________ were the high status group and the prisoners showed _____________ identification within their group, especially when the guards became a _____________ permeable group. As a consequence, the _____________ engaged in collective action to improve their conditions.

Studies such as Sherif *et al.* (1961)'s 'Robber's Cave' experiment show that _____________ can contribute to prejudice. Social identity theory, however, can explain how prejudice arises through group _____________ alone. This idea is supported by evidence from _____________ studies such as that by Tajfel (1970) who showed that boys allocating points to other boys will show favouritism to individuals in their _____________ group even when the groups are _____________ and there is no direct competition between them.

Poppe & Linssen (1999) demonstrated how Europeans of different nationalities held both _____________ views about other nationalities and held their own nationality in higher esteem than others. This latter finding illustrates the phenomenon of _____________. Levine *et al.* showed how group membership affects helping behaviour. Football fans who encountered an injured stranger were more likely to help them if the stranger was wearing the _____________ team colours than if they wore neutral colours or those of a _____________ football club.

Dobbs & Crano (2001) used a minimal groups study to show that asking people to justify their in-group favouritism changes prejudice. In members of the minority group, in-group favouritism _____________, whereas it _____________ in the majority group. This is more complex than social identity theory would predict, so is difficult to explain. There are also _____________ in prejudice that social identity theory cannot account for. Platow *et al.* (1990) found that participants who were very _____________ in nature tended to show less in-group favouritism than those who were very _____________.

Social identity theory *continued*

appearance
attitude
behaviour
better
categorise
collective action
compare
competition
competitive
cooperative
decreased
devalued
discrimination
ethnic group
gender
guards
identification
identify
impermeable
increased
individual differences
in-group favouritism
less
minimal groups
more
own
power
prejudice
prisoners
random
rival
same
self-esteem
status
stereotype
stereotyped
subordinate
Tajfel
Turner
violence

Social identity theory

Answers

Social identity theory was proposed by **Tajfel** & **Turner** (1979). It has many applications in social psychology, one of which is to explain **prejudice**. This can be defined as an **attitude** towards a group which causes the formation of an opinion about a person, based on a **stereotype**, before you have found out about them as an individual.

According to this theory, we use characteristics of ourselves and others to:

- **categorise** people as belonging to a range of social groups. These classifications might include **gender, ethnic group** and social class.
- **identify** ourselves as belonging to a group, actively adopting the identity of that group, for example by assuming the **appearance** or behaviour associated with the group. This identification has emotional significance; for example it is linked to our **self-esteem**.
- **compare** members of our own group to other people. We tend to judge our own group to be **better**, thus preserving our self-esteem. As a consequence, members of other groups are **devalued**.

As a result of social categorisation, identification and comparison, our **behaviour** towards members of our own and other groups differs, i.e. we show in-group favouritism, which causes **discrimination**. Devaluing the out-group leads to negative behaviours such as **violence**. However, because the dominant group has more **power**, the less powerful (**subordinate**) groups can suffer oppression. When the dominant group is seen as inaccessible or **impermeable** to others, and if the **status** of the dominant group seems unfair or changeable, the subordinate group is likely to work together against it. This is called **collective action**. This was demonstrated by Reicher & Haslam (2002) using an artificial prison situation. The **guards** were the high status group and the prisoners showed **more** identification within their group, especially when the guards became a **less** permeable group. As a consequence, the **prisoners** engaged in collective action to improve their conditions.

Studies such as Sherif *et al.* (1961)'s 'Robber's Cave' experiment show that **competition** can contribute to prejudice. Social identity theory, however, can explain how prejudice arises through group **identification** alone. This idea is supported by evidence from **minimal groups** studies such as that by Tajfel (1970) who showed that boys allocating points to other boys will show favouritism to individuals in their **own** group even when the groups are **random** and there is no direct competition between them.

Poppe & Linssen (1999) demonstrated how Europeans of different nationalities held both **stereotyped** views about other nationalities and held their own nationality in higher esteem than others. This latter finding illustrates the phenomenon of **in-group favouritism.** Levine *et al.* showed how group membership affects helping behaviour. Football fans who encountered an injured stranger were more likely to help them if the stranger was wearing the **same** team colours than if they wore neutral colours or those of a **rival** football club.

Social identity theory

Answers *continued*

Dobbs & Crano (2001) used a minimal groups study to show that asking people to justify their in-group favouritism changed prejudice. In members of the minority group, in-group favouritism **increased**, whereas it **decreased** in the majority group. This is more complex than social identity theory would predict, so is difficult to explain. There are also **individual differences** in prejudice that social identity theory cannot account for. Platow *et al.* (1990) found that participants who were very **cooperative** in nature tended to show less in-group favouritism than those who were very **competitive**.

Tajfel
Turner
prejudice
attitude
stereotype
categorise
gender
ethnic group
identify
appearance
self-esteem
compare
better
devalued
behaviour
discrimination
violence
power
subordinate
impermeable
status
collective action
guards
more
less
prisoners
competition
identification
minimal groups
own
random
stereotyped
in-group favouritism
same
rival
increased
decreased
individual differences
cooperative
competitive

Explaining and investigating prejudice

Gladys and Gwendoline live in a residential home because they are now too frail to look after themselves safely. They have spent a quiet life in a partnership together for the last 48 years and haven't really encountered any homophobic behaviour because they've kept themselves to themselves. In the home, however, they are subjected to negative comments from other residents and their visiting families.

1. What is meant by prejudice? [1 mark]
2. a) Describe **one** theory that attempts to explain how prejudice can arise. [4 marks]
   b) Explain how the theory described in part (a) would apply to the example of Gladys and Gwendoline. [3 marks]
   c) Evaluate the theory you have described in part (a) identifying at least **two** strengths and **two** weaknesses. [4 marks]
3. If Gladys and Gwendoline found another lesbian couple in the residential home, they could engage in collective action to improve the situation.
   a) What is collective action? [1 mark]
   b) When is collective action most likely to happen? [2 marks]
4. One way to find out about homophobic attitudes would be to conduct a survey.
   a) Describe what is meant by a survey. [2 marks]
   b) The management team at Gladys and Gwendoline's care home has decided to interview the residents and visitors. The team cannot decide whether to do a structured, unstructured or semi-structured interview.

      Describe the differences between these three approaches to interviewing. [2 marks]
   c) Choose one of these three approaches to interviewing and explain why you would recommend using it in this situation. [2 marks]

Prejudice and questionnaires

Warthogs is a famous school for wizards and witches. Some of the students are 'purebloods' – their parents were also magic folk – other are muggle-born, that is, their parents were ordinary people (muggles). Some of the 'purebloods' think that they are a better class of student and have been calling the muggle-born students nasty names (like 'mud-blood'). Other 'purebloods' are scared of the muggle-born students because they know that some, such as Bryony Danger, are very powerful witches so simply avoid them at all cost.

1. a) Draw a line from each box on the left to one box on the right to link the names for the three elements of prejudice with their descriptions.

cognitive	the way an individual responds to members of a group
affective	the beliefs an individual has, based on stereotypes, about a particular group
behavioural	the feelings an individual has towards members of a group

[3 marks]

   b) Identify how each of these elements is described in the prejucice shown by the 'pureblood' students. [3 marks]

2. a) Name and describe **one** theory of prejudice. [4 marks]

   b) Explain how the theory you have described in part (a) could explain how the prejudice has arisen in this situation. [3 marks]

   c) Evaluate the theory you have described in part (a) in terms of **one** strength and **one** weakness.

3. Professor Grumblebore has decided to conduct a survey to test whether plans to use the house system to reduce prejudice have been successful. He is going to measure levels of verbal bullying before and after the implementation of prejudice-reduction strategies.

   a) Describe **one** strength and **one** weakness of the survey as a research method. [4 marks]

   b) Professor Grumblebore has decided to use a questionnaire to conduct a survey. Write two questions that he could use. One must be a closed question, the other an open question. [2 marks]

   c) One way in which interviews and questionnaires differ is that questionnaires tend to use more closed questions than interviews. Describe one other way in which conducting a survey using a questionnaire would differ from conducting a survey using interviews. [1 mark]

Surveys

A survey is a way of conducting a _____________-scale data collection. The data may be obtained using questionnaires or interviews. In _____________, the participant answers questions on paper whereas in _____________ the questions are asked face-to-face. Surveys are useful for investigating people's attitudes or beliefs so they can be used to investigate prejudice and _____________. In a survey, a range of questioning techniques can be employed to produce different kinds of data. _____________ questions allow the respondent to give only a small selection of different answers, such as *yes/no/sometimes* or *agree/disagree.* _____________ questions give the respondent the opportunity to expand their answers, giving depth and detail. As a consequence, open questions readily produce _____________ data whereas closed questions produce _____________ data. Surveys can be structured, with _____________ questions in a predetermined order. Alternatively, surveys can be _____________, using open questions and being _____________, responding to what the participants say with new questions.

One of the strengths of surveys is that they can collect large amounts of data so their findings are likely to be more _____________ than those of studies using smaller samples. When closed questions are used the results are easy to collate, score and _____________. In contrast, when open questions are used, _____________ data can be obtained, giving insight into the reasons for people's attitudes or behaviour. Open questions can also supply information that is difficult to obtain through direct observation, e.g. _____________ can be accessed. When standardised techniques are used (such as closed questions), the results are highly _____________ and replicable.

There are, however, problems with using the survey method. One important weakness of _____________ interviews or questionnaires is that they lack flexibility. For example, closed questions do not allow participants to say exactly what they mean. As a result important information may be lost and results may not truly reflect _____________ or feelings. In any survey, responses may be affected by _____________, which makes participants respond in the way they think people ought to. This reduces the _____________ of the findings. Responses may also be affected by response biases; this is where participants respond in a set way. Sometimes people are _____________ and when they self-report their attitudes or behaviours they may not be very accurate so the findings of surveys may not be valid predictors. Finally, the sample of respondents in a survey may be _____________ because very similar people may be prepared to take part in interviews or to return questionnaires.

analyse	interviews	representative
biased	large	social desirability
closed	open	structured
detailed	opinions	subjective
discrimination	qualitative	unstructured
feelings	quantitative	validity
fixed	questionnaires	
flexible	reliable	

Surveys

Answers

A survey is a way of conducting a **large**-scale data collection. The data may be obtained using questionnaires or interviews. In **questionnaires**, the participant answers questions on paper whereas in **interviews** the questions are asked face-to-face. Surveys are useful for investigating people's attitudes or beliefs so they can be used to investigate prejudice and **discrimination**. In a survey, a range of questioning techniques can be employed to produce different kinds of data. **Closed** questions allow the respondent to give only a small selection of different answers, such as *yes/no/sometimes* or *agree/disagree*. **Open** questions give the respondent the opportunity to expand their answers, giving depth and detail. As a consequence, open questions readily produce **qualitative** data whereas closed questions produce **quantitative** data. Surveys can be structured, with **fixed** questions in a predetermined order. Alternatively, surveys can be **unstructured**, using open questions and being **flexible**, responding to what the participants say with new questions.

One of the strengths of surveys is that they can collect large amounts of data so their findings are likely to be more **representative** than those of studies using smaller samples. When closed questions are used the results are easy to collate, score and **analyse**. In contrast, when open questions are used, **detailed** data can be obtained, giving insight into the reasons for people's attitudes or behaviour. Open questions can also supply information that is difficult to obtain through direct observation, e.g. **feelings** can be accessed. When standardised techniques are used (such as closed questions), the results are highly **reliable** and replicable.

There are, however, problems with using the survey method. One important weakness of **structured** interviews or questionnaires is that they lack flexibility. For example, closed questions do not allow participants to say exactly what they mean. As a result important information may be lost and results may not truly reflect **opinions** or feelings. In any survey, responses may be affected by **social desirability**, which makes participants respond in the way they think people ought to. This reduces the **validity** of the findings. Responses may also be affected by response biases; this is where participants respond in a set way. Sometimes people are **subjective** and when they self-report their attitudes or behaviours they may not be very accurate so the findings of surveys may not be valid predictors. Finally, the sample of respondents in a survey may be **biased** because very similar people may be prepared to take part in interviews or to return questionnaires.

large	fixed	structured
questionnaires	unstructured	opinions
interviews	flexible	social desirability
discrimination	representative	validity
closed	analyse	subjective
open	detailed	biased
qualitative	feelings	
quantitative	reliable	

Ethical guidelines

Teacher notes

Print this table onto card, cut it up and ask students to match up the ethical guidelines, reasons and examples. A grid is provided to copy and give to students to keep a record of their work.

Ethical guideline	Reason for the guideline	Example of the guideline in practice
Consent	Participants should fully understand what they are agreeing to do. Their decision to participate should not be influenced by the power of the researcher or by payment.	In Meeus & Raaijmaker (1986) participants were given enough information to decide whether to join a study in which they had to cause stress to a job applicant. They therefore knew that the procedure would be unpleasant.
Deception	Generally, participants should not be deliberately misled about the purpose of a study. This should happen only when researchers have no other way to conduct the investigation and only if the participants are not likely to become distressed.	In Milgram (1963) the participants were misled into believing that it was an investigation into memory when it was actually about obedience.
Right to withdraw	Participants should be allowed to leave the study at any time and should know that they are able to do this. They should also be able to remove their data at the end of the study if they want to.	Slater *et al.* (2006) told participants in advance of starting their virtual reality obedience procedure that they could leave at any time without giving reasons.
Debriefing	If participants are aware that they have been in a study they should be given a full explanation of the research as soon as possible. They should leave the study feeling at least as good as when they came into it.	Hofling *et al.* (1966) interviewed each nurse within 48 hours of the ward incident. They were offered support and reassurance about the situation and reassured about their anonymity.
Competence	Researchers should only conduct studies for which they have sufficient experience, so participants should not be put at greater physical or psychological risk than they would encounter in their normal life. If a problem is identified with a participant, a researcher should not offer advice unless they are qualified to do so.	Reicher & Haslam (2002) ensured that the participants in their prison study were mentally healthy and non-aggressive. They also finished the study early to avoid the risk of violence.

Ethical guideline	Reason for the guideline	Example of the guideline in practice
Consent		
Deception		
Right to withdraw		
Debriefing		
Competence		

Stretch and challenge

Where your examples are of a guideline being broken, think about what the researchers could have done to overcome the ethical problem.

Sampling

Print this table onto card, cut it up and ask students to match up the sampling methods, descriptions and examples. A grid is provided to copy and give to students to keep a record of their work.

Sampling method	Description of sampling method	Example of sampling method in use
Opportunity sample	Asking people who are easily accessible to participate.	Hofling *et al.* (1966) used nurses who happened to be alone on a ward in nearby hospitals for the experimental part of their study.
Self-selected or volunteer sample	Finding participants by word of mouth or using requests such as placing cards in shop windows or on laboratory notice boards.	Milgram (1963) obtained his sample by placing a newspaper advertisement asking for males to participate in an experiment on memory.
Stratified sample	Choosing people from each type or group in the population. Within each type, selection is random and in proportion to the prevalence of that type in the population.	Racism could be investigated in a school. Children from each ethnic group would be randomly selected to participate. Each ethnic group would be represented by a different number of children relative to the number of members of that ethnic group in the school.
Random sample	Selecting participants so that each individual in the target population has an equal chance of being chosen.	Verkooijen *et al.* (2007) recruited participants by selecting the homes of about 2% of 16–20-year-olds so that every relevant address from the Danish Household Register was equally likely to be chosen.

Sampling

Sampling method	Description of sampling method	Example of sampling method in use
Opportunity sample		
Self-selected or volunteer sample		
Stratified sample		
Random sample		

Essays

Question 1

Teachers at Hill Top High School are worried about behaviour in Years 7 and 8. The children are normally well behaved and all of Year 11 are prefects so are responsible for telling children in lower years how to behave in the corridors and playground. The staff are concerned because there have been reports of older children being seen on the way home from school telling younger ones to kick passing cats and dogs. Two kittens have been killed and a small dog was badly injured.

Describe agency theory and use it to explain why the younger children may be behaving badly.

continue overleaf if necessary

Essays

Question 2

> Tabitha and her brother James have just moved house with their family. They have moved to a different part of the country and Tabitha notices that her accent is quite different from that of the other children in her new class. They notice too and exclude her and James from their games. The other children seem to make a point of carrying a certain type of bag that is different from Tabitha's and singing songs that Tabitha doesn't know. After a few days they start to call her names.

Using examples from the situation above, describe social identity theory. How can this theory explain the behaviour of the children in Tabitha's class?

....

....

....

....

....

....

....

....

....

....

....

....

....

....

....

....

....

....

....

....

....

continue overleaf if necessary

Murdered for being different

GOTH LOVERS ATTACKED

The Mirror, Friday 28 March 2008 (Edited)
Paul Byrne

DISTRAUGHT Robert Maltby told yesterday how he gazed at girlfriend Sophie Lancaster as she lay dying in her hospital bed – and said to himself: 'What have we done to deserve this?'

Robert, 21, and Sophie, 20, both suffered terrible injuries after a ferocious attack by five drunken teenage thugs who picked on them simply because they were goths. He survived – but emerged from a coma to discover Sophie was dying from massive head injuries.

Herbert and three other teenage boys. The gang, described in court as 'like a pack of wild animals', kicked and punched Robert then stamped on his head until he was unconscious. Sophie cried for them to stop as she cradled his head on her lap. But Herbert kicked her in the face and he and Harris then stamped on her head as she lay on the ground. Paramedics said the couple's injuries were so bad they could not tell them apart.

Judge Anthony Russell QC said he was duty bound to give Harris and Herbert life sentences.

Outside court Sophie's mum Sylvia, 52, said: 'Her voice was cruelly silenced in a single mindless act. Sophie's death was a tragedy in so many ways. It has also ruined the lives of those responsible as well as the lives of their families.' Sylvia, who yesterday released harrowing pictures of Sophie in a coma, added: 'On a wider scale it is a tragedy for a society which in the past prided itself on its tolerance. I am convinced Sophie was killed simply because of the way she looked. She did not conform to the ideals of those who took her life. We need to show respect, compassion and tolerance for those whose culture differs from our own.'

a) Use your understanding of the social approach to explain how this tragedy could have arisen.

b) Sophie's mother suggests that something could be learned from the tragedy. What help could psychological explanations offer to guide society in altering the views of young people?

Stretch and challenge

Look at the website below, which has photos of Sophie and two of her attackers. Identify how, according to social identity theory, the boys might categorise themselves as members of a different social group from Sophie.

http://www.express.co.uk/posts/view/39401/Teenage-boy-guilty-of-Goth-murder

What can social psychology tell us about hatred based on appearance?

Creative activities

1 School soccer anger stopper

What are your local football teams? The chances are that feelings between fans of these teams are not entirely positive. Imagine that both teams reach the semi-finals and the local secondary school is worried because aggressive behaviour between gangs of children supporting opposing teams has begun to get violent. Using your knowledge of social identity theory, design a programme to help the school to reintegrate the children and reduce tension between competing fans. You need to consider ways that you can reduce social categorisation, identification and comparison between groups and encourage social identification to a united group.

2 Major Milgram advises agency in the Army

You are a newly commissioned senior officer in the army and are keen to impress your commanding officer. The Army's current problem is rebellion in the ranks and you want to show that you can come up with well justified strategies. Write a proposal to your superiors describing explanations of obedience and suggesting how the issue might be tackled by increasing the sense of joint responsibility that individuals have to their platoon that will raise their likelihood of acting in an agentic way. Justify why this is an important idea.

Evidence of practice: conducting a survey

Agentic students

Hamilton & Sanders (1995) found that participants assigned more responsibility to a person who committed crimes in the workplace if they were acting independently than if they were following orders from a superior. You could conduct a survey to find out whether students feel the same about wrongdoing by fellow students at college. You could include situations where the student is acting on their own when following orders from a fellow student or member of staff.

Try to make the situations plausible but also think about potential ethical consequences of your survey. Don't use questions about drug-taking or bullying – and ask your teacher to check your questions before using them.

Sexist beliefs in school

In Unit 2 you will be looking at gender. You could begin to investigate whether there are differences in attitudes between boys and girls or between older and younger people. When you are designing your questions, try to make them neutral so that you don't lead the respondents to give the answers you expect. Remember also to keep an even balance between positive and negative statements or questions about men and women.

For ethical reasons do not try to find evidence of sexist practice in your school – you are not qualified to do so and remember that it should not be possible from your results to identify the attitudes of specific individuals.

Preparation

1. Choose who you are working with, and decide on a topic to investigate. Agree an aim for your group, then devise a suitable hypothesis.
2. Decide whether you will use an interview or a questionnaire and think about how you will collect both qualitative and quantitative data. Will you use a structured or unstructured design?
3. What is your target population and what sample size do you want? Think about how you will obtain a sample (by opportunity, volunteer, stratified or random sampling?).
4. Think carefully about the ethical issues your survey could raise and how you will avoid or resolve them. Some issues will be general ones, such as confidentiality; others may relate specifically to your target population (such as children).
5. Write a few questions each – compare how they have been written and the styles of questions you have used (e.g. open questions, closed questions and Likert scales). Combine the best ones and write any extras you need to cover the issues you want to investigate.
6. Is your survey valid? Is it testing what you want it to? How do you know?
7. Is your survey reliable? Would you get the same results if you used it twice?
8. Use your survey to collect data.
9. Analyse your qualitative data, for example by looking for general themes in people's responses and using one or two as examples.
10. Analyse your quantitative data, for example by counting the total number of responses that represent each viewpoint. If possible, work out measures of central tendency (averages) and measures of spread (e.g. the range) on your data.
11. Present some of these findings using tables and graphs. Make sure that you have titles and column and row headings on tables and headings of the axes of your graphs.

Obedience at school

Some researchers carried out an investigation into attitudes towards obedience. They asked 18 students from each year at their school, ten boys and eight girls. They were trying to find out whether the older children were more agentic as a result of having had more exposure to the socialising effects of school discipline.

> 10. What school year are you in? *Please tick one box.*
> Year 7 □ Year 8 □ Year 9 □ Year 10 □ Year 11 □ Year 12 □ Year 13 □
>
> 11. If a teacher tells you to tuck your shirt in, how likely are you to do it immediately?
> *Please circle one answer.*
> very unlikely quite unlikely not sure quite likely very likely
>
> 12. Students should always follow instructions they are given for homework exactly.
> *Please circle one answer to show how much you agree with this statement.*
> strongly agree agree don't know disagree strongly disagree
>
> 13. Describe one or more times that you have disobeyed an instruction from a teacher.
>
> 14. Sometimes students give orders to other students. Why do you think a student might obey a teacher but not another student?

1. Write a hypothesis that could have been used for this study. [1]
2. The sample was chosen because all the school year groups contained the same number of students and overall there were 1000 boys and 800 girls in the school.
   a) Name the sampling method that they were using. [1]
   b) Describe **one** advantage of this sampling method. [4]
3. In answering the questions 3 (a) and (b) and 4 (a) and (b) you may use each of the example questions 10, 11, 12, 13 and 14 once, more than once or not at all.
   a) Identify by question number, **one** open and **one** closed question from the questionnaire. [2]
   b) Questions 11 and 12 have the 'obedient' response at opposite ends. Why is this important? [2]
4. Some of the questions in the questionnaire produced qualitative data.
   a) Identify by question number **one** question above that would produce qualitative data. [2]
   b) Outline **one** advantage and **one** disadvantage of qualitative data. [2]
5. The researchers were concerned about the reliability of their questionnaire.
   a) What is meant by reliability? [1]
   b) Outline one way the researchers could check the reliability of their questionnaire. [2]
6. Some of the teachers gave the researchers information about general obedience levels in the school. They thought this would be helpful as the students' views about their own behaviour might be biased. What term is used to refer to this bias? [1]
7. Initially, the researchers intended to investigate the students' opinions about obedience by conducting interviews.
   a) In one design they had a fixed set of questions similar to questions 10, 11 and 12 above. What type of interview was this? [1]
   b) In another design, there were some questions like number 13 but the interviewers also had the freedom to introduce new questions of their own.
      i) What type of interview is this? [1]
      ii) Outline **one** advantage and **one** disadvantage of this type of interview. [2]

You've got mail: a survey about prejudice

Bushman & Bonacci (2004) conducted an investigation into discrimination directed at Arabs in America following the September 11 attacks on the World Trace Center in 2001. As part of this study 940 introductory level psychology students from Iowa State University completed several questionnaires which measured prejudiced attitudes towards Arab-Americans. A target group of European-Americans was chosen to participate.

1. Write a possible hypothesis for this study. [1]
2. Although they were only testing attitudes to Arab-Americans, there were questions about other ethnic groups, (see table). Why was this necessary? [2]
3. Part of the questionnaire was used to identify 'in-group' members, i.e. European-Americans, for the second part of the study. Write a closed question that could have been used to collect this information. [1]
4. a) The participants were students at the researchers' university so were readily available to do the questionnaire in class. Which sampling technique is this? [1]

   b) Of the original group described above, 194 men and 318 women were selected to participate. Comment on how representative this sample might be. [2]
5. One set of questions had 11 statements such as 'If I knew I had been assigned to live in a dorm room with an Arab-American, I would ask to change rooms'. For each, the participant had to choose a rating from 1 *(strongly disagree)* to 10 *(strongly agree)*.

   a) Is the example a closed or an open question? [1]

   b) Were the data produced by these questions qualitative or quantitative? [1]

   c) All the statements were negative; that is, they expressed anti-Arab views. Describe **one** advantage and **one** disadvantage of having all negative statements rather than a mixture of negative and positive. [4]

   d) The same 11 questions were asked about each of the five ethnic groups listed below. Totals were then added up to give scores for attitudes to each group. These were used to calculate an average. The results are given below:

Ethnic group	Arab-American	African-American	Asian-American	European-American	Hispanic-American
Average prejudice score of European-Americans towards each group	29.4	23.2	23.0	20.4	25.3

   Higher scores indicate greater prejudice. What do the findings show about prejudice in relation to the aim? [1]
6. Several ethical issues arose in this research which were resolved in different ways.

   a) One question asked whether the individual would participate in an unsolicited phone, email or door-to-door study. This allowed the researchers to find out who might participate in the second part of the study. Which ethical guideline were they following? [1]

   b) After the end of the second part of the study, participants were given a full explanation and offered the chance to contact a researcher if they had any questions. Which ethical guideline were they following and what is the purpose of this procedure? [2]
7. The 11-item questionnaire used questions from a scale previously used to assess people's prejudice towards Jews. The researchers could therefore be confident that it would measure prejudice accurately. Is this an indication of validity or reliability? [1]

The social approach quick quiz

1

a) Name one theory of prejudice.
b) Name two sampling methods.
c) What is a stereotype?
d) What is meant by subjectivity?
e) Define obedience.
f) What is meant by collective action?
g) Give one example of the influence of one person on the social behaviour of another.
h) What is meant by the agentic state?
i) Why are psychologists concerned about participants giving consent?
j) What is reliability?
k) Identify one study that supports social identity theory.
l) What is a survey?
m) Suggest one piece of evidence that contradicts agency theory.
n) What is a debrief?
o) What is meant by qualitative data?
p) Describe the key issue for the social approach.

2

a) Define prejudice.
b) Name one theory of obedience.
c) Is opportunity sampling representative?
d) What are the three stages in social identity theory?
e) What is meant by the autonomous state?
f) Give two groups that are targets of prejudice about whom you could describe studies.
g) Give one example of the influence of group membership on social behaviour.
h) What is validity?
i) Define moral strain.
j) What are the two methods that can be used to collect data in a survey?
k) Identify one study that supports agency theory.
l) What is stratified sampling?
m) Suggest one piece of evidence that contradicts social identity theory.
n) Identify two ethical guidelines.
o) What is meant by quantitative data?
p) Which four studies must you know in detail for the social approach?

The social approach quick quiz

Answers

1

a) Name one theory of prejudice. **Social identity theory**

b) Name two sampling methods. **Any two of: opportunity; volunteer (self-selected); random; stratified**

c) What is a stereotype? **A fixed, simplistic belief about a group which can underlie a prejudice**

d) What is meant by subjectivity? **Considering something only from your own perspective**

e) Define obedience. **Following the orders of an authority figure**

f) What is meant by collective action? **Efforts by an out-group to change attitudes within society**

g) Give one example of the influence of one person on the social behaviour of another. **e.g. an authority figure demanding obedience from another person**

h) What is meant by the agentic state? **Giving up our free will for the sake of our society**

i) Why are psychologists concerned about participants giving consent? **So that participants are able to make informed decisions about participating in studies**

j) What is reliability? **Consistency of results**

k) Identify one study that supports social identity theory. **e.g. Poppe & Linssen (1999)**

l) What is a survey? **A large-scale investigation based on questionnaire or interview data**

m) Suggest one piece of evidence that contradicts agency theory. **e.g. not all the participants in Milgram's/Hofling *et al.'s* studies obeyed**

n) What is a debrief? **Giving a full explanation to participants after a study and returning them to at least as positive a state as they were in before the study**

o) What is meant by qualitative data? **Descriptive information not in the form of numbers**

p) Describe the key issue for the social approach. **e.g. genocide/football hooliganism**

The social approach quick quiz

Answers *continued*

2

a) Define prejudice. **An attitude towards an individual or group based on a limited, stereotyped view of a group formed before getting to know individuals**

b) Name one theory of obedience. **Agency theory**

c) Is opportunity sampling representative? **No**

d) What are the three stages in social identity theory? **Social identification, categorisation, comparison**

e) What is meant by the autonomous state? **Having the free will to act as our conscience dictates**

f) Give two groups that are targets of prejudice about whom you could describe studies. **e.g. racism (Gee *et al.*, 2006), women (Hellerstein *et al.*, 2002), homosexuals (Stonewall, 2005; Bergan-Gander & von Kurthy, 2006; Koh & Ross, 2006)**

g) Give one example of the influence of group membership on social behaviour. **e.g. Levine *et al.* (2005) found that football supporters were more likely to help another person in the same football club colours as them**

h) What is validity? **The extent to which we are measuring what we set out to measure**

i) Define moral strain. **The unpleasant sensation that results from pressure to obey orders to commit an immoral act**

j) What are the two methods that can be used to collect data in a survey? **Questionnaire and interview**

k) Identify one study that supports agency theory. **e.g. Milgram (1963)**

l) What is stratified sampling? **A way to select participants so that the groups representing the different subgroups of a target population are in the same proportion in the sample as in the population**

m) Suggest one piece of evidence that contradicts social identity theory. **e.g. Dobbs & Crano (2001), Platow *et al.* (1990)**

n) Identify two ethical guidelines. **e.g. any two from: consent, deception, right to withdraw, competence**

o) What is meant by quantitative data? **Information in the form of numbers**

p) Which four studies must you know in detail for the social approach?

i) **Milgram (1963)**

ii) **Hofling *et al.* (1966)**

iii) **One of obedience from a country other than the USA, e.g. Slater *et al.*, (2006) (UK), Meeus & Raaijmakers (1986) (Holland)**

iv) **One on prejudice or obedience, chosen from: Sherif (1954/1961/1988), Tajfel (1970/1971) or Reicher & Haslam (2003/2006)**

Social test

Centre No.						Paper Reference							Surname	Initial(s)
Candidate No.						6	P	S	0	1	/	1	Signature	

Psychology Advanced Subsidiary

Unit 1: Social Psychology

Time: 50 minutes

Instructions to candidates

Answer ALL the questions.

Information for candidates

The total mark for this paper is 40.

Advice to candidates

Quality of written communication will be taken into account in the marking of your response to question 11. This question is indicated with an asterisk (*). Quality of written communication includes clarity of expression, the structure and presentation of ideas, and grammar, punctuation and spelling.

Question number	Leave blank
1	
2	
3	
4	
5	
6	
7	
8	
9	
10	
11	
Total	

SECTION A

Answer ALL questions.
You are advised to spend approximately 7 minutes on this section.

Choose answer A, B, C or D, and put a cross in the box (☒). If you change your mind, put a line through the box (~~☒~~) and then put a cross in another box (☒).

1. What percentage of the participants in the study conducted by Milgram (1963) administered 450V to the 'learner'?

☐ **A** 15%
☐ **B** 63%
☐ **C** 65%
☐ **D** 100% **(1)**

2. A survey is best defined as a way to:

☐ **A** collect data without having to do too much work
☐ **B** collect lots of data using questions that are spoken or on paper
☐ **C** investigate prejudice
☐ **D** test a hypothesis **(1)**

3. The ethical guideline of 'consent' means that:

☐ **A** researchers must take their idea to an ethical committee
☐ **B** participants can choose to leave the study whenever they like, even if they have been paid
☐ **C** people must know what will happen in a study so they can decide whether to participate
☐ **D** two researchers studying the same thing must agree on their definitions **(1)**

4. Social identity theory has three stages. They are:

☐ **A** categorisation, identification and comprehension
☐ **B** comprehension, identification and comparison
☐ **C** identification, comparison and discrimination
☐ **D** categorisation, identification and comparison **(1)**

5. In an argument, Sarah's older brother told her to pinch their younger brother. She said it would hurt him and refused.

Why did Sarah refuse? Because:

☐ **A** she was acting as an agent for the family group
☐ **B** all three siblings were part of the same in-group
☐ **C** she was in the autonomous state
☐ **D** all three siblings were part of the same out-group **(1)**

6. One problem with social identity theory is that:

☐ **A** people's behaviour changes when they identify with a group
☐ **B** people vary in their obedience
☐ **C** it cannot effectively explain racism
☐ **D** some people are more prejudiced than others **(1)**

(Total 6 marks)

TOTAL FOR SECTION A: 6 MARKS

SECTION B

Answer ALL questions.
You are advised to spend approximately 25 minutes on this section.

7. **(a)** Research in social psychology often raises ethical issues.

Name one ethical issue faced by Hofling *et al.* (1966) in their study of obedience and describe how they overcame this ethical problem.

....

....

....

.... **(2)**

(b) (i) Outline the procedure used by Milgram (1963) in his study of obedience.

....

....

....

....

....

....

.... **(4)**

(b) (ii) Identify an ethical issue that arose in Milgram's study that is **different** from the one you identified in 7(a). Describe how this could have affected Milgram's participants.

....

....

....

.... **(2)**

(c) For your course you will have learned about another study of obedience conducted in a different country from Milgram's. Describe the differences between these studies in terms of **either** the methodology **or** the findings.

....

....

....

.... **(2)**

(Total 10 marks)

8. The table below shows the results of an investigation into prejudice which asked 20 people how likely they would be to offer help to someone who was struggling with their shopping. The shopper was described in different ways and the participants responded on a scale that read: very likely/quite likely/possibly/quite unlikely/very unlikely.

	Total number of responses about helping				
Shopper described as	*very likely*	*quite likely*	*possibly*	*quite unlikely*	*very unlikely*
a scruffy young person in a hoodie top	0	2	2	13	3
a person speaking a foreign language	0	1	7	9	3
an elderly person	12	4	2	1	1

(a) The participants were given the questions printed on a sheet and responded by ticking boxes under each heading. Was this an interview or a questionnaire?

.... **(1)**

(b) Which groups were most and least likely to be helped?

Most likely to be helped: ....

Least likely to be helped: .... **(1)**

(c) Describe your conclusion from these findings.

....

....

....

.... **(2)**

(d) Reliability is often an issue in surveys.

(i) What is meant by the term 'reliability'?

....

.... **(1)**

(ii) How could the researchers test the reliability of this survey?

....

....

....

.... **(2)**

(Total 7 marks)

9. As part of the requirements for the Social Psychology part of your course you will have conducted a survey in which you collected both qualitative and quantitative data.

(a) What is meant by 'qualitative data'?

....

.... (1)

(b) Explain how you collected your qualitative data.

....

....

....

.... (2)

(Total 3 marks)

TOTAL FOR SECTION B: 20 MARKS

SECTION C

You are advised to spend approximately 18 minutes on this section.

Answer ALL questions.

10. You will have learned about one of the following studies from the social approach in your course:

Sherif (1954/1961/1988): 'Robber's Cave' study

Tajfel (1970/1971): Study of minimal groups

Reicher & Haslam (2003/2006): Learning from the experiment

Choose **one** study from the list above and evaluate **one** aspect of this study.

The study I am evaluating is: ....

....

....

....

.... (2)

(Total 2 marks)

***11.** The social approach to psychology can help us to understand how people behave in different situations. Read the description in the box below. Apply your understanding of the concepts and ideas from the social approach to explain this issue.

> A small town is having problems with violence between two rival gangs of youths. One group, the 'Squads', wear Army-style jackets and chant aggressively. The other group, the 'Hards', wear jeans and vest tops and have tattoos.

A 'Squad'

A 'Hard'

(Total 12 marks)

TOTAL FOR SECTION C: 14 MARKS

TOTAL MARKS FOR PAPER: 40 MARKS

Mark scheme

SECTION A

1. C 65% (1)

2. B collect lots of data using questions that are spoken or on paper (1)

3. C people must know what will happen in a study so they can decide whether to participate (1)

4. D categorisation, identification and comparison (1)

5. C she was in the autonomous state (1)

6. D some people are more prejudiced than others (1)

SECTION B

7. (a) *Name one ethical issue faced by Hofling* et al. *(1966) in their study of obedience and describe how they overcame this ethical problem.*

Possible distress at knowing they could have risked a patient's health/fears about job;
By (debriefing) telling the participants what had happened after whole procedure was over;
Confidentiality;
By ensuring that the names of the nurses and the hospitals were kept secret; (2)

(b) (i) *Outline the procedure used by Milgram (1963) in his study of obedience.*
Two marks for:
Gave verbal prods to make participants obey;
Measured obedience as maximum voltage reached;
A further two marks for any other methodological points, e.g:
Participant appeared to be randomly allocated to learner or teacher role;
One real shock given to participant (to make equipment seem authentic);
Required to give shocks to the 'learner' (but were not real);
Shock increased in 15V increments; (4)

(b) (ii) *Identify an ethical issue that arose in Milgram's study that is* different *from the one you identified in 7(a). Describe how this could have affected Milgram's participants.*
Deception;
Distress because they believed they were hurting someone when they weren't;
Lack of informed consent;
Some participants regretted having been involved so they had lasting negative effects; (2)

(c) *For your course you will have learned about another study of obedience conducted in a different country from Milgram's. Describe the differences between these studies in terms of* either *the methodology* or *the findings.*
e.g. Meeus & Raaijmakers (1986):
Methodology:
The participants were required to stress an interviewee rather than give (pretend) electric shocks;
There was a control condition in which no experimenter was present;
Findings:
The rate of maximum obedience (making all 15 comments) with the experimenter present was higher than in Milgram's study (92%);
The rate of maximum obedience with the experimenter absent was lower than in Milgram's study (0%); **(2)**

8. **(a)** *The participants were given the questions printed on a sheet and responded by ticking boxes under each heading. Was this an interview or a questionnaire?*
Questionnaire; **(1)**

(b) *Which groups were most and least likely to be helped?*
Most likely to be helped: **Elderly person**
Least likely to be helped: **Scruffy young person** **(1)**

(c) *Describe your conclusion from these findings. e.g.:*
Prejudice is greater towards scruffy young people and people speaking a foreign language than towards elderly people;
As a consequence discrimination against them is greater; **(2)**

(d) (i) *What is meant by the term 'reliability'?*
Consistency of findings; **(1)**

(ii) *How could the researchers test the reliability of this survey?*
e.g. test–retest:
Give out the questionnaire and collect data, then do the same again (with the same people);
If very similar results are obtained the questionnaire is reliable; **(2)**

9. **(a)** *What is meant by 'qualitative data'?*
Results in a detailed, descriptive form; **(1)**

(b) *Explain how you collected your qualitative data.*
1 mark can be awarded for each detail, such as:
Stating the question(s) asked;
Identifying the type of question or technique (e.g. open questions/unstructured interview);
Saying how the qualitative data were analysed; **(2)**

SECTION C

10. *Choose **one** study from the list above and evaluate **one** aspect of this study.*

Sherif (1954/1961/1988): 'Robber's Cave' study
Tajfel (1970/1971): Study of minimal groups
Reicher & Haslam (2003/2006): Learning from the experiment

e.g. Tajfel

The boys were told it was a study of visual judgements so did not know it was about prejudice;

So they would not have been affected by demand characteristics;

The boys believed they were in 'over-estimators' or 'under-estimators' groups but allocation was random;

So any differences between their responses was caused by believing in the groups, not actual differences between the boys; **(2)**

***11.** *Apply your understanding of the concepts and ideas from the social approach to explain this issue.* **(12)**

Level	Mark	Descriptor
		AO1: Knowledge and understanding of psychological concepts. AO2: Application of psychological concepts.
1	0	No content worth of marks.
2	1–3	A brief, simple answer with some relevance to the question but with little application of ideas to the situation given. Answer lacks clarity and/or organisation. Little use of relevant terminology and poor spelling, punctuation and/or grammar.
3	4–6	An answer which is simple but largely relevant and accurate with limited application of ideas to the situation given. Limited clarity and/or organisation. Some use of relevant terminology. Frequent spelling, punctuation and/or grammatical errors.
4	7–9	The answer contains both relevant and accurate evidence (from studies and/or theories) and has some effective application of ideas to the situation given. Clarity of expression and organisation are competent with some use of relevant terminology. Some spelling, punctuation and/or grammatical errors are likely to be present.
5	10–12	The answer contains accurate evidence (from studies and/or theories) and effectively applies relevant ideas to the situation given. Evidence and application are well balanced. Clarity of expression and organisation are effective and the candidate makes good use of relevant terminology. Few spelling, punctuation or grammatical errors are present.

Indicative content:

- **Social identity theory (SIT) says that people classify others into groups, this is social classification; (AO1)**
- **The boys could do this using clothing; (AO2)**
- **SIT says we identify with our own group and show that we belong, this is social identification; (AO1)**
- **'The Hards' do this by having tattoos; (AO2)**
- **SIT says social comparison causes people to judge other groups; (AO2)**
- **When the boys do this they decide their own group is best; (AO2)**
- **This is one cause of their violent behaviour as they lose respect for the other group; (AO2)**

Resources

See PowerPoint file 2-24 *Resources*.

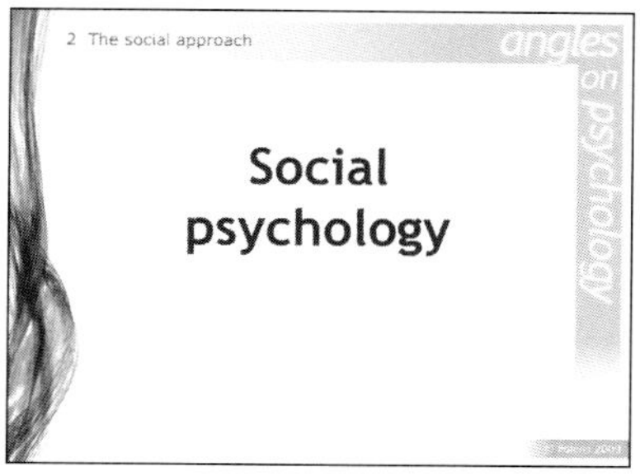

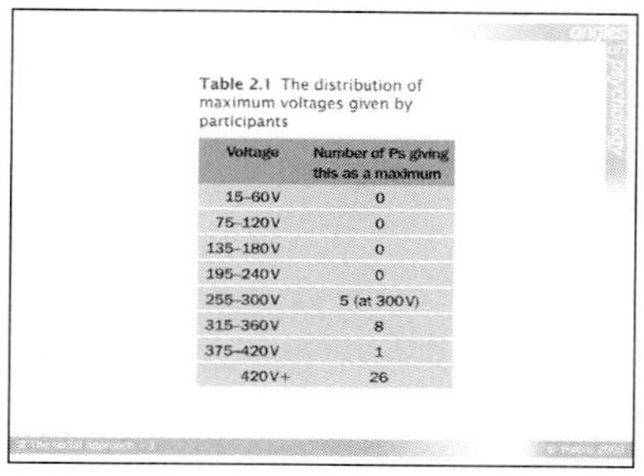

Table 2.1 The distribution of maximum voltages given by participants

Voltage	Number of Ps giving this as a maximum
15–60V	0
75–120V	0
135–180V	0
195–240V	0
255–300V	5 (at 300V)
315–360V	8
375–420V	1
420V+	26

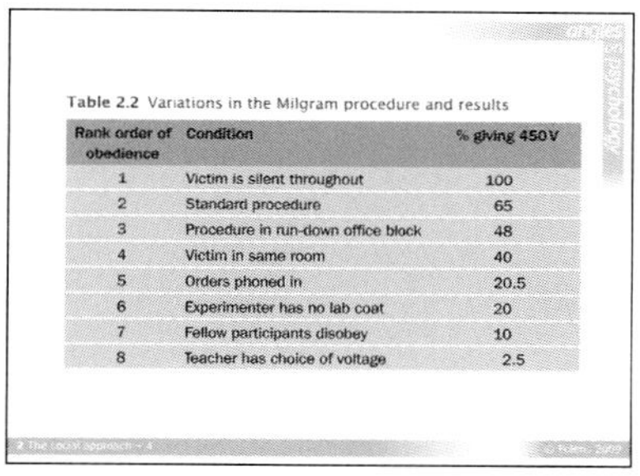

Table 2.2 Variations in the Milgram procedure and results

Rank order of obedience	Condition	% giving 450V
1	Victim is silent throughout	100
2	Standard procedure	65
3	Procedure in run-down office block	48
4	Victim in same room	40
5	Orders phoned in	20.5
6	Experimenter has no lab coat	20
7	Fellow participants disobey	10
8	Teacher has choice of voltage	2.5

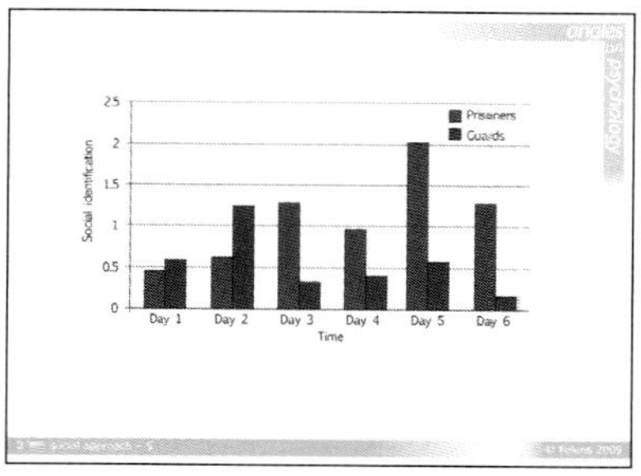

References

Bushman, B.B. & Bonacci, A.M. (2004) 'You've got mail: Using e-mail to examine the effect of prejudiced attitudes on discrimination against Arabs'. *Journal of Experimental Social Psychology*, 40: 753–59.

Geher, G., Bauman, K.P., Hubbard, S.E.K. & Legare, J.R. (2002) 'Self and other obedience estimates: Biases and moderators'. *Journal of Social Psychology*, 142(6): 677–89.

Chapter 3

The cognitive approach

Activity number	Activity title	Activity/file type
The cognitive approach		
3.1	Introduction	ST PP
3.2	Levels of processing theory	CE SC A
3.3	Kim's game: a test of short-term memory capacity	ST CA PP TN
3.4	Features of short-term memory	CA PP TN
3.5	The multi-store model	CE A
3.6	Cue-dependent theory of forgetting	CE A
3.7	Applying theories of memory to advertising	SAQ SC
3.8	Applying theories of learning to improving memory	SAQ SC
3.9	Applying theories of forgetting	SAQ
3.10	Cognitive psychology and revision	SAQ
3.11	Cognitive theories	WM SC A
3.12	Godden & Baddeley (1975)	CE A
3.13	Cognitive snap!	WM TN prep CA
3.14	Amnesia	MW
3.15	The experimental method	CE A
3.16	LoP game	CA TN prep
3.17	Interactive quiz	CA PP
3.18	Essays: Questions 1 and 2	LAQ
3.19	What makes adverts work?	ET SAQ
3.20	Creative activities: 1 and 2	KI
3.21	Evidence of practice: short experiment	RM
3.22	Memory for faces	RM
3.23	Instant recall	RM
3.24	The cognitive approach quick quiz	QQ A
3.25	Cognitive test	AT A
3.26	Resources	PP
3.27	References	

Introduction

See PowerPoint 3-1 *Introduction*.

This brief slideshow introduces aspects of cognition and memory.

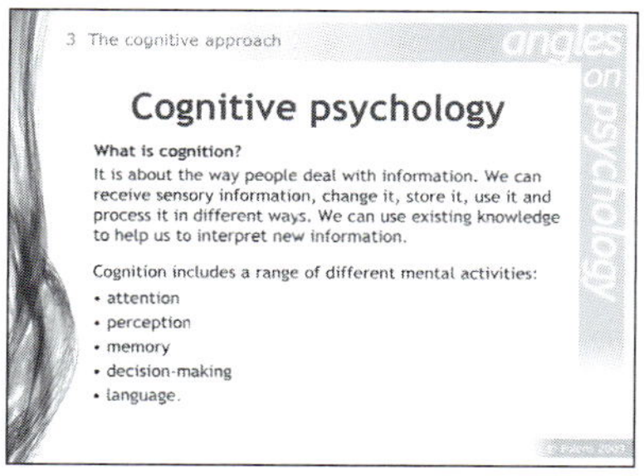

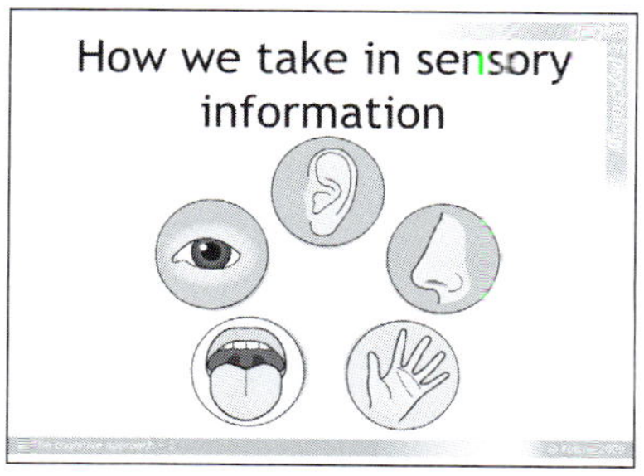

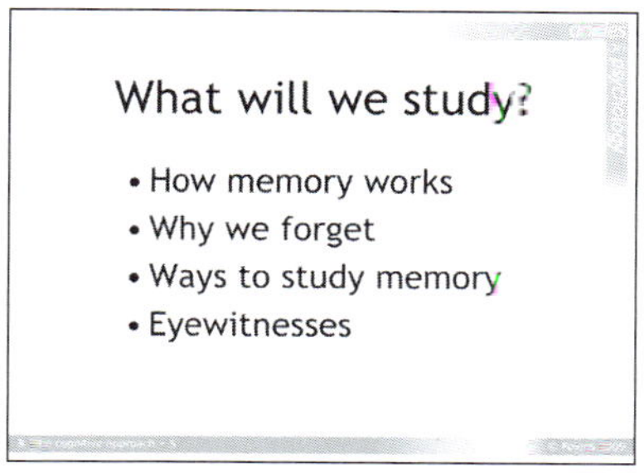

Levels of processing theory

Levels of processing is a ____________ that attempts to explain why we can recall some memories more easily than others. It was proposed by ____________ & ____________ (1972). It suggests that ____________ processing causes better memory than ____________ processing. So it is saying that when we encode information and use it, the more we have to *do* with that information, the better we will recall it. This is because memory is a ____________ of processing. The best encoding or processing usually requires us to deal with ____________, and is sometimes called semantic processing. An example of this kind of processing would be that required when we consider the question: 'Is a boat a kind of food?' The encoding that results in the poorest recall often results from processes such as looking at the shape of stimuli, and is called ____________ processing. An example of this would be answering the question: 'Is the word GHOST in capital letters?' Intermediate between these two is ____________ processing, which involves the sound of the stimulus, such as whether two words ____________. An example of a question causing this type of processing would be 'Does the word lamb rhyme with dram?'

by-product	meaning	structural
Craik	phonemic	theory
deep	rhyme	
Lockhart	shallow	

Stretch and challenge

1. There are many ways to elicit the different levels of processing. For example, you could show people pictures of animals like the ones below and ask them three types of question:
   a) is the animal ...? dangerous / edible / fast moving
   b) does the noise it makes rhyme with ...? glue / star / muck
   c) is the colour of its coat ...? brown / white / yellow
2. Which of the questions above tests each of the levels of processing?
3. Create at least one alternative way to test levels of processing.

Levels of processing theory

Answers

Levels of processing is a **theory** that attempts to explain why we can recall some memories more easily than others. It was proposed by **Craik** & **Lockhart** (1972). It suggests that **deep** processing causes better memory than **shallow** processing. So it is saying that when we encode information and use it, the more we have to do with that information, the better we will recall it. This is because memory is a **by-product** of processing. The best encoding or processing usually requires us to deal with **meaning**, and is sometimes called semantic processing. An example of this kind of processing would be that required when we consider the question: 'Is a boat a kind of food?' The encoding that results in the poorest recall often results from processes such as looking at the shape of stimuli, and is called **structural** processing. An example of this would be answering the question: 'Is the word GHOST in capital letters?' Intermediate between these two is **phonemic** processing, which involves the sound of the stimulus, such as whether two words **rhyme**. An example of a question causing this type of processing would be 'Does the word lamb rhyme with dram?'

theory	shallow	phonemic
Craik	by-product	rhyme
Lockhart	meaning	
deep	structural	

Kim's game: a test of short-term memory capacity

See PowerPoint 3-3 *Kim's game*. This could be run in PowerPoint, or could be used as a pack of cards printed from the presentation.

To run the PowerPoint presentation in class

Provide each student with paper and a pen. You might like to warn them that it is a memory test but that they must not write anything down until they are instructed. The sequence of instructions and images is timed until the end of the images, where it will pause. To continue from the screen saying 'Now write down as many of the items that you have just seen as you can' you will need to left-click the mouse.

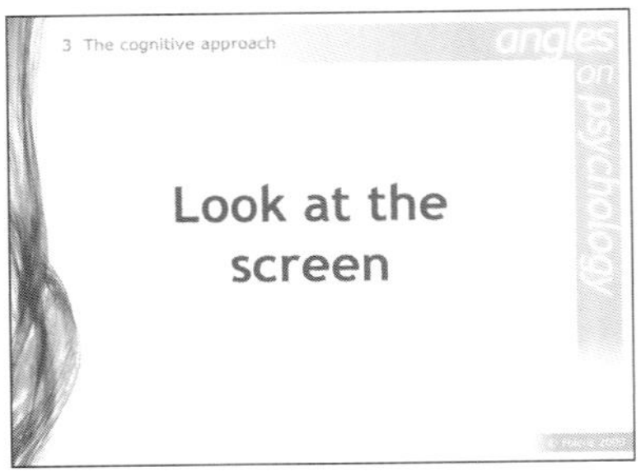

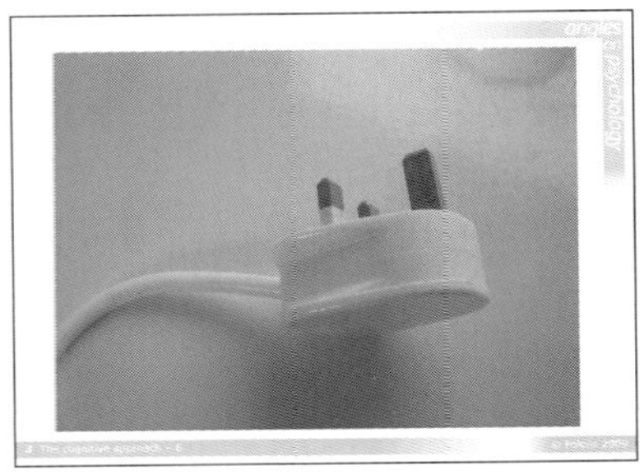

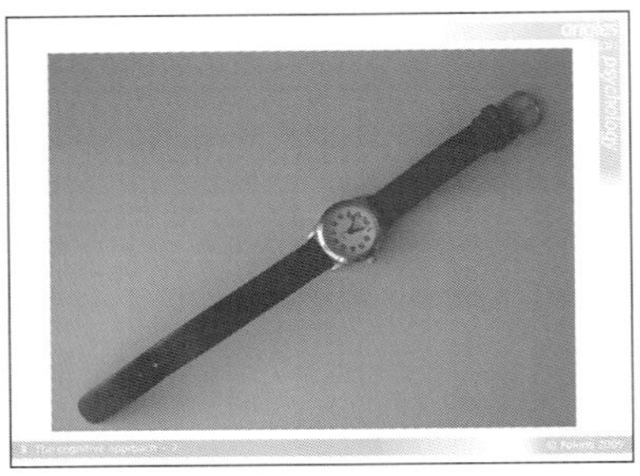

Kim's game: a test of short-term memory capacity *continued*

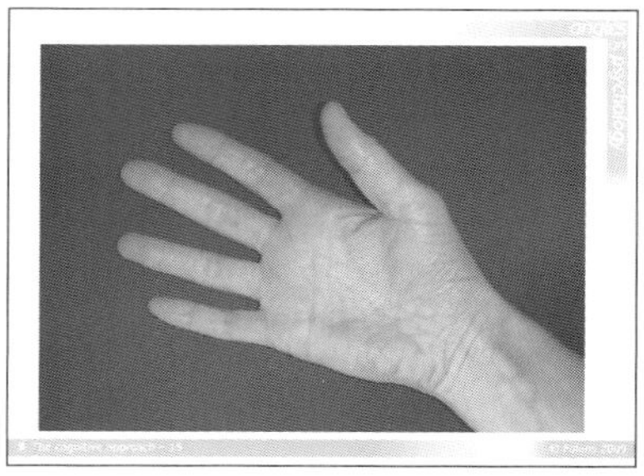

Wait for the next instruction.

Now write down as many of the items that you have just seen as you can. They do not have to be in order.

Click to check answers

Now check how many of them you remembered:

- Leaf
- Tape
- Cotton (reel)
- Robin
- Plug
- Watch
- Pony
- Apple
- Key
- Car
- Rabbit
- Frog
- Butterfly
- Hand
- Cockerel
- Toadstool
- Balloon
- Orange
- Cow
- Teapot
- Flower

Features of short-term memory

See PowerPoint 3-4 *STM displacement*. This could be run in PowerPoint, or could be used as a pack of cards printed from the presentation.

To run the PowerPoint presentation in class

The slides show an animation of Peterson & Peterson's (1959) graph, an animation of displacement and end with a replication of Baddeley (1960). To do the latter, students need to be provided with paper and pen. They will be warned that it is a memory test. A single screen of words follows. The students are then prompted for immediate recall (from STM). You should then leave a 20-minute gap (or longer) for recall from LTM. The list of words can then be presented again, with the words in categories so that the students can see if they have made more sound-alike errors on immediate recall and similar meaning errors on long-term recall.

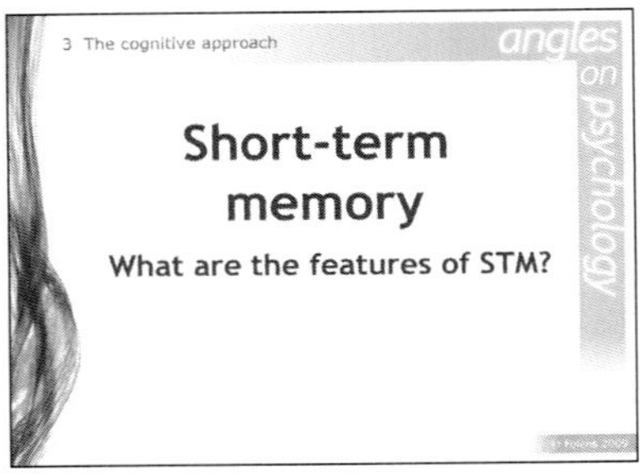

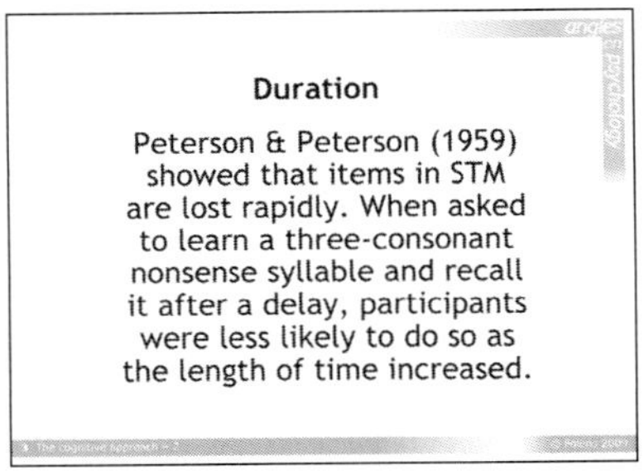

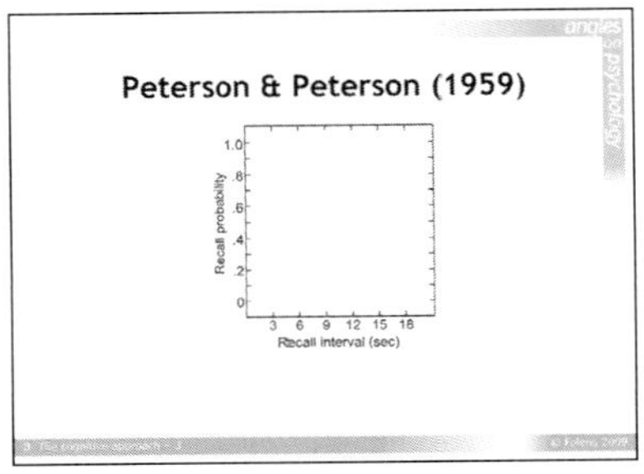

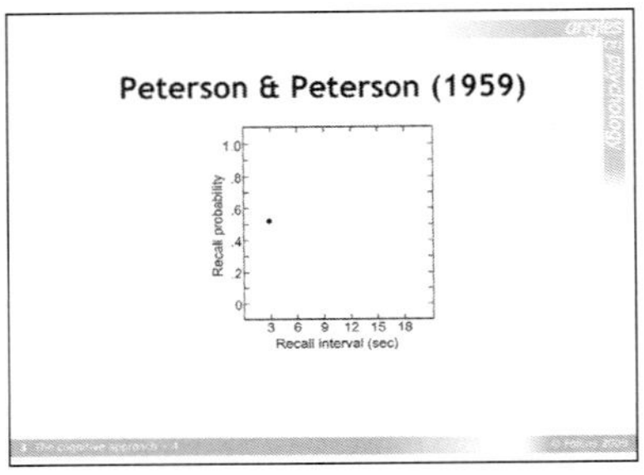

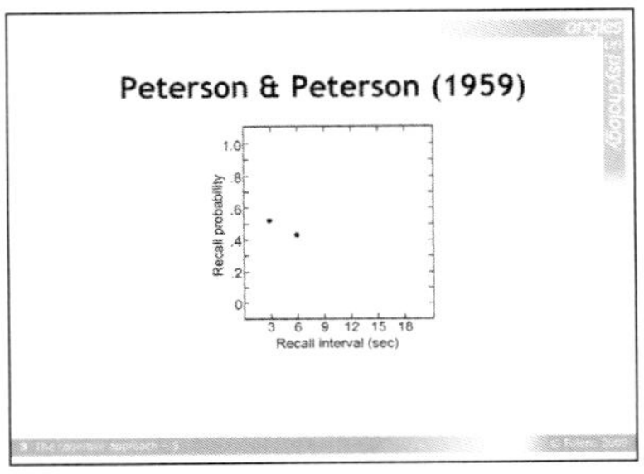

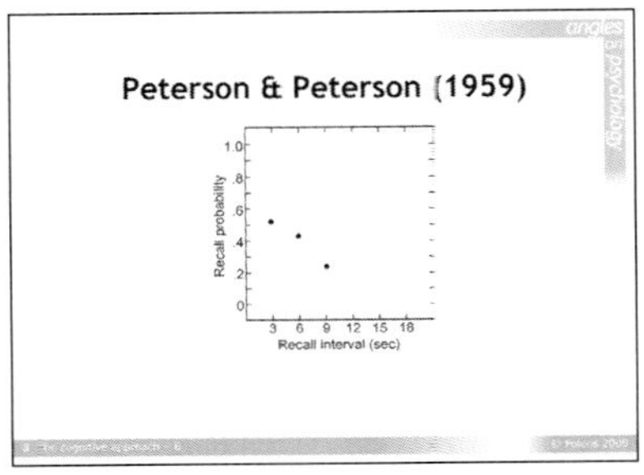

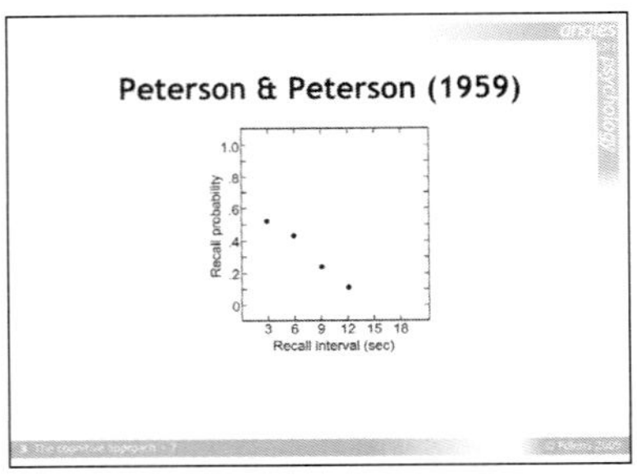

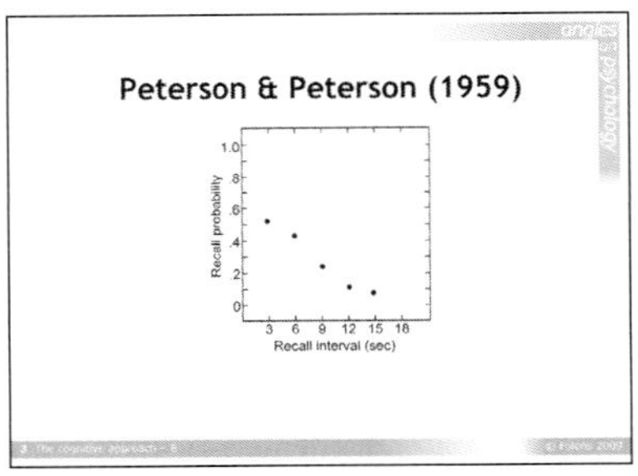

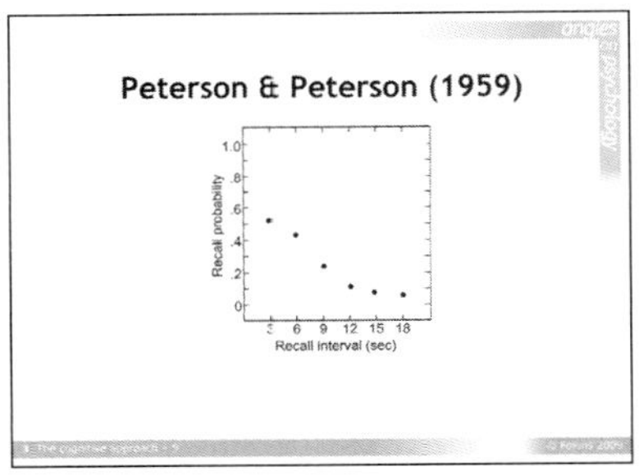

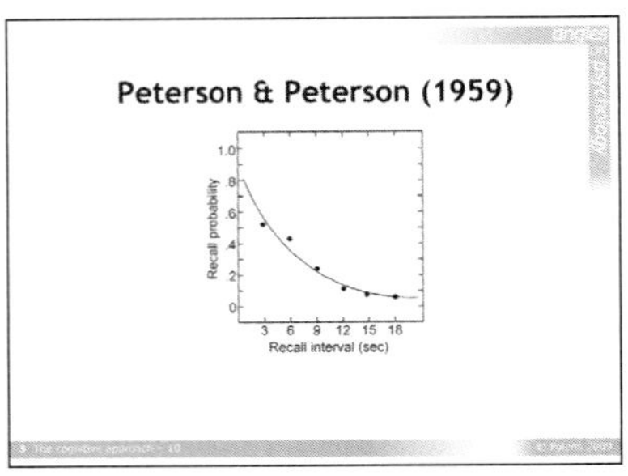

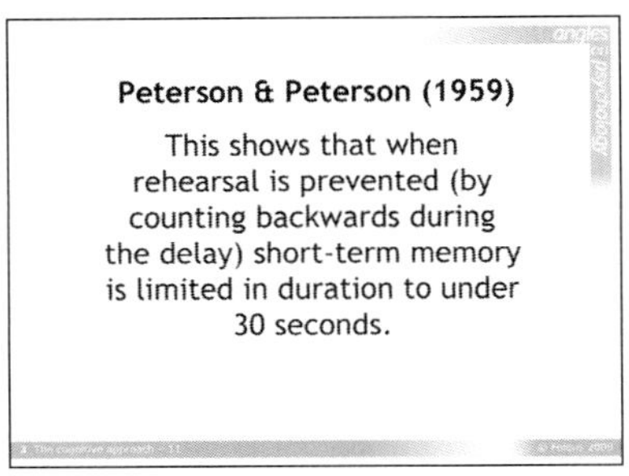

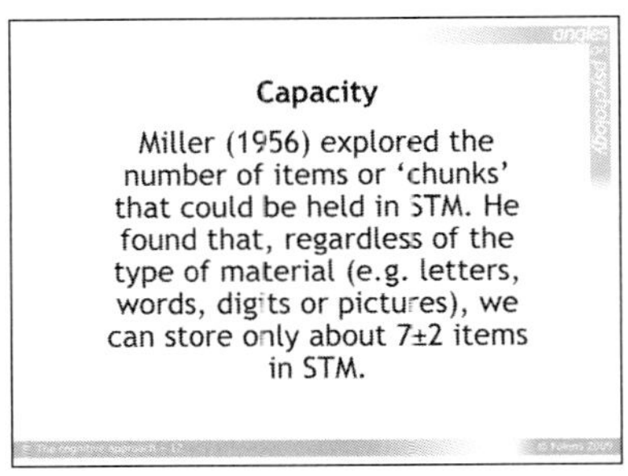

Features of short-term memory *continued*

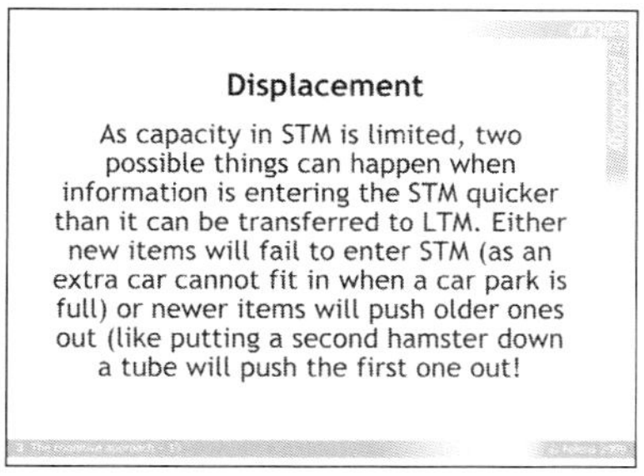

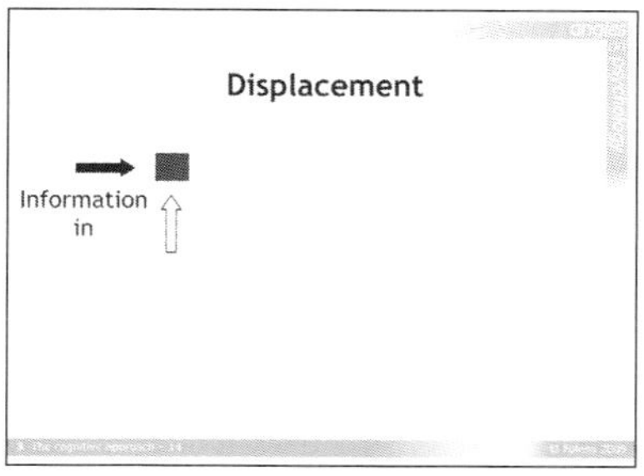

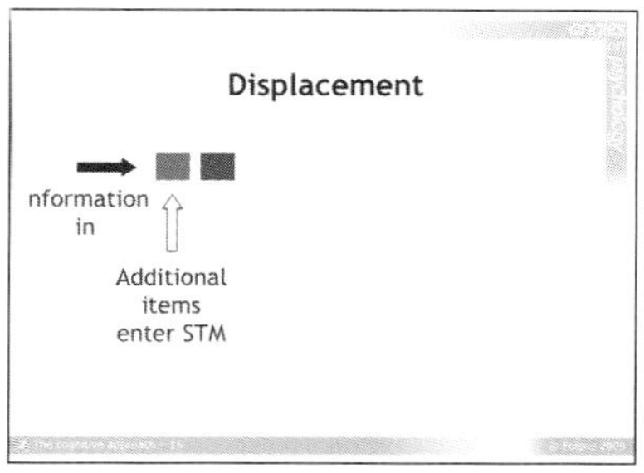

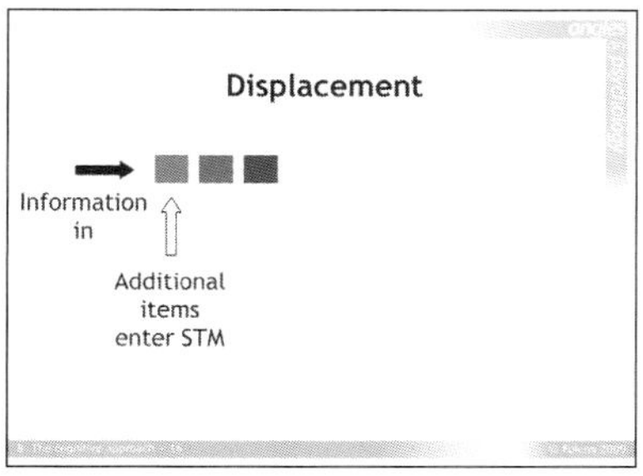

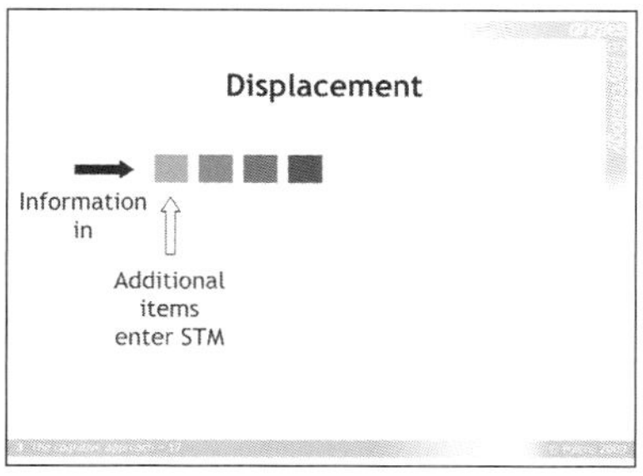

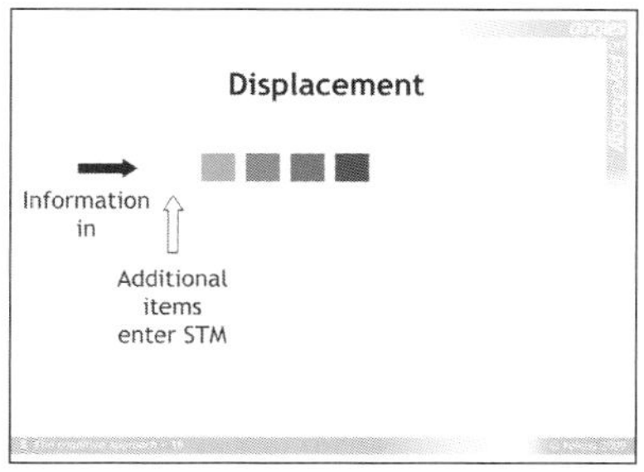

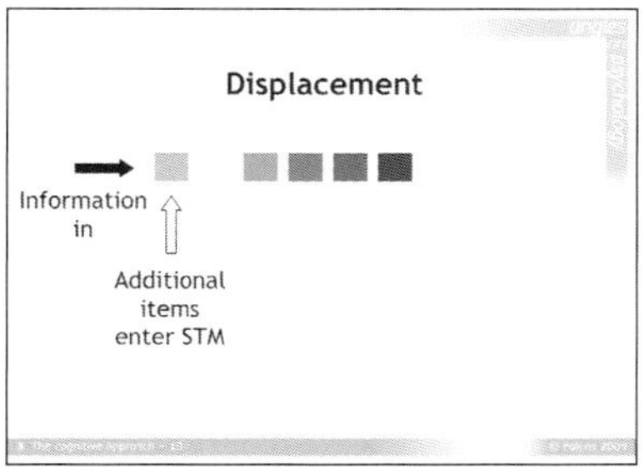

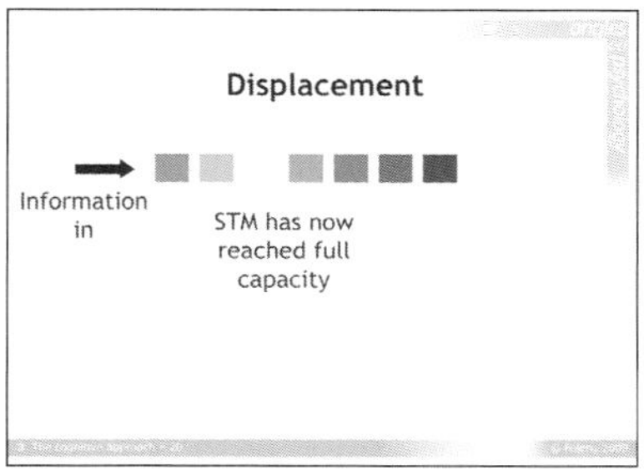

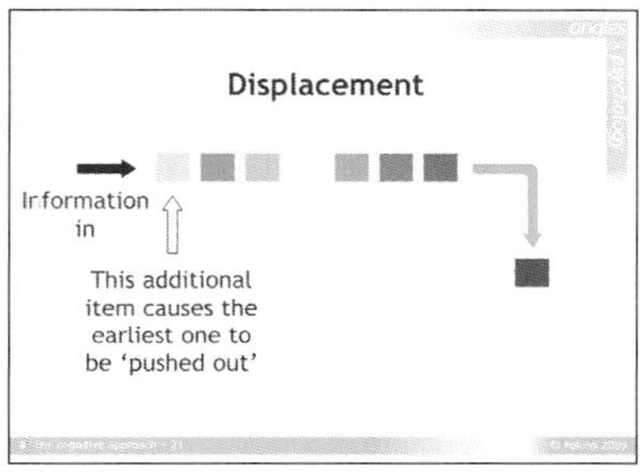

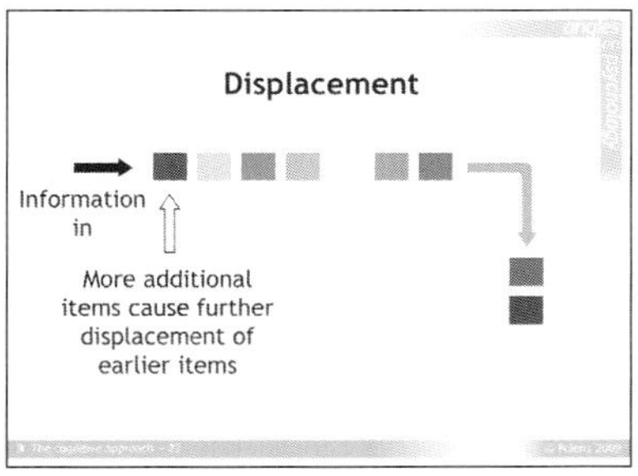

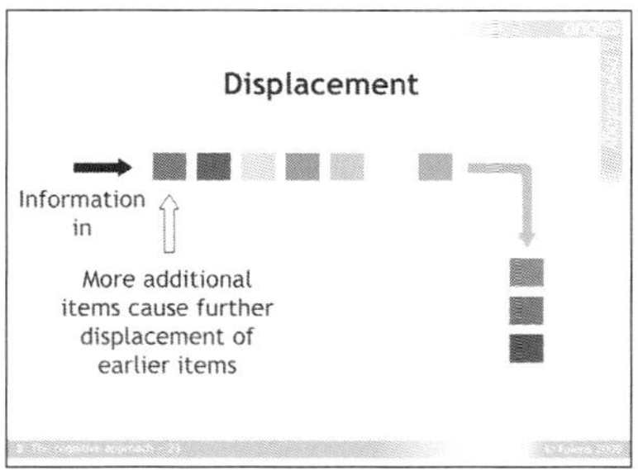

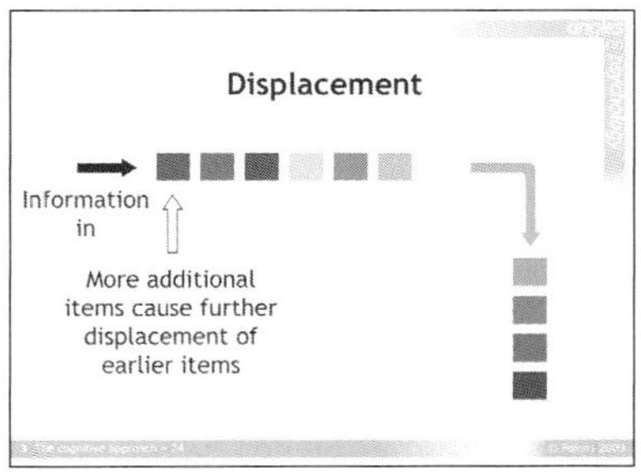

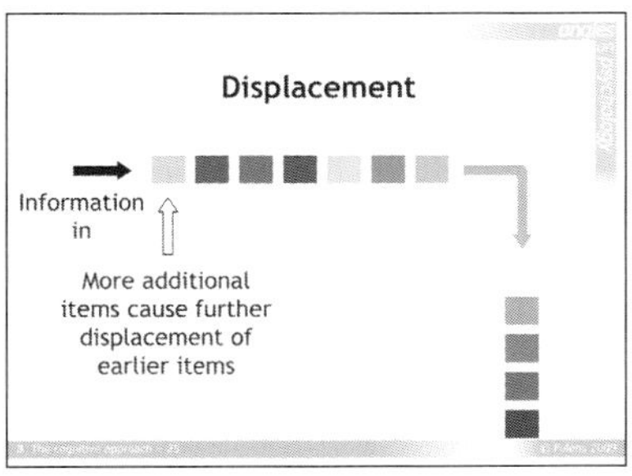

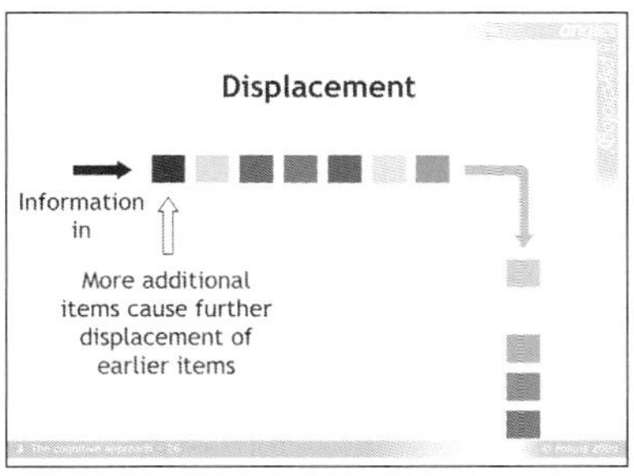

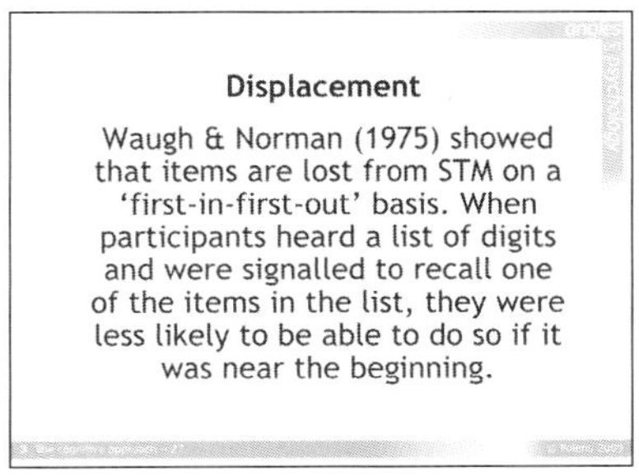

Features of short-term memory *continued*

Encoding

Baddeley (1966) showed that items in STM tended to become muddled when they sounded similar. When asked to learn and immediately recall a list of words, participants made more errors on those that sounded alike.

Encoding

Try this test.

A list of words will appear. Read them carefully, as you will have to recall them.

Have a pen and paper ready.

mad	day	tall
big	late	man
pen	mat	broad
map	strong	hot
can	foul	cap
wide	safe	great
cat	large	bar
old	pit	high

Now write down as many words as you can.

We will talk about the results later.

pause

Write down as many words as you can from the list you saw earlier.

pause

mad	day	tall
mat	late	big
man	pen	broad
map	strong	wide
cat	hot	great
can	foul	high
cap	safe	large
	bar	
	pit	
	old	

Acoustically Similar	Control	Semantically Similar
mad	day	tall
mat	late	big
man	pen	broad
map	strong	wide
cat	hot	great
can	foul	high
cap	safe	large
	bar	
	pit	
	old	

The multi-store model

The multi-store model (MSM) was proposed by _____________ & _____________ (1972). It is a structural model of memory because it suggests that our memory can be understood in terms of different memory stores. The three proposed memory stores are as follows:

_____________ (STSS): This receives incoming information from the senses and is _____________; that is, information from each sensory system is encoded in the corresponding sensory format (for example, visual stimuli are encoded as visual signals). Three types of STSS have been investigated. These are the _____________ memory – for vision, the _____________ memory – for hearing and the _____________ memory – for touch. The duration of memories in STSS is very _____________ . The capacity of STSS seems to be surprisingly large, with some information being remembered in its entirety; for example, Sperling (1960) demonstrated this for the visual STSS using a matrix array. His results suggested that retrieval was virtually perfect for a very short time. Forgetting therefore occurs by decay, although it may also happen because information that has not been _____________ to will never have been encoded.

_____________ (STM): This store receives information from STSS and it uses _____________ to transfer information to LTM. It has a limited capacity of 7 ± 2 _____________ or items and a limited duration of 30 _____________. If information enters STM more quickly than it can be consolidated and transferred to LTM, then forgetting occurs by displacement. Much of STM is encoded in an _____________ form, although this is not the case for all STM functions.

_____________ (LTM): This store has the greatest duration and capacity; nevertheless, forgetting still occurs – at least we seem to be unable to access all our memories. Encoding in LTM is _____________; that is, information is stored on the basis of meaning. Retrieval from LTM may use several mechanisms including various kinds of _____________, such as context and state.

acoustic	haptic	semantic
Atkinson	iconic	Shiffrin
attended	long-term memory	short
chunks	modality specific	short-term memory
cues	rehearsal	short-term sensory store
echoic	seconds	

The multi-store model

Answers

The Multi Store Model (MSM) was proposed by **Atkinson** & **Shiffrin** (1968). It is a structural model of memory because it suggests that our memory can be understood in terms of different memory stores. The three proposed memory stores are as follows:

Short-term sensory store (STSS): This receives incoming information from the senses and is **modality specific**; that is, information from each sensory system is encoded in the corresponding sensory format (for example, visual stimuli are encoded as visual signals). Three types of STSS have been investigated. These are the **iconic** memory – for vision, the **echoic** memory – for hearing and the **haptic** memory – for touch. The duration of memories in STSS is very **short**. The capacity of STSS seems to be surprisingly large, with some information being remembered in its entirety; for example, Sperling (1960) demonstrated this for the visual STSS using a matrix array. His results suggested that retrieval was virtually perfect for a very short time. Forgetting therefore occurs by decay, although it may also happen because information that has not been **attended** to will never have been encoded.

Short-term memory (STM): This store receives information from STSS and it uses **rehearsal** to transfer information to LTM. It has a limited capacity of 7 ± 2 **chunks** or items and a limited duration of 30 **seconds**. If information enters STM more quickly than it can be consolidated and transferred to LTM, then forgetting occurs by displacement. Much of STM is encoded in an **acoustic** form, although this is not the case for all STM functions.

Long-term memory (LTM): This store has the greatest duration and capacity; nevertheless, forgetting still occurs – at least we seem to be unable to access all our memories. Encoding in LTM is **semantic**; that is, information is stored on the basis of meaning. Retrieval from LTM may use several mechanisms including various kinds of **cues**, such as context and state.

Atkinson	haptic	seconds
Shiffrin	short	acoustic
short-term sensory store	attended	long-term memory
modality specific	short-term memory	semantic
iconic	rehearsal	cues
echoic	chunks	

Cue-dependent theory of forgetting

Tulving (1972) suggested that *cues* are extra pieces of information that help to locate an item in ____________. According to his theory, these cues must be encoded at the ____________ time as the memory itself, i.e. as key information to help retrieval. If cues are *absent* when recall is attempted, ____________ will occur. Context cues are features of the ____________ that trigger the location of a memory (e.g. a smell, sight or place). State cues are ____________ triggers; they may be ____________ (e.g. another memory), ____________ (e.g. a drug) or ____________ (e.g. a mood).

There is evidence to support cue dependency, e.g. the ____________ conducted by Godden & Baddeley (1975). In this study the independent variable was whether the participants were in the same context or a different context when learning and recalling. They were either on ____________ or in the ____________. The dependent variable was the number of ____________ they recalled from a list. Their findings showed that recall was ____________ when the participants were in a different situation, regardless of where they were. Experiments such as this are well ____________ so the researchers can be sure that it is the effect of the absence of cues that causes forgetting, rather than some other variable. This certainty is an indicator of the ____________ of the study.

Similar results were produced by Baker *et al.* (2004). They showed that when participants learn while ____________ they then recall ____________ when they can do this again than if they cannot. The important factor is that the cues that are encoded during learning are also present during recall otherwise forgetting is likely to occur as it is more difficult to ____________ the memories.

Furthermore, cue dependency has practical applications. For example Abernethy (1940) showed that context could help in education. She found that students performed better when they sat their exams in the ____________ room as they had learned their work. Similarly, Jerabek & Standing (1992) showed that context reinstatement during exams, where students simply imagined the classroom, also improved ____________. This idea has also been used to help solve crimes. Eyewitnesses are more likely to remember events they have observed if they imagine the scene, as this provides cues for recall. This technique has been applied to help the police. It can be used in both ____________ reconstruction and in the cognitive interview where questions are used to help witnesses to find alternative paths to the memory.

One criticism of the cue-dependency theory is that context and state effects may not be ____________; it may simply be that particular ____________ evoke corresponding ____________, so all effects are, in fact, ____________ -dependent. For example, a nervous student in an exam may visualise their classroom as a way to reinstate context. However, this may actually work because imagining the classroom returns them to a relaxed but alert state of mind and it is this that acts as a ____________ and triggers their recall. Another criticism is that the theory fails to account for the fact that some emotionally charged memories appear to be very ____________ remembered (e.g. flashbulb memories) while others are ____________ completely (e.g. in repression).

Cue-dependent theory of forgetting *continued*

better
chewing gum
cognitive
contexts
controlled
crime scene
cue
different
emotional
environment
field experiment
forgetting
forgotten
internal
land
LTM
physiological
recall
retrieve
same
same
state
states
validity
water
well
words
worse

Cue-dependent theory of forgetting

Answers

Tulving (1972) suggested that *cues* are extra pieces of information that help to locate an item in **LTM**. According to his theory, these cues must be encoded at the **same** time as the memory itself, i.e. as key information to help retrieval. If cues are *absent* when recall is attempted, **forgetting** will occur. Context cues are features of the **environment** that trigger the location of a memory (e.g. a smell, sight or place). State cues are **internal** triggers; they may be **cognitive** (e.g. another memory), **physiological** (e.g. a drug) or **emotional** (e.g. a mood).

There is evidence to support cue dependency, e.g. the **field experiment** conducted by Godden & Baddeley (1975). In this study the independent variable was whether the participants were in the same context or a different context when learning and recalling. They were either on **land** or in the **water**. The dependent variable was the number of **words** they recalled from a list. Their findings showed that recall was **worse** when the participants were in a different situation, regardless of where they were. Experiments such as this are well **controlled** so the researchers can be sure that it is the effect of the absence of cues that causes forgetting, rather than some other variable. This certainty is an indicator of the **validity** of the study.

Similar results were produced by Baker *et al.* (2004). They showed that when participants learn while **chewing gum** they then recall **better** when they can do this again than if they cannot. The important factor is that the cues that are encoded during learning are also present during recall otherwise forgetting is likely to occur as it is more difficult to **retrieve** the memories.

Furthermore, cue dependency has practical applications. For example Abernethy (1940) showed that context could help in education. She found that students performed better when they sat their exams in the **same** room as they had learned their work. Similarly, Jerabek & Standing (1992) showed that context reinstatement during exams, where students simply imagined the classroom, also improved **recall**. This idea has also been used to help solve crimes. Eyewitnesses are more likely to remember events they have observed if they imagine the scene, as this provides cues for recall. This technique has been applied to help the police. It can be used in both **crime scene** reconstruction and in the cognitive interview where questions are used to help witnesses to find alternative paths to the memory.

One criticism of the cue-dependency theory is that context and state effects may not be **different**; it may simply be that particular **contexts** evoke corresponding **states,** so all effects are, in fact, **state**-dependent. For example, a nervous student in an exam may visualise their classroom as a way to reinstate context. However, this may actually work because imagining the classroom returns them to a relaxed but alert state of mind and it is this that acts as a **cue** and triggers their recall. Another criticism is that the theory fails to account for the fact that some emotionally charged memories appear to be very **well** remembered (e.g. flashbulb memories) while others are **forgotten** completely (e.g. in repression).

Cue-dependent theory of forgetting

Answers *continued*

LTM
same
forgetting
environment
internal
cognitive
physiological
emotional
field experiment
land
water
words
worse
controlled
validity
chewing gum
better
retrieve
same
recall
crime scene
different
contexts
states
state
cue
well
forgotten

Applying theories of memory to advertising

Kristen is a graphic artist working in a team planning an advertising campaign for ice cream. She has come up with a series of possible billboard designs. One version, called 'Ices', depicts a grinning child with an ice cream cone in each hand; another called 'Whippo' has a scene under the midday sun with a cowboy on a horse, lassoing an ice cream vendor selling 'Whippo', and a third, called 'Charlie's Chilly Choc Ice', shows children queuing at a van above which an aeroplane flies bearing a banner saying 'Children choose Charlie's cheap 'n' cheerful Chilly Chocs'.

1. a) Kristen's designs are based on a theory of memory suggested by a colleague. Identify and outline the theory of memory that best explains Kristen's choices. [3 marks]

   b) Describe how the theory of memory you have outlined in part (a) can explain how each of the advertisements Kristen has designed would work. [3 marks]

2. a) Which of the advertisements would you expect to be most effective? [1 mark]

   b) Justify your answer to part (a) using the findings of psychological research. [4 marks]

Stretch and challenge

1. Look through a magazine such as a Sunday supplement for advertisements.

   a) Find three advertisements, one using each of the levels of processing to improve product retention by potential consumers.

   b) i) Which advertisement do you think will be the most effective?

      ii) Why do you think it will be effective?

      iii) Which level of processing does it use?

      iv) Does it use more than one memory aid?

2. Either invent a product or choose a product for which you have not seen adverts.

   Design three advertisements, each using one of the three levels of processing.

Applying theories of learning to improving memory

Dennis has just started a part-time job and is finding it difficult to remember the names of all the different hair products at the beauty salon. He asks Kate, one of his friends at college who is studying psychology, if she knows of any techniques that might help him. At first, she suggests repeating the names over and over again; then, when this doesn't help much, she recommends trying to find things he can remember that rhyme with each product. Finally, she says that the best way to memorise them is to use meaning, trying to think about what each one is for.

1. Identify **two** theories of memory that Kate might be using to make her recommendations and justify your choices. [4 marks]
2. Why does Kate suggest that using meanings would be more effective than using rhymes? [2 marks]
3. Suggest **one** other way that Kate could help Dennis to remember the product names and explain, using any theory of memory or forgetting, how this would help him. [3 marks]

Stretch and challenge

1. Consider the practical challenges faced by people at your school or college.
   - Are there new staff or students?
   - Do they need to learn a new timetable?
   - Is it an unfamiliar site, so do they need to find their way around?
   - Have you had to learn new names? Your teachers are certainly likely to need to.

   a) Select **two** problems such as these and devise different strategies for each one.

   b) Think about the evidence you would use to justify those strategies.

Applying theories of forgetting

> The local DIY shop is looking for new staff. Erica has applied for a job and is worried because she knows that she will have to learn the entire contents of each aisle in the store. She has walked up and down the rows looking at the products and doesn't know where to begin.

1. Erica thinks that by the time she gets to the interview she will have forgotten everything she has already learned about the products. Identify a theory that could account for this problem and why Erica may indeed have forgotten everything when she gets to the interview. [3 marks]
2. When Erica attends her interview there are three interviewers in the room. The store manager asks her a question and then one of the other people ask her another. By the time she has answered the second question she has completely forgotten the first. Why? [3 marks]
3. Erica gets the job! On her first day she is walked up and down the aisles and told the product names. A couple of hours later she is on her own and is approached by a customer who asks where to find batteries. She tries to remember but can't, so walks along the ends of the aisles until she remembers where the batteries are located. Identify an appropriate theory and explain why Erica can't remember where the batteries were located until she finds the right aisle. [4 marks]
4. During her first few days in her new job Erica is very scared but learns a great deal about the shop's layout. After the first week she finds that she is less scared but can remember even less! Why might this be? [2 marks]

Cognitive psychology and revision

> Megan is revising for her AS examinations. She has tried re-reading her notes and repeating them to herself. Her friend Stephanie suggests that she might try using mnemonics such as rhymes and writing out questions so that someone else can ask Megan what she understands.

1. What is the purpose of re-reading notes? [2 marks]
2. Identify a theory that could account for the effectiveness of rhyming memory aids. [1 mark]
3. Explain how the use of rhyming memory aids could help Megan to learn according to the theory you identified in question 2. [3 marks]
4. Describe **one** strength and **one** weakness of the theory you have identified and described. [4 marks]

Cognitive theories

Hannah is doing work experience at a local residential home. Some of the residents have memory problems and she is trying to help them by applying what she knows about theories of memory and forgetting.

Use lines to pair up the following ideas correctly.

Theory
Cue-dependent forgetting
Multi-store model
Levels of processing
Displacement

Explanation
One resident, Betty, is trying to remember to collect several items from the kitchen. Hannah has suggested that Betty doesn't try to remember more than seven items at one time.
Following a fall, Godfrey has suffered amnesia. He keeps forgetting where he has put things down. Hannah's recommendation is to walk back to each room he has visited rather than just sitting still and worrying.
An elderly resident, Flo, can't remember the order in which she is supposed to press the buttons on the mobile phone her grandson has bought her in order to call up the phone book. Hannah is helping her by asking her to demonstrate it each morning and afternoon.
Hector has suffered a stroke and is experiencing difficulty with the names of the care workers. He is good at writing poems, so they have worked out little rhymes that each includes the name of a member of staff and a description of their appearance.

Stretch and challenge

Design a leaflet for Hannah's residential home explaining to new staff various ways that they could help to improve the residents' memories. Include the other two levels of processing that Hannah has not employed. Justify your recommendations with evidence.

Cognitive theories

Answers

Theory
Cue-dependent forgetting
Multi-store model
Levels of processing
Displacement

Explanation
One resident, Betty, is trying to remember to collect several items from the kitchen. Hannah has suggested that Betty doesn't try to remember more than seven items at one time.
Following a fall, Godfrey has suffered amnesia. He keeps forgetting where he has put things down. Hannah's recommendation is to walk back to each room he has visited rather than just sitting still and worrying.
An elderly resident, Flo, can't remember the order in which she is supposed to press the buttons on the mobile phone her grandson has bought her in order to call up the phone book. Hannah is helping her by asking her to demonstrate it each morning and afternoon.
Hector has suffered a stroke and is experiencing difficulty with the names of the care workers. He is good at writing poems, so they have worked out little rhymes that each includes the name of a member of staff and a description of their appearance.

Godden & Baddeley (1975)

Godden & Baddeley (1975) investigated _____________-dependent memory. They were testing the idea that recall of _____________ when the _____________ and recall environments were the same would be better than when they were different.

The participants were 13 male and 5 female _____________ divers, each using their own scuba equipment. This ensured that the participants were not at any _____________ risk than they would have been in their normal life, so satisfied the ethical guideline which states that participants have a right to be protected from _____________. The participants learned word lists presented on _____________ either on land or _____________ feet under water. The words were heard in blocks of 3 at a rate of one word every 2 seconds. There was a 4-second gap between blocks so the divers could breathe without the noise of their apparatus interfering with their _____________. They practised this breathing pattern before each testing session. The list of words was presented twice, with a 10-second gap in between. Finally the participant heard 15 digits which they copied down, followed by an instruction (e.g. to return to the shore), then _____________ for 4 minutes. They then _____________ the words either in the same or the other environment by writing them in pencil on a plastic-covered board. They were allowed 2 minutes to recall the words in any order. Each participant was tested in each of the _____________ possible combinations of environments: land/land, land/water, water/water, water/land. The research method was therefore a _____________ with a _____________ design. There were approximately 24 hours between sessions for each individual. The two levels of the independent variable were whether the environments were _____________ or _____________.

Participants were tested at the end of a day's diving so that they all began testing in approximately the same _____________, i.e. cold and wet. In the 'under water' condition, the divers were heavily weighted so that they could _____________ easily on the bottom. In the 'on land' condition, the participants sat at the edge of the water with their scuba equipment _____________ but with their masks tipped back and breathing tubes _____________. These controls helped to ensure that _____________, comfort and noise were similar in both environments. Some unavoidable situational variables arose. Most of the 'under water' testing was done in the sea, although at various locations, and for two participants, a freshwater site was used. For _____________ and equipment failure reasons, gaps between testing were not always 24 hours. During one session, a participant was nearly run over by an ex-army amphibious truck!

Recall was not affected by whether the words had initially been _____________ on land or under the water. Accuracy was similar for 'learn and recall on land' (mean 13.5 words) and 'learn and recall in water' (mean 11.4 words). However, when recall took place in a different location from learning, more words were _____________: 'learn in water and recall on land' (mean 8.4 words) and 'learn on land and recall in water' (mean 8.6 words).

This difference could have been due to the _____________ of changing environment so 16 more participants were tested in the land/land condition. The procedure was either the same as before (_____________) or, during the waiting time, the participants were instructed to enter the water, _____________ a short distance, _____________ to about 20 feet and return (_____________). The mean scores were: non-disrupted 8.44 words, disrupted 8.69 words. This difference was very _____________ and in _____________ direction to that expected if disruption, rather than the effect of context, were the reason for the difference seen in the main experiment. Therefore it can be concluded that context cues provided by the physical environment do improve recall.

Godden & Baddeley (1975) *continued*

4	field experiment	off	state
20	forgotten	on	swim
audiotape	greater	physical harm	the opposite
context	health	position	the same
different	hearing	recalled	trained
disrupted	learned	repeated measures	waited
disruption	learning	sit	words
dive	non-disrupted	small	

Godden & Baddeley (1975)

Answers

Godden & Baddeley (1975) investigated **context**-dependent memory. They were testing the idea that recall of **words** when the **learning** and recall environments were the same would be better than when they were different.

The participants were 13 male and 5 female **trained** divers, each using their own scuba equipment. This ensured that the participants were not at any **greater** risk than they would have been in their normal life, so satisfied the ethical guideline which states that participants have a right to be protected from **physical harm**. The participants learned word lists presented on **audiotape** either on land or **20** feet under water. The words were heard in blocks of 3 at a rate of one word every 2 seconds. There was a 4-second gap between blocks so the divers could breathe without the noise of their apparatus interfering with their **hearing**. They practised this breathing pattern before each testing session. The list of words was presented twice, with a 10-second gap in between. Finally the participant heard 15 digits which they copied down, followed by an instruction (e.g. to return to the shore), then **waited** for 4 minutes. They then **recalled** the words either in the same or the other environment by writing them in pencil on a plastic-covered board. They were allowed 2 minutes to recall the words in any order. Each participant was tested in each of the **4** possible combinations of environments: land/land, land/water, water/water, water/land. The research method was therefore a **field experiment** with a **repeated measures** design. There were approximately 24 hours between sessions for each individual. The two levels of the independent variable were whether the environments were **the same** or **different**.

Participants were tested at the end of a day's diving so that they all began testing in approximately the same **state**, i.e. cold and wet. In the 'under water' condition, the divers were heavily weighted so that they could **sit** easily on the bottom. In the 'on land' condition, the participants sat at the edge of the water with their scuba equipment **on** but with their masks tipped back and breathing tubes **off**. These controls helped to ensure that **position**, comfort and noise were similar in both environments. Some unavoidable situational variables arose. Most of the 'under water' testing was done in the sea, although at various locations, and for two participants, a freshwater site was used. For **health** and equipment failure reasons, gaps between testing were not always 24 hours. During one session, a participant was nearly run over by an ex-army amphibious truck!

Recall was not affected by whether the words had initially been **learned** on land or under the water. Accuracy was similar for 'learn and recall on land' (mean 13.5 words) and 'learn and recall in water' (mean 11.4 words). However, when recall took place in a different location from learning, more words were **forgotten**: 'learn in water and recall on land' (mean 8.4 words) and 'learn on land and recall in water' (mean 8.6 words).

This difference could have been due to the **disruption** of changing environment so 16 more participants were tested in the land/land condition. The procedure was either the same as before (**non-disrupted**) or, during the waiting time, the participants were instructed to enter the water, **swim** a short distance, **dive** to about 20 feet and return (**disrupted**). The mean scores were: non-disrupted 8.44 words, disrupted 8.69 words. This difference was very **small** and in **the opposite** direction to that expected if disruption, rather than the effect of context, were the reason for the difference seen in the main experiment. Therefore it can be concluded that context cues provided by the physical environment do improve recall.

Godden & Baddeley (1975)

Answers *continued*

context	hearing	state	disruption
words	waited	sit	non-disrupted
learning	recalled	on	swim
trained	4	off	dive
greater	field experiment	position	disrupted
physical harm	repeated measures	health	small
audiotape	the same	learned	the opposite
20	different	forgotten	

Cognitive snap!

Teacher sheet

The cards below should be printed onto card and cut out. Remember that if the students themselves cut them out they will see them correctly paired up. They can then be used in a number of different ways:

- a single individual can use them as revision, pairing them up and checking their answers against the original, complete printed sheet
- pairs of students can use them to test one another
- each student in a small group can be given a card, face down, which they hold up to their forehead. The rest of the group provide them with clues until they can guess what the card says
- each member of the class can be issued with a card (making sure that only whole 'pairs' are used) and they have to find their 'match' by moving around the classroom.

Godden & Baddeley (1975)	cue-dependent forgetting (divers)
Craik & Tulving (1975)	levels of processing (sentences)
Peterson & Peterson (1959)	STM duration (trigrams)
Ramponi *et al.* (2004)	LoP (age, associations and involuntary recall)
Nyberg (2002)	levels of processing (brain scan)
Gardiner *et al.* (2006)	levels of processing (case study)
Reber *et al.* (1994)	levels of processing (emotional words)
Glanzer & Cunitz (1966)	STM and LTM (serial position curve)
Smythe & Costall (2003)	STM and LTM (mobile phones)
Seitz & Schumann-Hengsteler (2000)	STM coding (auditory and visual)
Bartlett (1932)	reconstructive memory (*War of the Ghosts*)
Allport & Postman (1947)	stereotypes and schema (white/black)
Carli (1999)	stereotypes and schema (story endings)

Wynn & Logie (1998)	stereotypes and schema (no schema for university)
Tulving & Pearlstone (1966)	cue-dependent forgetting (category headings)
Baker *et al.* (2004)	context-dependent forgetting (chewing gum)
Duka *et al.* (2001)	state-dependent forgetting (alcohol)
Jerabek & Standing (1992)	context-dependent forgetting (exam room)
Cassaday *et al.* (2002)	state-dependent forgetting (relaxation)
Mystkowski *et al.* (2003)	state-dependent forgetting (caffeine and spider phobia)
Koehler *et al.* (2002)	repression (GSR)
Walker *et al.* (1997)	repression (diary)
Berntsen (2002)	repression (shocking events recalled)
Hadley & MacKay (2007)	repression (taboo words recalled)
Loftus (1975)	leading questions (barn)
Memon & Wright (1999)	post-event information (Oklahoma bombing)
Paterson & Kemp (2006)	leading questions (co-witnesses)
Yuille & Cutshall (1986)	leading questions (real robbery)
Riniolo *et al.* (2003)	leading questions (*Titanic*)

Amnesia

media watch

The Mirror 23 October 2006 [edited]

EMERGING from his coma, a terrible knowledge that something was horribly wrong made Richard Hammond panic.

He said: 'My mind was like an office that had been utterly ransacked. All the filing cabinets were knocked over. It was a total mess and I couldn't find my way around any more. My own mind was like a foreign place. I didn't know where anything was. I was standing there and watching everything I knew disappear through my fingers up to the point where I could barely hold on to my own name.'

The first two days after Richard's near-fatal 288mph jet car crash at York were critical. As Richard slowly regained consciousness two days after the crash he refused to believe he had had an accident, though wife Mindy, 36, reminded him every day.

He said: 'For two weeks I simply didn't believe I'd been in a crash. Mindy kept telling me over and over, but I refused to believe it.'

'I'm dimly aware of a time when I was in intensive care, of bits of conversations, of a sense of people being around, a sense of urgency. That feeling went on for quite some time. I'd wake up and be very lucid, then pass out and forget it.'

He said: 'I'd no recollection of the crash so was quite happy. But what followed that was feeling increasingly aware that there was a problem. I'd sit down on a bench here for a good think, and then "Aaagh!" As soon as I wandered off it wasn't familiar any more. It was horrible. My conversations were rambling and every now and then I'd stop, look out of the window and start again. Every meal was a surprise, even though I'd ordered them myself. The doctors came in each morning and asked what day it was, what was their name?'

'I couldn't remember. It was the most awful feeling. There was nothing there in my head. I'd try and cheat and write things down on my hand so I'd know.'

'I regressed into a little boy. All my emotions became very childlike, very fragile. The last time I was in hospital was when I was five. My mind flashed back to that time. My needs became very basic. All I wanted was a penknife and a comic book with Spitfires on it.'

It wasn't until Richard was moved to a private hospital two weeks after the crash that the situation began to sank in.

He said: 'Mindy came into the room and I said "I've had a really bad crash, haven't I?" It was in childish terms because I had to break it down into the simplest possible way.'

'I wasn't supposed to make phone calls so I stole one and rang round my friends. I couldn't tell you what I'd had for lunch, but I could find and rebuild a mobile phone! I came very close to trying to escape. I still can't watch any sort of violence on a DVD. I just disintegrate into tears.'

Questions

1. a) Identify two pieces of evidence that suggests Richard can still recall from his long-term memory.
   b) Identify one piece of evidence that suggests he has lost some long-term memory ability.
2. a) Identify two pieces of evidence that suggest Richard is suffering from loss of short-term memory.
   b) Identify two pieces of evidence that suggest he has not lost all short-term memory function.
   c) Explain why each meal was a surprise even though he'd ordered it.
3. a) Identify one case of amnesia that you have studied.
   b) Describe how the memory problems experienced by the amnesic you have studied differ from those described for Richard.

The experimental method

There are three kinds of experiment. The ____________ experiment is conducted in a contrived environment such as a room in a psychology department. This allows the experimenter to ____________ extraneous variables that might affect the participants. They can also easily manipulate the ____________ variable – the factor that is changed to create two or more conditions in the experiment. There may also be special equipment to measure the ____________ variable, that is, the changes in the participants. Alternatively, the experimenter may set up the experimental conditions in the participants' normal surroundings – this would be a ____________ experiment. Examples of suitable settings include ____________ schools for investigating young children or ____________ for studying working life. This may be a better way to conduct an experiment as it may be ____________ typical of natural behaviour because the participants are in a familiar situation. If so, the results would be ____________ to other natural settings whereas results from a study in an artificial setting might not be. These methods are true experiments as the researcher controls the IV. This is not the case in a ____________ experiment in which the researcher can only record the dependent variable in different situations which happen to exist. They have ____________ control over the experimental situation; for example they cannot ____________ participants to conditions.

Variables in field experiments are ____________ to control than in laboratory experiments. However, participants are likely to be ____________ that they are in an experiment. This is good because they are unlikely to respond to ____________; that is, clues from the experimental setting that could tell them what the experimenter expects to happen.

In any experiment, one of three ____________ is used. This is the way that the participants are allocated to conditions. In a/an ____________ design, there is a different group of participants for each level of the IV (condition). This makes it ____________ to hide the aim of the experiment but there may be ____________ between the participants which could disrupt the results. In a/an ____________ design, the same group of participants performs in each level of the IV (condition). This overcomes the problem of individual differences but means that there may be ____________. For example, participants may get better on a task as they do it more than once (____________ effect), or may get bored or tired so perform worse (____________ effect). One way to overcome these problems is to use ____________. This is where the group of participants performing in each level of the IV is subdivided so that some do the conditions in each possible order. This means that any ____________ or disadvantage arising from doing a condition first or last is balanced out across the subgroups. In a/an ____________ design, the researcher finds individuals who are alike in important ways. These are divided up so that for each member of one group there is a similar person in the other group. They may be similar in terms of age, occupation and health but in different groups according to their gender.

Experiments tend to produce ____________ data, because they are rigorously controlled so the experimenter can be sure that they could obtain the same results again as they could replicate exactly the same circumstances. Experimental results also tend to be highly ____________, as the researcher can 'stand back' from the situation rather than getting involved with the participants.

The degree of control in an experiment can make the setting or task unlike real life. This is one reason why results may not generalise, causing the study to lack ____________. Another possible ____________ is ____________; for example when the researcher treats participants in different levels of the IV differently, creating bias.

The experimental method *continued*

benefit	experimenter effects	individual differences	offices
control	fatigue	laboratory	order effects
counterbalancing	field	less	practice
demand characteristics	generalisable	matched pairs	problem
dependent	harder	more	randomly allocate
easier	independent	natural	reliable
experimental designs	independent groups	nursery	repeated measures
		objective	unaware
			validity

The experimental method

Answers

There are three kinds of experiment. The **laboratory** experiment is conducted in a contrived environment such as a room in a psychology department. This allows the experimenter to **control** extraneous variables that might affect the participants. They can also easily manipulate the **independent** variable – the factor that is changed to create two or more conditions in the experiment. There may also be special equipment to measure the **dependent** variable, that is, the changes in the participants. Alternatively, the experimenter may set up the experimental conditions in the participants' normal surroundings – this would be a **field** experiment. Examples of suitable settings include **nursery** schools for investigating young children or **offices** for studying working life. This may be a better way to conduct an experiment as it may be **more** typical of natural behaviour as the participants are in a familiar situation. If so, the results would be **generalisable** to other natural settings whereas results from a study in an artificial setting might not be. These methods are true experiments as the researcher controls the IV. This is not the case in a **natural** experiment in which the researcher can only record the dependent variable in different situations which happen to exist. They have **less** control over the experimental situation; for example they cannot **randomly allocate** participants to conditions.

Variables in field experiments are **harder** to control than in laboratory experiments. However, participants are likely to be **unaware** that they are in an experiment. This is good because they are unlikely to respond to **demand characteristics**; that is, clues from the experimental setting that could tell them what the experimenter expects to happen.

In any experiment, one of three **experimental designs** is used. This is the way that the participants are allocated to conditions. In an **independent groups** design, there is a different group of participants for each level of the IV (condition). This makes it **easier** to hide the aim of the experiment but there may be **individual differences** between the participants which could disrupt the results. In a **repeated measures** design, the same group of participants performs in each level of the IV (condition). This overcomes the problem of individual differences but means that there may be **order effects**. For example, participants may get better on a task as they do it more than once (**practice** effect), or may get bored or tired so perform worse (**fatigue** effect). One way to overcome these problems is to use **counterbalancing**. This is where the group of participants performing in each level of the IV is subdivided so that some do the conditions in each possible order. This means that any **benefit** or disadvantage arising from doing a condition first or last is balanced out across the subgroups. In a **matched pairs** design, the researcher finds individuals who are alike in important ways. These are divided up so that for each member of one group there is a similar person in the other group. They may be similar in terms of age, occupation and health but in different groups according to their gender.

Experiments tend to produce **reliable** data, because they are rigorously controlled so the experimenter can be sure that they could obtain the same results again as they could replicate exactly the same circumstances. Experimental results also tend to be highly **objective**, as the researcher can 'stand back' from the situation rather than getting involved with the participants.

The degree of control in an experiment can make the setting or task unlike real life. This is one reason why results may not generalise, causing the study to lack **validity**. Another possible **problem** is **experimenter effects**; for example when the researcher treats participants in different levels of the IV differently, creating bias.

The experimental method

Answers *continued*

laboratory
control
independent
dependent
field
nursery
offices
more
generalisable
natural
less
randomly allocate
harder
unaware
demand characteristics
experimental designs
independent groups
easier
individual differences
repeated measures
order effects
practice
fatigue
counterbalancing
benefit
matched pairs
reliable
objective
validity
problem
experimenter effects

LoP game

The triangular cards on the next page should be printed onto card and cut out. Remember that if the students themselves cut them out they will see them correctly paired up.
They can then be used in a number of different ways:

- a single individual can use them as revision
- groups of students can work with the whole pack
- three groups can work on separate parts and then combine their results.

LoP game *continued*

Processing is meaning-based

Processing at deepest level

Lab experiment comparing recall of people judged using processing that was shallow or deep

Lab experiment comparing recall of words in different types of questions

BOWER & KARLIN

SEMANTIC PROCESSING

CRAIK & TULVING (1975)

Faces processed for honesty were better recalled than those judged on gender

Produces best recall

Words processed more deeply were recalled better

Processing is visually-based

Produces poorest recall

Used brain scans

Measured brain activity during different types of processing

STRUCTURAL PROCESSING

NYBERG (2002)

Shallowest level of processing

Frontal and temporal lobes were more active during semantic processing

levels of processing theory

Medium level of depth

Processing is sound-based

Case study of Jon

CRAIK & LOCKHART (1972)

PHONEMIC PROCESSING

GARDINER *et al.* (2006)

Suggests that recall is a by-product of processing

Intermediate recall

Semantic processing helps amnesics learning

Age and LoP affect recall but not for highly associated words under involuntary recall

Tested recall of high and low emotion words

Tested recall of words judged for shape, syllables or pleasant meaning

Deep processing helps recall of low but not high emotion words

RAMPONI *et al.* (2004)

REBER *et al.* (1994)

Interactive quiz

See PowerPoint 3-17 *Cognitive interactive quiz*

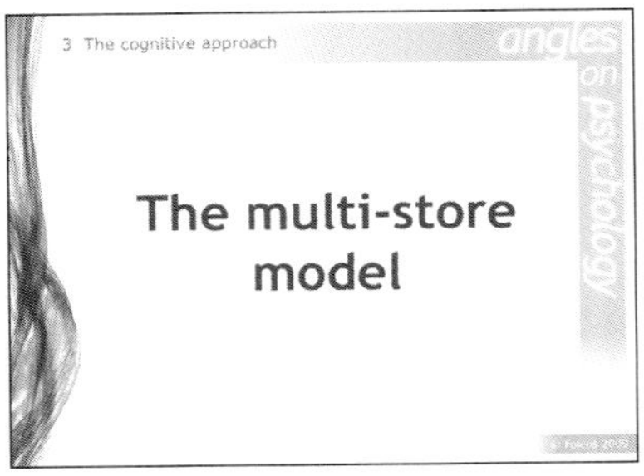

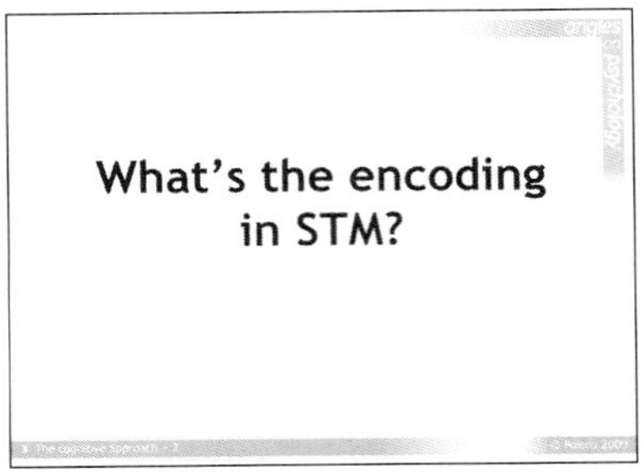

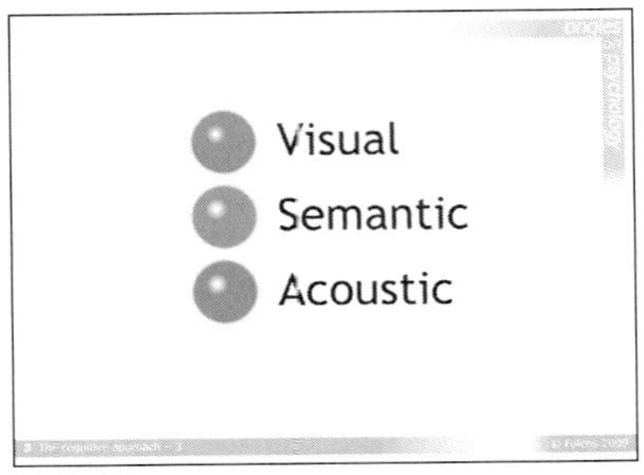

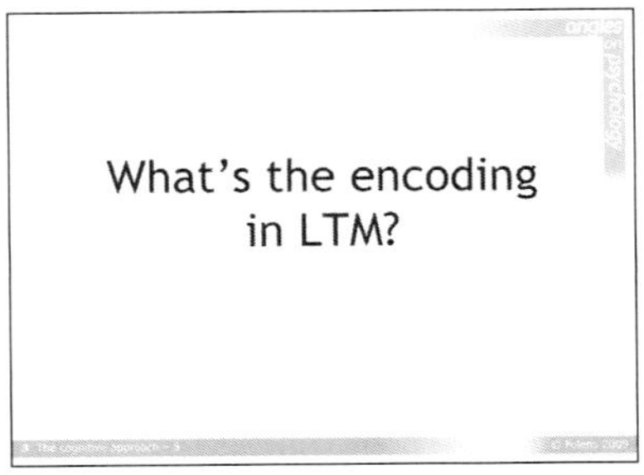

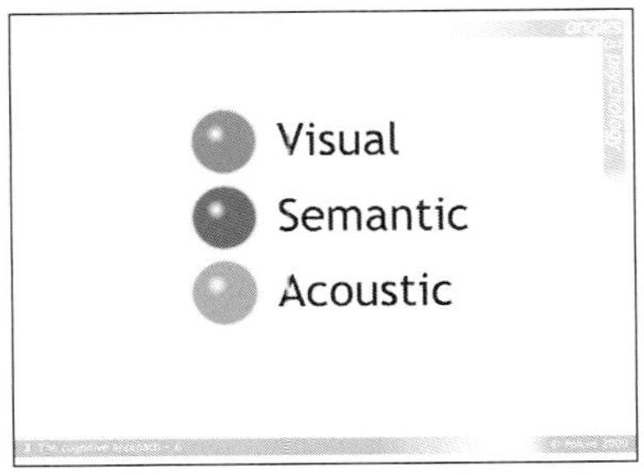

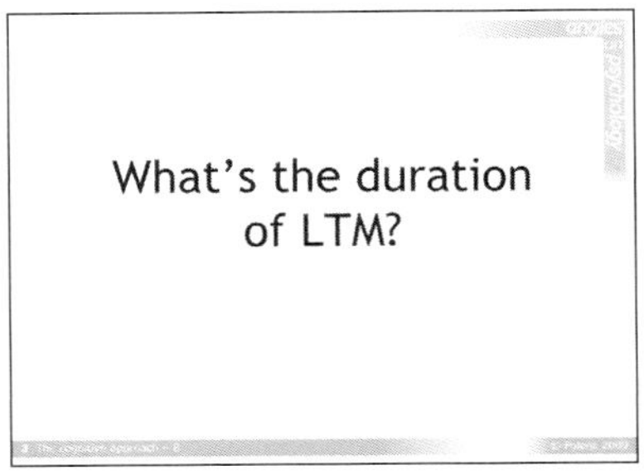

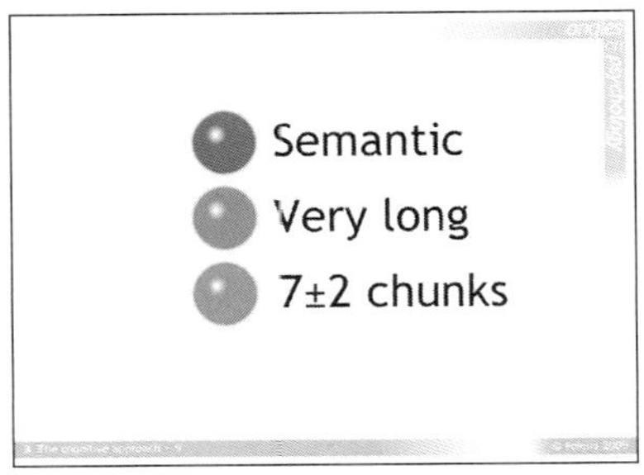

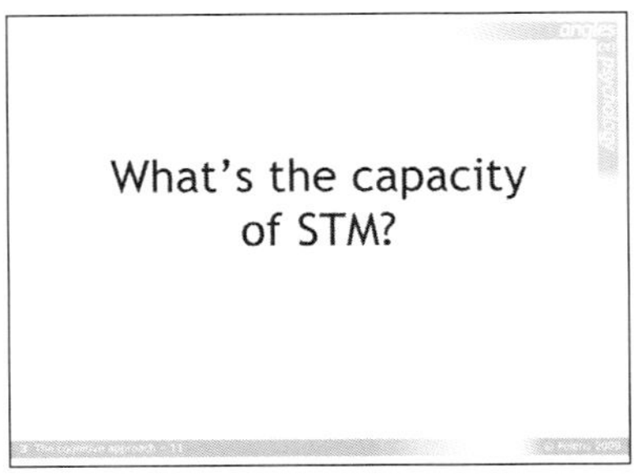

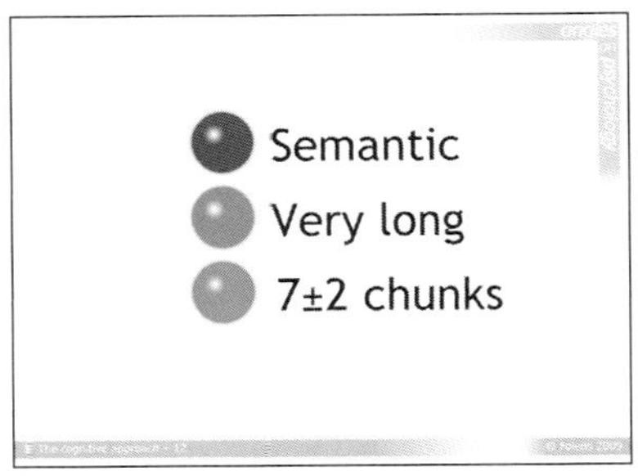

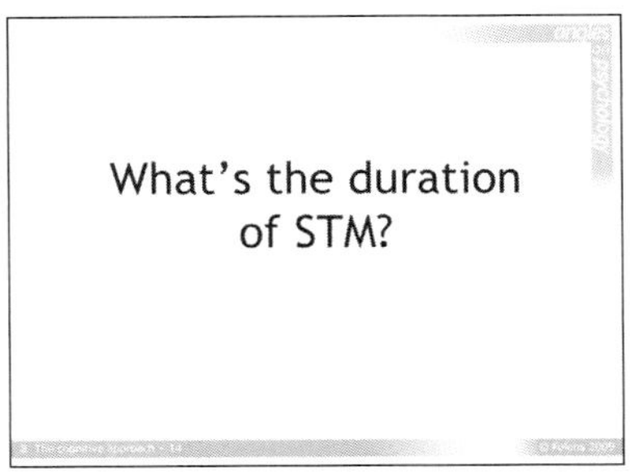

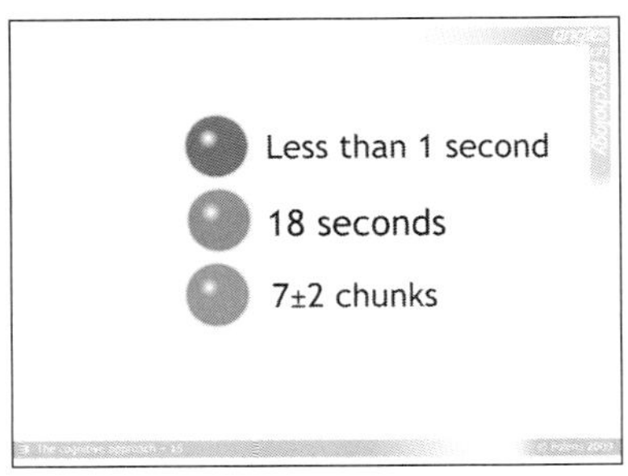

Interactive quiz *continued*

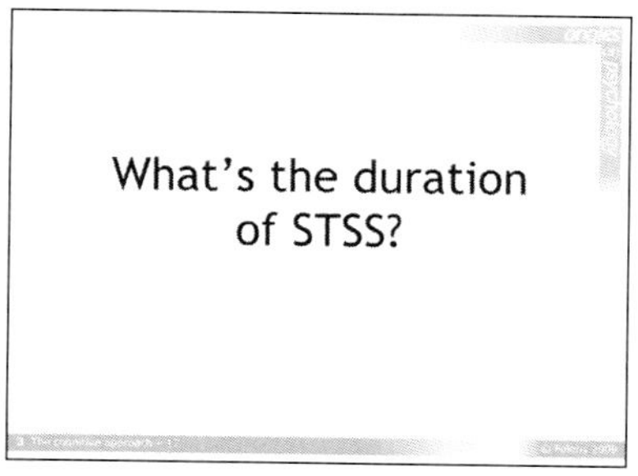

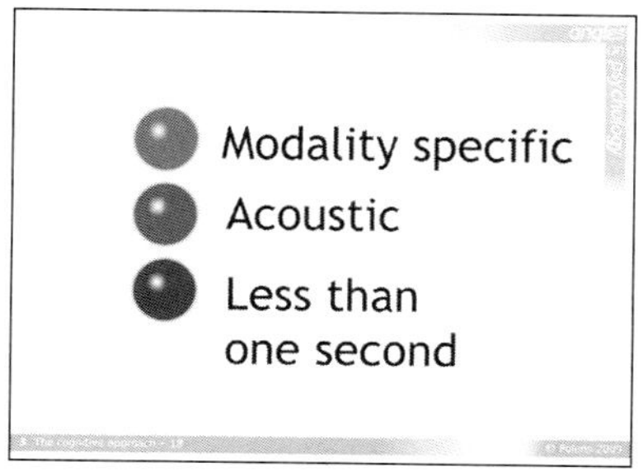

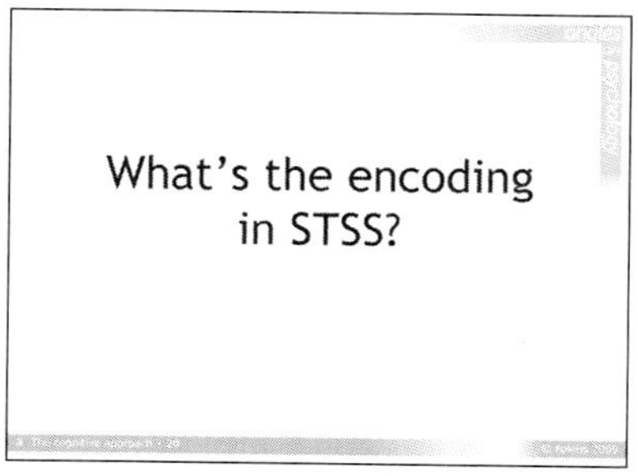

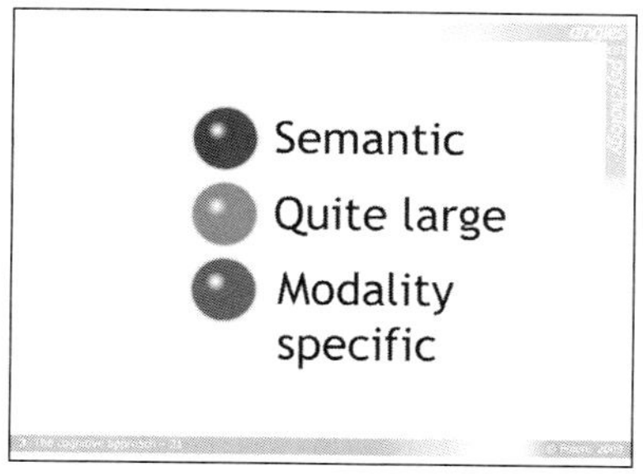

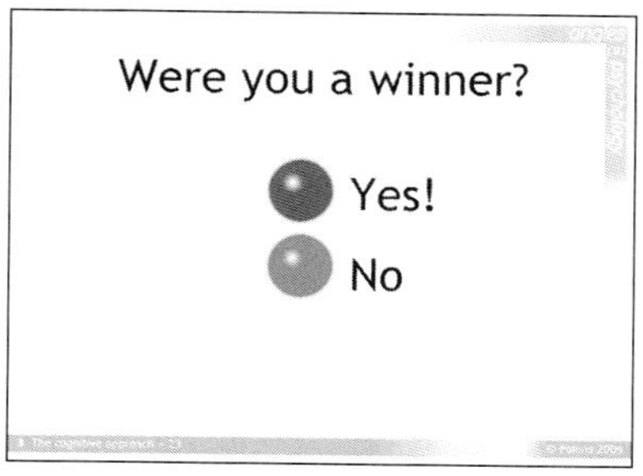

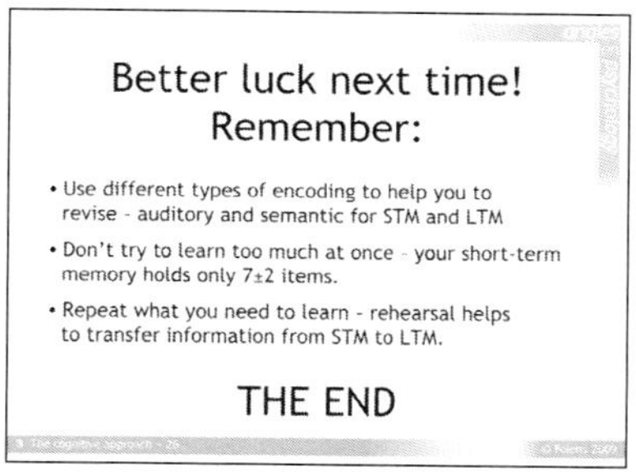

Essays

Question 1

> Mrs Barker has just started teaching at a new school. She will have to learn the names of many new students and remember her way around the buildings.

Outline **one** theory of memory and use this theory to explain how Mrs Barker's memory could be assisted. Consider the effectiveness of these ideas using psychological research.

continue overleaf if necessary

Essays

Question 2

> It has recently been observed that some people remember web addresses very easily and others find them very difficult to recall. Some researchers have suggested that this may be because they are using different strategies to try to remember them whilst others have suggested that some addresses are simply easier to remember than others and maybe people are just learning different ones.

Using **two** or **more** theories of memory or forgetting, discuss psychological evidence that could explain why differences in recall for web addresses might arise. You can base your answer on the suggestions in the box or use other ideas.

....

....

....

....

....

....

....

....

....

....

....

....

....

....

....

....

....

....

....

....

....

continue overleaf if necessary

What makes adverts work?

research now: Shopping for Gogey and Latuk

Berg & Lippman (2001) aimed to test the effect of humour on radio advertising. Sixty undergraduate psychology students listened to simulated radio shows containing advertisements for grocery items with fictitious brand names. The advertisements included either humorous or non-humorous statements. Participants were later asked to recognise visually presented brand names and were given a true–false test for associations between products and brand names such as 'Gogey is bread' or 'Latuk is soap'. They found that humour did not affect recall of brand names themselves but it did increase recognition of brand name and product type associations.

1. What conclusion would you draw from the findings of this study?
2. Think about the strengths and weaknesses of this study. How could it have been improved?
3. One explanation for these findings is that humorous and non-humorous material is processed differently. How would levels of processing theory account for this?
4. Alternatively, we may remember funny advertisements better because we tend to think about them again and again. What theory would account for this effect on memory and how would it explain the effect that was demonstrated?

research now: Brainy TV commercials

Rossiter *et al.* (2001) used brain scans to investigate how people respond to TV advertising. Thirty-five right-handed women aged 25–45, who were the main shoppers for their families, watched TV programmes containing commercial breaks. They watched an 18-minute documentary with 12 30-second advertisements. These were previously unseen commercials for established brands of consumer products. A week later they were tested on recognition of scenes from the commercials whilst having their brains scanned. They found that scenes that were shown for longer than 1.5 seconds were better recognised than ones shown for less time. They also found that scenes that caused brain activity in the left side of the brain were remembered better. This suggests that advertisers should try to produce adverts that are processed by the left hemisphere as they are more likely to be effective.

1. The second finding was surprising as it is believed that pictorial information is processed by the right side of the brain. However, there are also differences in the way men and women, and left- and right-handed people process information. What other tests should Rossiter *et al.* have conducted?
2. In terms of the multi-store model, what process appears to be happening in the left side of the brain?

Resources

Full text of Berg & Lippman (2001): http://64.233.169.104/search?q=cache:nJGk7E-0KUsJ:road.uww.edu/road/eamond/Research/GenderJokes(DK1)/References%2520and%2520info/Humor%2520in%2520advertising.htm+louis+g+lippman+Gojey&hl=en&ct=clnk&cd=2&gl=uk

Creative activities

Creative activity 1

research now: Alliterating ads, mizspeling, and memory

Lowery *et al.* (2003) investigated the effect of many different linguistic features (word and letter patterns) on recall of product names; for example, alliteration and rhyme. Their findings showed that five factors were important, and were more so for less familiar brands than familiar ones. Some of these factors were:

- unusual spellings, e.g. Kool-Aid (a drink)
- semantic appositeness – that is, having meaningful relevance, e.g. WD-40 (a technical product – oil)
- initial plosives – that is, starting with a harsh, sharp sound, e.g. Comet (a cleanser).

1. Produce a long list of real brand names and identify different ways that they attempt to assist recall to make the product memorable. Include some unusual items that are less likely to be remembered. Devise a survey to investigate people's recall of these products. You could either ask participants to identify the type of product from the brand name, or to recall as many brand names as they can for a particular type of product (or a mixture of the two).
2. Compare your results to those above. How are they similar or different?
3. Write memos to two of the companies suggesting ways to improve the memorability of their products. Justify your arguments with evidence.

Resource

This website provides free articles on advertising: http://www.ameritest.net/resources/

Creative activity 2

Donald and Sheehan are psychology students in the sixth form at school and are trying to learn all the road signs for their driving theory test. They are using what they know about the psychology of memory and forgetting to help them. They have tried drawing the signs out and showing them to each other and making up rhymes like this:

Warning ones have three corners,
Banning ones are blue,
But if you wrong a red one,
It'll be very bad news for you.

They have also tried applying logic, like 'from a motorway you can see lots of sky, so the signs are blue; from a major road you can see fields, so the signs are green and from a local road you can see newspaper shops, so the signs are black and white'. They are trying not to use visual and spatial information at the same time, so either they look at pictures of signs or they imagine the road layout. They have set up a computer so it looks like the ones at the test centre and are spending time sitting there learning. Finally, they are doing all of these things over and over again.

Take any two of Donald and Sheehan's ideas and justify them using your knowledge of cognitive psychology.

Evidence of practice: short experiment

Leading questions

Elizabeth Loftus has conducted many studies about eyewitness testimony that demonstrate similar effects to the one you are going to explore (e.g. Loftus, 1975 and Loftus & Palmer, 1979). One important way in which eyewitnesses can be misled is through the wording of questions used to ask them about what they believe they have seen. Using specific examples, and the definite article (the) rather than open ended questions and the indefinite article (a), tend to result in unreliable witness accounts.

You can demonstrate this effect using photographs or a short film clip. The photos on page 100 are also available on slides 8–11 of PowerPoint 3-26.

Preparation

1. Collect some large, complex, high quality colour pictures, e.g. from advertisements in magazines. Choose six and copy them on A4 card or put them into a powerpoint presentation. Write down why you rejected the pictures you have decided not to use.
2. For each picture, devise two sets of questions: one containing some leading questions, the other containing none (this is your IV). In each set, some correct answers should be 'yes' and others 'no'. Try to avoid a pattern in these answers. (Use the examples provided as a guide). Make the leading and non-leading questions similar, e.g. 'Did you see a ...' and 'Did you see the ...'. There will also need to be some 'filler' questions. Think about why these issues are important in terms of validity and reliability.
3. You will need to decide on a group of potential participants who do not know about leading questions (e.g. non-psychology students). How will you select them?
4. Will it be better to use the same or different people for the two sets of questions? If each participant answers both types this is a repeated measures design, if they answer only one type, it is an independent groups design. Record and justify your decision.
5. Organise how you will show the pictures for a very short time (e.g. 5-10 seconds per picture). You might do this by putting the cards in a stack and telling the participants to turn over when you say 'next' every 10 seconds, or put them in a timed presentation. Write down the reasons for your choice. Think about experimenter effects.
6. Think about the order of the pictures and questions. This is important to avoid confusion between pictures. Think again about experimenter effects. Make copies of the questions.
7. Decide what to tell the participants at the start and the end. Ensure that what you do is ethical without giving too much away. Think about demand characteristics, consent and the right to withdraw. Record your decisions about ethics.
8. Conduct a pilot study to check timings etc., then collect your data.
9. Add up the total number of correct and incorrect answers given to leading questions and non-leading questions (the DV). Ignore the fillers. Work out the mean, median and modal number of errors made in response to the leading and non-leading questions. Calculate the range for each group.
10. Select one of the measures of central tendency and plot a bar chart. What labels do you need on the axes? Why is a bar chart the most appropriate graph?
11. Consider using familiar versus unfamiliar scenes or staging a mock 'event'. The latter would be a field experiment and would present many methodological and ethical problems. Think about why you chose the method you did and record your justification.

Resources

- http://www.seweb.uci.edu/faculty/loftus/ – this site provides many free full-text journal articles on eyewitness testimony
- http://faculty.washington.edu/eloftus/ – some additional articles are available here, including those from less academic sources
- http://www.metacafe.com/watch/44768/car_theft/ – CCTV of a car theft
- http://video.google.com/videoplay?docid=2061842890783782238 – CCTV of a laptop theft

Question sheet

1. Was he holding the controls?
   Were the lines on the tarmac white?
   Did you see the hat he was wearing?
1. Was he holding the controls?
   Did you see the white lines on the tarmac?
   Did you see the hat he was wearing?

2. Was the little girl carrying a bag?
   Was there any writing on the balloons?
   Did you see a red balloon?
2. Was the little girl carrying a bag?
   Was there any writing on the balloons?
   Did you see the red balloon?

3. Was the pony white or black?
   Did you see a 'sale' sign in the window?
   Were the flowers red or white?
3. Was the pony white or black?
   Did you see the 'sale' sign in the window?
   Were the flowers red or white?

4. How many books were there on the table?
   Did you see the American flag?
   Was he wearing boots?
4. Did you see the two books on the table?
   Did you see the American flag?
   Did you see the boots he was wearing?

Memory for faces

Bower & Karlin (1974) carried out an experiment to test levels of processing theory. They showed 12 participants 144 pictures of faces that they were asked to judge either for sex (shallow processing) or either likeableness or honesty (both deep processing). To do this they pressed a button (but it was not connected to anything as this was not really part of the experiment). Immediately afterwards, the participants were shown 144 test slides, some of which they had seen before. They were asked to write down which ones they recognised.

1. The independent variable in this study was the level of processing. What were the two conditions and how was each one operationalised? [3 marks]
2. What was the dependent variable? [2 marks]
3. The participants were university students who were fulfilling a requirement to participate in studies as part of their introductory psychology course. What type of sampling is this? [1 mark]
4. At the beginning of the study, the participants were told that the researchers were interested in how fast people could make different kinds of judgements. They were also asked whether they had ever been 'in any reaction-time experiments before' and were instructed to 'be sure and press the button firmly so that the responses are properly recorded'.
   a) Why was it necessary to give the participants this information? [2 marks]
   b) Identify **one** ethical issue this procedure raises. [1 mark]
   c) How might the researchers have overcome this ethical issue? [2 marks]
5. The faces used in the slides were all taken from a Yale University yearbook. Half were of males and half of females. Any photos of people with unusual characteristics, such as large earrings or hats, were not used. All the pictures were of Caucasians and the men were wearing ties. Why were these particular photographs selected? [2 marks]
6. The participants each answered all three types of questions. The order of the different question types was organised so that some questions in each possible order were answered by some participants.
   a) What was the experimental (participant) design in this experiment? [1 mark]
   b) Why was it necessary to present the question types in each possible order and what is this arrangement called? [2 marks]

Instant Recall

INSTANT RECALL Dr Miriam Stoppard

The Mirror, 22 December 2006 (Edited)

Dear Miriam,

I'VE always been a bit forgetful but, at 54, it's worse than ever. I go into a room and forget why I've gone there.

I've read you can take supplements to make your brain smarter. Do you know of any?

Miriam replies,

THERE are some smart drugs but they're only available on prescription.

Most over-the-counter products have no science to back them up. Neurozan contains bio-elements to help maintain brain function and performance. It helps support brain and nerve health. Also a four-month course of ginkgo biloba, 120mg daily, improves short-term memory.

1. If a psychologist wanted to test the claim that a four-month course of ginkgo biloba was best for improving memory they might conduct an experiment.
   a) What would the IV be? [1 mark]
   b) If you were going to conduct this experiment, comparing two conditions, suggest how you would operationally define these. [2 marks]
   c) Would a laboratory or field experiment be best? Justify your choice. [2 marks]
2. Design an experiment to test whether Neurozan improves memory over a four-month period. You are not required to investigate different doses (amounts). [5 marks]
3. Experiments such as these involving drugs raise ethical issues for researchers.
   a) Identify **three** ethical issues that would be important in experiments such as these. [3 marks]
   b) Explain why each of the issues you identified in part (a) would be important. [3 marks]
   c) For **one** of these issues, describe how a researcher should attempt to minimise the potential risk for participants. [3 marks]

The cognitive approach quick quiz

1

a) Name two theories of forgetting.
b) What is 'storage'?
c) What theory were Godden and Baddeley (1975) testing?
d) What level of processing are we using when we are just looking?
e) What is meant by validity?
f) What is meant by phonemic processing?
g) What is context-dependent forgetting?
h) Which theory says that memory is a by-product of processing?
i) Name two measures of spread.
j) What is the difference between a laboratory experiment and a natural experiment?
k) Name a theory of memory other than levels of processing.
l) What was the DV in Godden and Baddeley's (1975) divers experiment?
m) What is an independent measures design?
n) What is the key issue for Cognitive Psychology?

2

a) Name the three levels of processing according to Craik and Lockhart.
b) What was the IV in Godden and Baddeley's (1975) divers experiment?
c) What is 'retrieval'?
d) What is meant by reliability?
e) Name two measures of central tendency.
f) What do we do when we process semantically?
g) What is counterbalancing?
h) What is state-dependent forgetting?
i) What is the difference between a laboratory experiment and a field experiment?
j) What are demand characteristics?
k) Name a theory of forgetting other than cue-dependent forgetting.
l) What did Godden and Baddeley (1975) find?
m) What is a matched pairs design?
n) What was your short experiment for Cognitive Psychology about?

The cognitive approach quick quiz

Answers

1

a) Name two theories of forgetting. **Cue-dependent forgetting; displacement/decay/interference, etc.**

b) What is 'storage'? **Retaining information in memory so that it can be used later**

c) What theory were Godden and Baddeley (1975) testing? **Levels of processing**

d) What level of processing are we using when we are just looking? **Structural**

e) What is meant by validity? **Being sure that you are testing what you intended to test**

f) What is meant by phonemic processing? **Sound-based encoding of information resulting in moderately good recall, according to levels of processing theory**

g) What is context-dependent forgetting? **Increased likelihood of failing to recall items because remembering is attempted in a different place from encoding**

h) Which theory says that memory is a by-product of processing? **Levels of processing**

i) Name two measures of spread. **Range, standard deviation**

j) What is the difference between a laboratory experiment and a natural experiment? **Whether or not the experimenter actively manipulates the IV**

k) Name a theory of memory other than levels of processing. **e.g. multi-store model, working memory model**

l) What was the DV in Godden and Baddeley's (1975) divers experiment? **Number of words recalled (and recognition of words)**

m) What is an independent measures design? **One in which a different group of participants is used in each level of the IV**

n) What is the key issue for Cognitive Psychology? **This will depend on your chosen topic, e.g. eyewitness testimony/recovered memory**

The cognitive approach quick quiz

Answers *continued*

2

a) Name the three levels of processing according to Craik and Lockhart. **Structural, phonemic, semantic**

b) What was the IV in Godden and Baddeley's (1975) divers experiment? **Same or different location**

c) What is 'retrieval'? **Accessing information previously stored in memory**

d) What is meant by reliability? **Being able to get the same results again**

e) Name two measures of central tendency. **Mean/median/mode**

f) What do we do when we process semantically? **Understand the meaning of the item to be remembered**

g) What is counterbalancing? **Conducting conditions in an experiment in different orders on different groups of participants in a repeated measures design**

h) What is state-dependent forgetting? **Increased likelihood of failing to recall items because remembering is attempted in a different mood or physiological condition**

i) What is the difference between a laboratory experiment and a field experiment? **A lab experiment is conducted in a controlled, artificial situation whereas a field experiment is done in the participants' normal environment**

j) What are demand characteristics? **Features of an experiment that give away the aims to particpants making them behave differently**

k) Name a theory of forgetting other than cue-dependent forgetting. **e.g. decay/ displacement/interference**

l) What did Godden and Baddeley (1975) find? **That forgetting was worse when participants were in a different environment during recall from during encoding**

m) What is a matched pairs design? **One in which participants are selected in pairs matched on important variables for the study and one of each pair is allocated to each condition**

n) What was your short experiment for Cognitive Psychology about? **This will depend on your chosen topic e.g. eyewitness testimony**

Cognitive test

Centre No.						Paper Reference							Surname	Initial(s)
Candidate No.						6	P	S	0	1	/	1	Signature	

Psychology Advanced Subsidiary

Unit 1: Cognitive psychology

Time: 50 minutes

Instructions to candidates

Answer ALL the questions.

Information for candidates

The total mark for this paper is 40.

Advice to candidates

Quality of written communication will be taken into account in the marking of your response to question 11. This question is indicated with an asterisk (*). Quality of written communication includes clarity of expression, the structure and presentation of ideas, and grammar, punctuation and spelling.

Question number	Leave blank
1	
2	
3	
4	
5	
6	
7	
8	
9	
10	
11	
Total	

SECTION A

Answer ALL questions.
You are advised to spend approximately 7 minutes on this section.

Choose answer A, B, C or D, and put a cross in the box (☒). If you change your mind, put a line through the box (~~☒~~) and then put a cross in another box (☒).

Sven conducts an experiment on recall of words with odd or normal spellings.

1. Sven uses a repeated measures design. This is where:

☐ **A** each participant is tested in only one condition
☐ **B** the researcher replicates the study to improve reliability
☐ **C** all the participants are tested in all the conditions
☐ **D** participants get fatigued and withdraw from the study **(1)**

2. Sven wants to be fair to all the participants when he decides which words are spelled correctly. He wants to avoid being more generous about spelling on the odd words. Sven is trying to make sure that he is:

☐ **A** objective
☐ **B** operational
☐ **C** subjective
☐ **D** random **(1)**

3. A natural experiment differs from a field experiment because:

☐ **A** natural experiments are always conducted in the natural environment but field experiments are not
☐ **B** natural experiments do not have an independent variable and field experiments do
☐ **C** in natural experiments participants cannot be randomly allocated to conditions but in field experiments they can
☐ **D** in natural experiments there is no dependent variable but in field experiments there is always one **(1)**

4. Retrieval happens in many different ways. These include:

☐ **A** recall and rehearsal
☐ **B** recall and recognition
☐ **C** rehearsal and recognition
☐ **D** rehearsal and repetition **(1)**

5. The levels of processing theory says there are three levels of processing. These are:

☐ **A** iconic, phonological and semantic
☐ **B** iconic, phonemic and semantic
☐ **C** structural, phonemic and echoic
☐ **D** structural, phonemic and semantic **(1)**

6. In the cognitive approach, the idea of 'information processing' suggests that information flows from input to output. Which description of Peter best illustrates this? Peter:

☐ **A** recalls the moment when he crashed his car
☐ **B** imagines his sister and wonders what she is doing
☐ **C** looks through the pages of an old photograph album
☐ **D** sees a friend, remembers their name and says hello **(1)**

(Total 6 marks)

TOTAL FOR SECTION A: 6 MARKS

SECTION B

Answer ALL questions.
You are advised to spend approximately 25 minutes on this section.

7. **(a)** Describe the procedure used by Godden & Baddeley (1975) in their study of cue-dependent memory.

....

....

....

....

....

.... **(3)**

(b) Outline the findings (results and/or conclusions) of Godden & Baddeley's (1975) study.

....

....

....

....

....

.... **(3)**

(c) Evaluate Godden & Baddeley's (1975) study in terms of **one** strength **or one** weakness.

....

....

....

.... **(2)**

(Total 8 marks)

8. The levels of processing model of memory (Craik & Lockhart, 1972) suggests that we remember deeply encoded information better than information that has been encoded only in a shallow way.

Outline **one** strength **and one** weakness of this theory.

....

....

....

....

.... **(6)**

(Total 6 marks)

9. As part of the requirements for the Cognitive Psychology part of your course you will have conducted an experiment.

State the topic that you investigated: ....

Name the experimental (participant) design you used ....

(a) Explain why you chose this experimental (participant) design.

....

.... **(1)**

(b) Operationalise the dependent variable that you measured.

....

.... **(1)**

(c) Operationalise the independent variable that you tested.

....

....

....

....

....

....

.... **(1)**

(d) Describe how you analysed and presented your data.

....

....

....

....

....

....

.... **(3)**

(Total 6 marks)

TOTAL FOR SECTION B: 20 MARKS

SECTION C

Answer ALL questions.
You are advised to spend approximately 18 minutes on this section.

10. The cognitive approach to psychology can be used to explain many issues in psychology.

Jon is sitting downstairs in the kitchen. He decides to go upstairs to get a book. On the way he sees some clothes that belong upstairs so carries them up and puts them away. He comes down again having forgotten to get the book and doesn't remember until he goes back into the kitchen.

Use the cue-dependent theory to explain why Jon forgot about the book, then remembered again.

....

....

....

.... **(2)**

(Total 2 marks)

***11.** In the cognitive approach to psychology, you will have learned about a theory of memory **other than** the levels of processing theory and cue-dependent theory.

Describe and evaluate this theory.

The theory I am describing and evaluating is: ....

....

....

....

....

....

....

....

....

....

....

....

(Total 12 marks)

TOTAL FOR SECTION C: 14 MARKS

TOTAL MARKS FOR PAPER: 40 MARKS

Mark scheme

SECTION A

1. **C** all the participants are tested in all the conditions **(1)**
2. **A** objective **(1)**
3. **C** in natural experiments participants cannot be randomly allocated to conditions but in field experiments they can **(1)**
4. **B** recall and recognition **(1)**
5. **D** structural, phonemic and semantic **(1)**
6. **D** sees a friend, remembers their name and says hello **(1)**

SECTION B

7. (a) *Describe the procedure used by Godden & Baddeley (1975) in their study of cue-dependent memory.*

IV same environment or different environments for learning and recall;

Two environments were land and water;

DV number of words recalled from word list;

Also tested recognition of words; **(3)**

(b) *Outline the findings (results and/or conclusions) of Godden & Baddeley's (1975) study.*

40% fewer words recalled when the learning and recall environments were different;

No effect of changing environment on recognition;

Recall in the same environment as learning for land and underwater was no different; **(3)**

(c) *Evaluate Godden & Baddeley's (1975) study in terms of* **one** *strength or* **one** *weakness.*

Strength:

They tested recognition and compared all combinations of land and water;

So they could be sure that the differences were due to the change in recall environment, not the disruptive effects of changing location;

Weakness:

It isn't possible to tell whether the effects are context-dependent or state-dependent;

It might be that on land the participants felt calmer and under the water more nervous or excited and these effects caused differences in recall when they changed location; **(2)**

8. *(Craik & Lockhart, 1972): Outline* **one** *strength and* **one** *weakness of this theory.*

Strength:

It is supported by experimental evidence such as Craik & Tulving (1975);
who found that shallow processed words were remembered less than deeply processed ones;

This was a good experiment because they compared all three levels of processing, structural, phonemic and semantic/they controlled factors such as time spent rehearsing each word;

Weakness:

Factors other than the depth of processing matter;
such as emotions and strong associations with words;

e.g. Ramponi *et al.* found that words with strong associations were recalled better regardless of how they were processed; **(6)**

9. *As part of the requirements for the Cognitive Psychology part of your course you will have conducted an experiment. State the topic that you investigated:*

What experimental (participant) design did you use?

Depends on student's own study. Must be one of:

Repeated or related measures or within groups;

Independent or unrelated measures/independent or between groups;

Matched pairs;

(a) Explain why you chose this experimental (participant) design.
Depends on answer above.
e.g. repeated measures:
to avoid participant variables such as (must be relevant to study, e.g. differences in recall ability);

e.g. independent groups:

to avoid order effects such as (must be relevant to study, e.g. remembering stimuli from previous test); **(1)**

(b) Operationalise the dependent variable that you measured.

Depends on student's own study.

e.g. <u>number</u> of words recalled from a list; **(1)**

(c) Operationalise the independent variable that you tested.

Accept any definition that provides two or more conditions relevant to cognitive psychology, e.g. structural/phonemic/semantic processing with different types of questions.)

(d) Describe how you analysed and presented your data.

Depends on student's own study. Should include reference to tables and/or charts and at least one measure of central tendency and at least one measure of dispersion. **(3)**

SECTION C

10. *Use the cue-dependent theory to explain why Jon forgot about the book, then remembered again.*

The downstairs room was a context cue during encoding/learning;

When he was upstairs this context cue was absent (which made remembering more difficult);

But when he was downstairs again the learning and recall contexts matched again so he could remember; **(2)**

***11.** *In the cognitive approach to psychology, you will have learned about a theory of memory* **other than** *the levels of processing theory and cue-dependent theory. Describe and evaluate this theory.* **(12)**

Level	Mark	Descriptor
		AO1: Knowledge and understanding of psychological concepts. AO2: Application of psychological concepts.
1	0	No content worth of marks.
2	1–3	A brief, simple answer giving some details of a relevant theory. Answer lacks clarity and/or organisation. Little use of relevant terminology and poor spelling, punctuation and/or grammar.
3	4–6	An answer which is simple but which provides largely accurate information relating to a relevant and named or identifiable theory. At the top of the band there will be some attempt at evaluation. Limited clarity and/or organisation. Some use of relevant terminology. Frequent spelling, punctuation and/or grammatical errors.
4	7–9	The answer contains accurate description and evaluation of a relevant theory although some of this may be limited. At the top of the band the evaluation will include some evidence. Clarity of expression and organisation are competent with some use of relevant terminology. Some spelling, punctuation and/or grammatical errors are likely to be present.
5	10–12	The answer contains both detailed and accurate description and effective evaluation of a relevant theory. Description and application are well balanced. Evaluation uses evidence. Clarity of expression and organisation are effective and the candidate makes good use of relevant terminology. Few spelling, punctuation or grammatical errors are present.

Likely theories are:

Reconstructive memory

Multi-store model

Working memory model

Spreading-activation

Indicative content (for multi-store model):

Possible (AO1) points:

- **There are three memory stores, the sensory register, STM and LTM (with different functions and properties);**
- **There is a different sensory register for each sense and they have a very short duration;**
- **The STM stores 7 ± 2 items for under 30 seconds and uses an auditory code;**
- **The LTM has a large capacity and duration and uses a semantic code;**
- **Rehearsal transfers information from STM to LTM;**

Possible (AO2) points:

- **Peterson & Peterson (1959) showed that STM lasts under 18 seconds by seeing how long participants could remember trigram for;**
- **Glanzer & Cunitz (1966) showed that STM and LTM are different because items at the beginning and end of a list are remembered better than the middle ones which have been displaced;**
- **Evidence from amnesics shows that STM and LTM are different, e.g. HM had a normal STM but could not make new LTMs;**
- **However Forde & Humphreys (2002) found that the amnesic FK could process information in his STM semantically, suggesting that STM doesn't only use an acoustic code;**
- **The LTM also seems to consist of different stores, such as procedural, semantic and episodic because HM could learn new procedural information but not make new semantic or episodic memories;**

Resources

See PowerPoint 3-26 *Resources*.

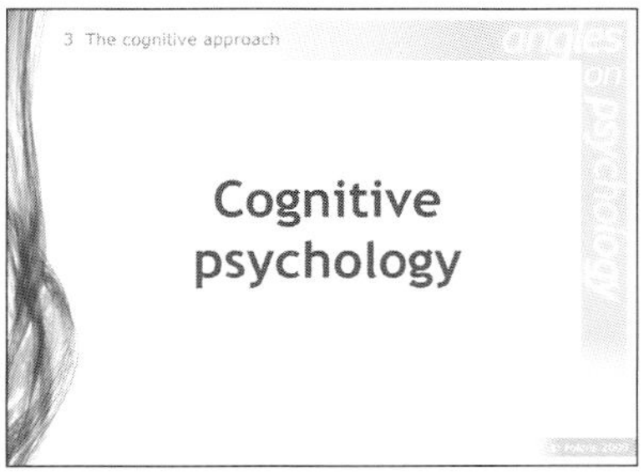

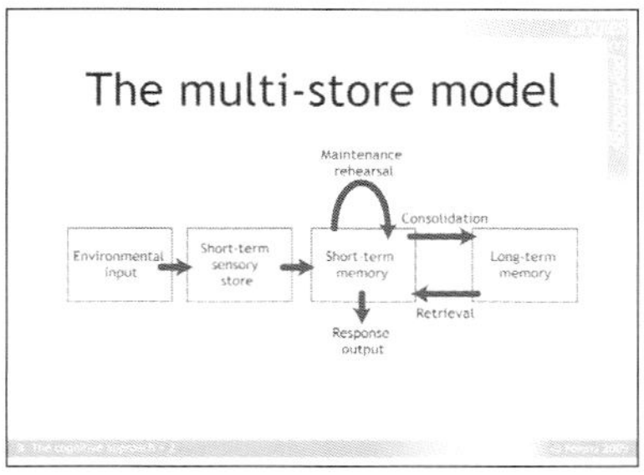

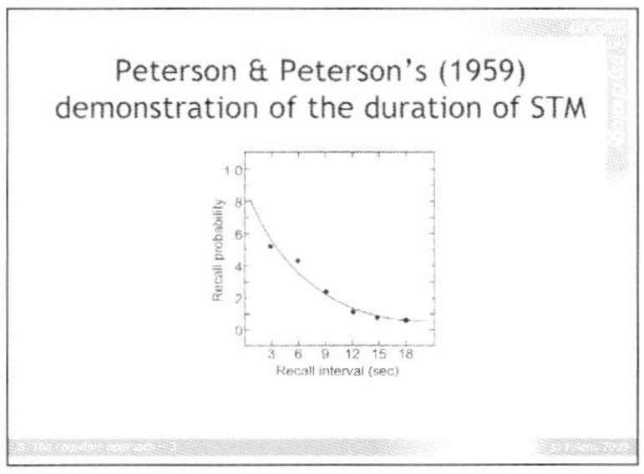

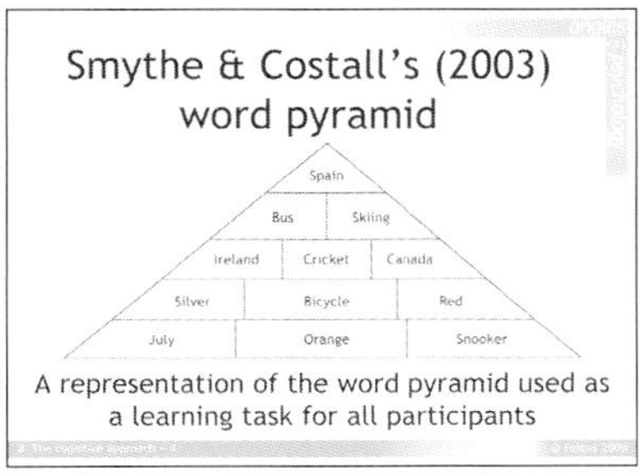

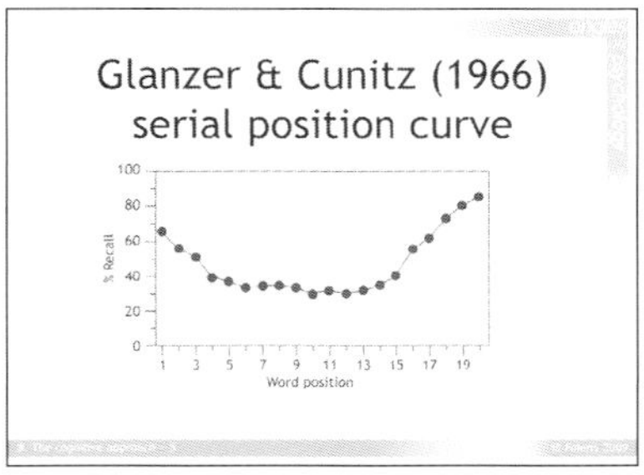

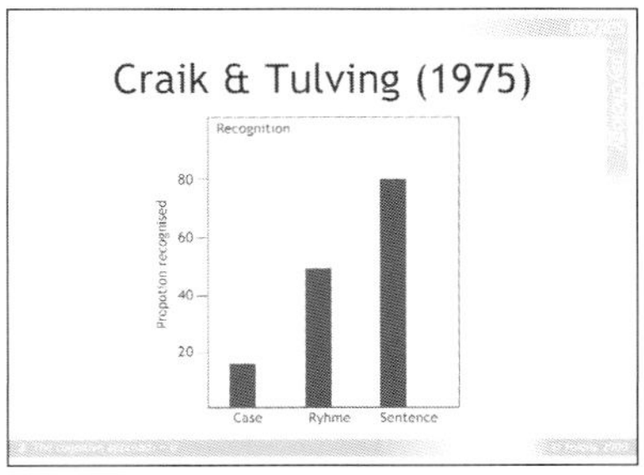

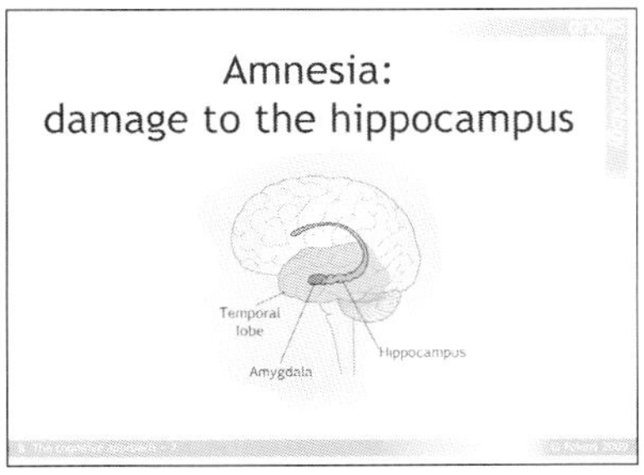

References

Abernethy, E.M. (1940) 'The effect of changed environmental conditions upon the results of college examinations'. *Journal of Psychology*, 10:293–301.

Berg, E.M. & Lippman, L.G. (2001) 'Does humor in radio advertising affect recognition of novel product brand names?' *Journal of General Psychology*, 128(2): 194–205.

Bower, G.H. & Karlin, M.B. (1974) 'Depth of processing pictures of faces and recognition memory'. *Journal of Experimental Psychology*, 103: 751–57.

Loftus, E.F. & Palmer, J.C. (1974) 'Reconstruction of automobile destruction: an example of the interaction between learning and memory'. *Journal of Verbal Learning and Behavior*, 13: 585–89.

Lowery, T.M., Shrum, L.J. & Dubitsky, T.M. (2003) 'The relation between brand-name linguistic characteristics and brand-name memory'. *Journal of Advertising*, 32(3): 7–17.

Rossiter, J.R., Silberstein, R.B., Harris, P.G. & Nield, G. (2001) 'Brain-imaging detection of visual scene encoding in long-term memory for TV commercials'. *Journal of Advertising Research*, March/April: 41: 13–21.

Sperling, G. (1960) 'The information available in brief visual presentations'. *Psychology Monographs: General and Applied*, 74(11).

Chapter 4

The psychodynamic approach

Activity number	Activity title	Activity/file type
The psychodynamic approach		
4.1	Introduction	ST PP
4.2	The unconscious mind	WM SC A
4.3	Case studies	CE A
4.4	Defence mechanisms	CA prep
4.5	Defence mechanisms	SAQ SC
4.6	Adolescent identity and defence mechanisms	SAQ
4.7	Psychosexual development and the structural model	SAQ SC
4.8	Freud (1905): Little Hans	CE A
4.9	Correlations	CE A
4.10	Psychosexual development	MW
4.11	Starter: gender	ST PP
4.12	Gender and the superego	SAQ
4.13	Gender	CA TN prep A
4.14	Essays: Questions 1 and 2	LAQ
4.15	Do dreams have meaning?	ET SAQ
4.16	Creative activities: 1 and 2	KI
4.17	Evidence of practice: conducting and analysing a correlational study	RM
4.18	Oral personalities and the Rorschach test	RM
4.19	Testing with TAT	RM SC
4.20	The psychodynamic approach quick quiz	QQ A
4.21	Psychodynamic test	AT A
4.22	Resources	PP
4.23	References	

Introduction

See PowerPoint 4-1: *Introduction*.

A brief slide show which uses images and questions to illustrate a range of issues which can be understood through the psychodynamic approach.

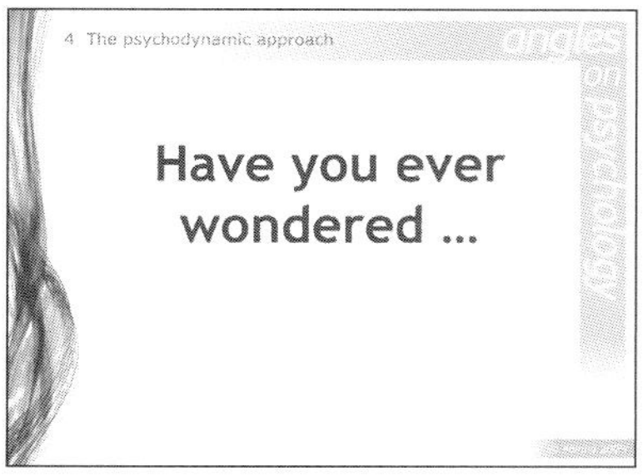

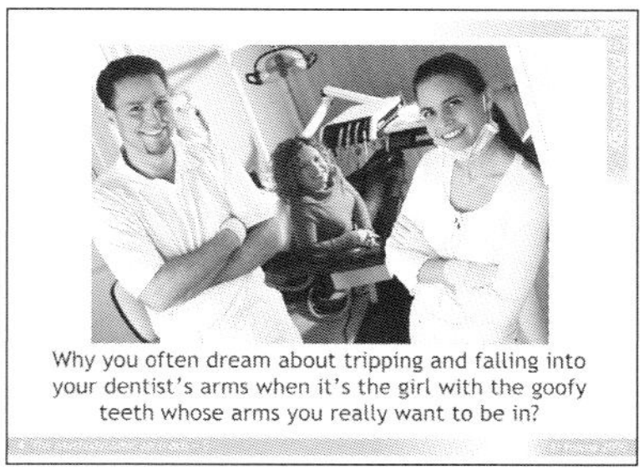

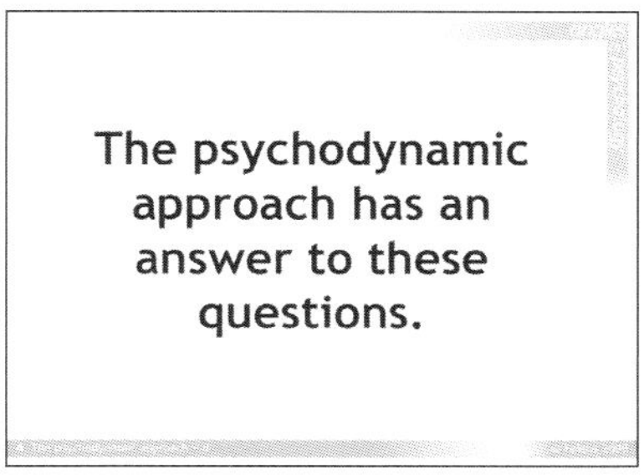

The unconscious mind

Draw a line to pair up correctly the terms on the left with the definitions on the right.

Freudian term
Catharsis
The conscious mind
Libido
The preconscious
Thanatos
The unconscious
Psychic energy

Definition
An unconscious instinct that is positive and makes itself apparent through sexuality
The release of stored psychic energy that can reduce negative effects such as symptoms of mental illness
The consequence of instincts and emotions that enables them to motivate behaviour as they build up and discharge
Mental processes of which we are fully aware, such as how we are feeling 'now'
Mental processes such as feelings, motives and memories of which we normally have no awareness
An unconscious motive that is negative and makes itself apparent through aggression
Mental processes such as memories that can be called to mind and are not represented symbolically

Stretch and challenge

1. In the cognitive approach, a useful way to understand the mind is to consider it in terms of information processing and computers. In Freud's day, the harnessing of hydraulic forces was one of the dominant technological advances (Draaisma, 2000). To what extent might Freud's thinking have been affected or limited by his knowledge of technological inventions?
2. Think back to the idea of schemas from the cognitive approach. Could our own understanding be limited by our technology?

The unconscious mind

Freudian term	Definition
Catharsis	An unconscious instinct that is positive and makes itself apparent through sexuality
The conscious mind	The release of stored psychic energy that can reduce negative effects such as symptoms of mental illness
Libido	The consequence of instincts and emotions that enables them to motivate behaviour as they build up and discharge
The preconscious	Mental processes of which we are fully aware, such as how we are feeling 'now'
Thanatos	Mental processes such as feelings, motives and memories of which we normally have no awareness
The unconscious	An unconscious motive that is negative and makes itself apparent through aggression
Psychic energy	Mental processes such as memories that can be called to mind and are not represented symbolically

Case studies

Case studies are detailed, _____________ investigations of a _____________ instance, such as one person or family. This is used to provide others with accounts of interesting individuals with the purpose of illustrating a point rather than finding something out although they may be based on a particular theory so may be used as evidence. They produce _____________ data from a range of techniques, such as observation, _____________ or questionnaires. The researcher, who may also be a therapist, asks the participant questions and listens to their replies, e.g. about their past experiences and their current problems. The role of the researcher is to _____________ this information to develop an understanding of complex relationships such as between members of a family or between current symptoms and early childhood experiences.

A case study produces in-depth information because the individual is allowed to talk _____________ so provides 'rich' data that could not be gained through the _____________ techniques used in the experimental method. This means that the researcher is less likely to overlook aspects of the data that might not be recorded in a more rigorously controlled setting. Case studies also enable researchers to investigate how factors _____________ in complex situations, such as the role of individual differences in development or the effect of trauma on later mental health. It is an _____________ way to investigate traumatic experiences as it is not necessary to deliberately cause distress by generating an unpleasant event as it would be in an experiment. The reality of the situation also gives case studies _____________ validity in this respect as the findings relate directly to an individual in a _____________ context. Validity can be increased further by _____________, the use of several different techniques to research the same phenomenon; for example, conducting interviews with a patient, sending _____________ to their family and making observations. Importantly, a case study may be the only way to investigate atypical instances that are _____________. This enables researchers to access information that is very unusual.

However, there are also problems with this research method. The researcher is likely to get to know the participant well and, as a result, they may become less _____________. The researcher may be _____________ because they will have a particular theoretical bias, such as a strongly cognitive or psychodynamic perspective. This may cause them to see, record or interpret examples that fit their expectations and overlook ones that do not. This reduces validity. Another problem with validity is that there is unlikely to be a source of baseline measures, such as how happy someone was generally before they became depressed, so comparisons are difficult to make. _____________ is also threatened by the process of interpretation – as we cannot be sure that an interpretation is correct. This is a particular problem for psychodynamic psychologists as they study the unconscious and this cannot be accessed directly so interpretations are impossible to verify. The issue of interpretation also affects _____________ because it is possible for two individuals to interpret the same information, such as a report of a dream, in different ways. This is specifically an example of _____________ inter-rater reliability. The findings of case studies are unlikely to _____________ to other people because the experiences or problems of two people are never identical.

descriptive	high	low	questionnaires	single
ethical	interact	objective	rare	subjective
freely	interpret	qualitative	real-life	triangulation
generalise	interviews	quantitative	reliability	validity

Case studies

Answers

Case studies are detailed, **descriptive** investigations of a **single** instance, such as one person or family. This is used to provide others with accounts of interesting individuals with the purpose of illustrating a point rather than finding something out although they may be based on a particular theory so may be used as evidence. They produce **qualitative** data from a range of techniques, such as observation, **interviews** or questionnaires. The researcher, who may also be a therapist, asks the participant questions and listens to their replies, e.g. about their past experiences and their current problems. The role of the researcher is to **interpret** this information to develop an understanding of complex relationships such as between members of a family or between current symptoms and early childhood experiences.

A case study produces in-depth information because the individual is allowed to talk **freely** so provides 'rich' data that could not be gained through the **quantitative** techniques used in the experimental method. This means that the researcher is less likely to overlook aspects of the data that might not be recorded in a more rigorously controlled setting. Case studies also enable researchers to investigate how factors **interact** in complex situations, such as the role of individual differences in development or the effect of trauma on later mental health. It is an **ethical** way to investigate traumatic experiences as it is not necessary to deliberately cause distress by generating an unpleasant event as it would be in an experiment. The reality of the situation also gives case studies **high** validity in this respect as the findings relate directly to an individual in a **real-life** context. Validity can be increased further by **triangulation**, the use of several different techniques to research the same phenomenon; for example, conducting interviews with a patient, sending **questionnaires** to their family and making observations. Importantly, a case study may be the only way to investigate atypical instances that are **rare**. This enables researchers to access information that is very unusual.

However, there are also problems with this research method. The researcher is likely to get to know the participant well and, as a result, they may become less **objective**. The researcher may be **subjective** because they will have a particular theoretical bias, such as a strongly cognitive or psychodynamic perspective. This may cause them to see, record or interpret examples that fit their expectations and overlook ones that do not. This reduces validity. Another problem with validity is that there is unlikely to be a source of baseline measures, such as how happy someone was generally before they became depressed, so comparisons are difficult to make. **Validity** is also threatened by the process of interpretation – as we cannot be sure that an interpretation is correct. This is a particular problem for psychodynamic psychologists as they study the unconscious and this cannot be accessed directly so interpretations are impossible to verify. The issue of interpretation also affects **reliability** because it is possible for two individuals to interpret the same information, such as a report of a dream, in different ways. This is specifically an example of **low** inter-rater reliability. The findings of case studies are unlikely to **generalise** to other people because the experiences or problems of two people are never identical.

descriptive	interpret	ethical	questionnaires	validity
single	freely	high	rare	reliability
qualitative	quantitative	real-life	objective	low
interviews	interact	triangulation	subjective	generalise

Defence mechanisms

The two right-hand columns can be photocopied and cut into cards to fit into the table blank on the next page.

	Definition	Example
Repression	Recall of a traumatic event, or the feelings linked to it, are unconsciously blocked, hiding the painful memory	Someone is unable to remember the last few moments before a car accident
Displacement	The redirection of an emotion from the cause to another object	You come home and shout at the dog because you've had a bad day at school
Denial	Refusal to accept that events are happening or have happened	An alcoholic denies that they have a drink problem
Reaction	Denied feelings are replaced by the adoption of an attitude that is the opposite of our genuine feelings	A girl is overly pleasant to someone who bullied her years before
Intellectualisation	The 'explaining away' of uncomfortable thoughts in a logical manner in order to master them	You lose a favourite scarf and say you didn't really like it anyway
Projection	An individual's own undesirable characteristics or feelings are attributed to others, so alleviating blame	A violent lad shouts 'What's your problem? Looking for a fight?' to an innocent stranger
Regression	Behaving in a child-like way when under emotional pressure	An examination candidate sucks her thumb
Sublimation	Redirecting negative energy to do something positive	A poet writes beautifully when sad but his ideas dry up when he's cheerful

	Definition	Example
Repression		
Displacement		
Denial		
Reaction		
Intellectualisation		
Projection		
Regression		
Sublimation		

Defence mechanisms

Camilla has heard that there is a big animal like a wild cat that roams the streets of her town at night. One night, walking home from a friend's house, she hears a horrible noise like a lion's roar, then a person screaming. She is terrified and runs the rest of the way. Although she was very frightened by the experience at the time, she seems to have calmed down. Her mother, however, is concerned that she is just hiding her fear.

1. Pair up each of the explanations for Camilla being unaware of her fear with one Freudian defence mechanism from the list below. Each explanation is a different defence mechanism.

   displacement, reaction, regression, intellectualisation, repression, denial

Explanation	Defence mechanism
Whenever Camilla sees a picture of a cat in a magazine she gets excited and says how much she likes big cats.	
Camilla suddenly starts to say that she is frightened of dogs, even though she hadn't been before.	
When asked if she is afraid of cats, Camilla says 'No, of course I'm not'.	
At college the next day her friend says she heard a weird noise like a big animal just after Camilla left. Camilla doesn't remember hearing the same sound.	
If Camilla encounters a cat when they are out, she starts to cry and hides behind her mother until it's gone away.	

[5 marks]

2. What is the purpose of defence mechanisms? [1 mark]
3. a) Describe how the defence mechanism of repression operates. [1 mark]
   b) Describe how **one other** of the defence mechanisms listed above operates. [1 mark]
4. Camilla's mother has heard about a study of phobias at a local university. They are asking parents of adolescents with phobias to consider participating in a case study but Camilla's mother doesn't know what would be involved.
   a) Describe what Camilla and her mother might expect to happen if Camilla was chosen to be a participant in a case study. [3 marks]
   b) Explain **one** strength and **one** weakness of the case study method used in the psychodynamic approach. [strength = 2, weakness = 2]

Stretch and challenge

Create another scenario in which two or more defence mechanisms are displayed.

Adolescent identity and defence mechanisms

Dave, Penelope and Jacklyn are at college together. Dave sometimes comes to college dressed conventionally, in jeans and a t-shirt, but sometimes dressed like a Goth. He occasionally ignores Jacklyn altogether and goes to sit with the computer geeks in the ICT lab. He has no idea what he wants to do when he leaves college.

Penelope, in contrast, has applied for nursing and intends to train as a midwife. She is ardently anti-abortion and is always off on rallies with her parents. Her mum is a counsellor who supports pregnant young women and her father is a vicar.

Jacklyn watches them both with faint amusement. They seem to be as odd as she was at school. First she tried out being a nerdy hard-working and sporty sort, then flipped and stopped doing anything at all, just deliberately hanging out with people her parents didn't like. She's settled into a set of friends she really likes and has a place at uni for psychology, her favourite subject.

1. Marcia (1980) described four identity states in adolescents:
   - identity diffusion
   - identity foreclosed
   - identity moratorium
   - identity achieved

   a) Decide which of these states Dave, Penelope and Jacklyn are in. [3 marks]

   b) Define *identity moratorium* and *identity foreclosed.* [2 marks]

2. Cramer (1997) studied adolescent identity states and defence mechanisms.

   a) Describe the sample she used. [2 marks]

   b) Outline the procedure used to classify the identity state of each participant. [2 marks]

   c) The tendency of each participant to use two defence mechanisms, denial and projection, was assessed using a thematic apperception test (TAT). Describe how the TAT test is administered and how the results are interpreted. [3 marks]

   d) The scores for identity state and use of defence mechanisms were correlated. Which identity state was correlated:
      - positively with both denial and projection [1 mark]
      - with denial only [1 mark]
      - negatively with both denial and projection [1 mark]
      - with neither denial nor projection [1 mark]

3. Evaluate the use of the TAT as a measure of defence mechanisms. [3 marks]

Psychosexual development and the structural model

Ineka is bored in a meeting and is looking around the table at her colleagues. Gisela is arranging her pen and pencils in order from smallest to largest, Gerry is biting his nails and Brian is arguing with the boss. Ineka vaguely remembers learning about fixation in her Psychology AS Level and is trying to decide which of the three earliest of Freud's stages of development might account for the behaviour of each colleague.

1. a) What is meant by the term *fixation*? [1 mark]

   b) (i) Each of Ineka's colleagues has fixated at a different stage. Which stage is most likely for each of these three people?

   Gisela .... [1 mark]

   Gerry .... [1 mark]

   Brian .... [1 mark]

   (ii) Explain how fixation at early stages of development could account for the behaviour of each colleague. [6 marks]

2. According to Freud's structural model there are three parts to the mind, the id (it), ego (I) and superego (above-I).

   a) Pair up each of these three parts with the correct principle on which it operates:

Part of the mind	operating principle
Id	
Ego	
Superego	

[3 marks]

   b) Each of the three early stages of Freud's theory of psychosexual development is particularly associated with one aspect of the mind. Identify the part of the mind that characterises each stage and explain why it is important at that time. [6 marks]

   c) Evaluate the structural model in terms of **one** strength and **one** weakness. [4 marks]

Stretch and challenge

1. Imagine three people with different personalities doing their weekly shopping. How might their fixations become apparent?

2. a) Imagine that three people with different personalities are considering taking up a new hobby or sport. Assume that their fixations affect their choice and describe the three people and their interests.

   b) Explain your choices.

Freud (1905): Little Hans

Aim: To interpret a five-year-old boy's phobia and help him to overcome his problems.

Procedure: Information about the boy, Hans, came mainly from Hans' ____________ in weekly reports and a description of Hans' ____________ life. He was taken to Freud aged five years so would have been in the ____________ stage of psychosexual development.

Findings: from age three, Hans was interested in his penis. Several things happened:

- Hans' mother threatened to cut it off if he didn't stop ____________ with it.
- Hans' father objected to Hans getting into ____________ with his parents.
- Hans developed a ____________ of horses, fearing that they would bite him.

Hans' fear seemed to be linked to the horse's large ____________. The phobia worsened and Hans was unwilling to go out in case he met a horse. The phobia then improved, relating only to horses with black harnesses over their noses, which Hans' father interpreted as his own ____________, i.e. it was a ____________. The end of the phobia coincided with two fantasies. In one, he had imaginary children. When asked who their mother was, Hans said 'Mummy, and you're their Granddaddy'. In the second, a plumber fitted him with a ____________ penis.

Conclusion: Freud's interpretation was that Hans' fear of horses related to the ____________ , symbolising his ____________ fear of his father (because they had black harnesses and big penises). The conflict arose over access to the parents' bed as this allowed Hans' father, but not Hans, access to his mother (because Hans would want to be attached to his ____________ but see his father as a ____________). Freud believed that Hans resolved this conflict as he fantasised himself with a big penis and ____________ to his mother. This would mean that Hans could overcome his ____________ anxiety and identify with his father.

Strengths

The case study allowed ____________ data to be gathered so a range of information, such as descriptions of fears, wishes and fantasies, could be gathered and interpreted.

Freud's case studies, such as this, provided evidence for his theories, such as the stages of psychosexual development, and for the techniques he used for helping patients using ____________, which is still used to treat people effectively.

Weaknesses

Most of the data was not obtained ____________ from Hans and Hans' father could have been biased by his relationship with his son.

Hans' father may have been ____________ as he knew Freud so would have been aware of his ideas, e.g. the Oedipus complex.

The most obvious explanation for Hans' fear of horses – that he had seen one collapse and ____________ in the street – was ignored by Freud which reduces the ____________ of the findings.

In general, Freud's idea that children have sexual feelings, even unconscious ones, such as fearing castration, seem unlikely so this aspect of the case lacks ____________.

Freud (1905): Little Hans *continued*

bed	die	Oedipus complex
believability	directly	phallic
biased	early	phobia
bigger	father	playing
castration	married	psychoanalysis
credibility	mother	rival
detailed	moustache	symbol

Freud (1905): Little Hans

Answers

Aim: To interpret a five-year-old boy's phobia and help him to overcome his problems.

Procedure: Information about the boy, Hans, came mainly from Hans' **father** in weekly reports and a description of Hans' **early** life. He was taken to Freud aged five years so would have been in the **phallic** stage of psychosexual development.

Findings: from age three, Hans was interested in his penis. Several things happened:

- Hans' mother threatened to cut it off if he didn't stop **playing** with it.
- Hans' father objected to Hans getting into **bed** with his parents.
- Hans developed a **phobia** of horses, fearing that they would bite him.

Hans' fear seemed to be linked to the horse's large **penis**. The phobia worsened and Hans was unwilling to go out in case he met a horse. The phobia then improved, relating only to horses with black harnesses over their noses, which Hans' father interpreted as his own **moustache**, i.e. it was a **symbol**. The end of the phobia coincided with two fantasies. In one, he had imaginary children. When asked who their mother was, Hans said 'Mummy, and you're their Granddaddy'. In the second, a plumber fitted him with a **bigger** penis.

Conclusion: Freud's interpretation was that Hans' fear of horses related to the **Oedipus complex**, symbolising his **unconscious** fear of his **father** (because they had black harnesses and big penises). The conflict arose over access to the parents' bed as this allowed Hans' father, but not Hans, access to his **mother** (because Hans would want to be attached to his **mother** but would see his father as a **rival**). Freud believed that Hans resolved this conflict as he fantasised himself with a big **penis** and **married** to his mother. This would mean that Hans could overcome his **castration** anxiety and identify with his father.

Strengths

The case study allowed **detailed** data to be gathered so a range of information, such as descriptions of fears, wishes and fantasies, could be gathered and interpreted.

Freud's case studies, such as this, provided evidence for his theories, such as the stages of psychosexual development, and for the techniques he used for helping patients using **psychoanalysis**, which is still used to treat people effectively.

Weaknesses

Most of the data was not obtained **directly** from Hans and Hans' father could have been biased by his relationship with his son.

Hans' father may have been **biased** as he knew Freud so would have been aware of his ideas, e.g. the Oedipus complex.

The most obvious explanation for Hans' fear of horses – that he had seen one collapse and **die** in the street – was ignored by Freud which reduces the **credibility** of the findings.

In general, Freud's idea that children have sexual feelings, even unconscious ones, such as fearing castration, seem unlikely so this aspect of the case lacks **believability**.

Freud (1905): Little Hans

Answers *continued*

father	penis	rival	biased
early	moustache	married	die
phallic	symbol	castration	credibility
playing	bigger	detailed	believability
bed	Oedipus complex	psychoanalysis	
phobia	mother	directly	

Correlations

Correlational designs propose a link or ____________ between two ____________. The two factors are ____________ rather than ____________. As a consequence, a single correlation cannot be used to determine whether a change in one factor is the ____________ of a change in another one, as can be done in ____________ studies. On the positive side, however, a correlation can sometimes be used when an experimental study could not be conducted. This is because it may be possible to measure existing variations in individuals and look for links between the variables when it would be impractical or unethical to induce such variations deliberately. For example, there are obvious ____________ problems with experimental studies on stress and illness – few people would volunteer to be severely stressed in order to find out if this makes them sick. Similarly, if we suspect a link between viewing violent TV in childhood and behaviour in adulthood, parents are unlikely to allow their children to be ____________ exposed to high levels of aggressive programmes for an experiment. It is, however, possible to investigate such patterns using a correlational design.

Two different relationships can be identified using a correlational design. For example, a researcher might predict that as the variable of stress level increases, so would the likelihood of illness. Note the absence of ____________ in this statement – we cannot say that the higher stress level *causes* the increased risk of illness. A relationship such as this, in which both variables increase together, is called a ____________ correlation. This is the kind of association we would predict between ____________ and harsh early parenting. Harsher parenting and ____________ anality scores would be expected to occur together. An alternative relationship which can be demonstrated is a ____________ correlation, for example in repression. On the basis of repressed memories we would predict that the greater the trauma associated with an event, the ____________ the individual's recall will be.

Identify which of the following you would expect to be positive and which negative correlations:

1. Severity of early loss and the personality trait of dependency
2. Number of times a parent tells off a child during potty training and how tidy they are in adulthood
3. How strongly a child identifies with the same-sex parent and their attachment to the opposite-sex parent
4. How guilty a person feels about a failed relationship and the number of dreams they have which contain symbols of their former partner
5. The strength of a researcher's belief in a concept and their objectivity when observing examples of that concept

anality	ethical	manipulated	relationship
causality	experimental	measured	variables
cause	higher	negative	
deliberately	lower	positive	

Correlations

Answers

Correlational designs propose a link or **relationship** between two **variables**. The two factors are **measured** rather than **manipulated**. As a consequence, a single correlation cannot be used to determine whether a change in one factor is the **cause** of a change in another one, as can be done in **experimental** studies. On the positive side, however, a correlation can sometimes be used when an experimental study could not be conducted. This is because it may be possible to measure existing variations in individuals and look for links between the variables when it would be impractical or unethical to induce such variations deliberately. For example, there are obvious **ethical** problems with experimental studies on stress and illness – few people would volunteer to be severely stressed in order to find out if this makes them sick. Similarly, if we suspect a link between viewing violent TV in childhood and behaviour in adulthood, parents are unlikely to allow their children to be **deliberately** exposed to high levels of aggressive programmes for an experiment. It is, however, possible to investigate such patterns using a correlational design.

Two different relationships can be identified using a correlational design. For example, a researcher might predict that as the variable of stress level increases, so would the likelihood of illness. Note the absence of **causality** in this statement – we cannot say that the higher stress level *causes* the increased risk of illness. A relationship such as this, in which both variables increase together, is called a **positive** correlation. This is the kind of association we would predict between **anality** and harsh early parenting. Harsher parenting and **higher** anality scores would be expected to occur together. An alternative relationship which can be demonstrated is a **negative** correlation, for example in repression. On the basis of repressed memories we would predict that the greater the trauma associated with an event, the **lower** the individual's recall will be.

Identify which of the following you would expect to be positive and which negative correlations:

1. Severity of early loss and the personality trait of dependency +
2. Number of times a parent tells off a child during potty training and how tidy they are in adulthood +
3. How strongly a child identifies with the same-sex parent and their attachment to the opposite-sex parent –
4. How guilty a person feels about a failed relationship and the number of dreams they have which contain symbols of their former partner +
5. The strength of a researcher's belief in a concept and their objectivity when observing examples of that concept –

relationship	cause	causality	negative
variables	experimental	positive	lower
measured	ethical	anality	
manipulated	deliberately	higher	

Psychosexual development

media watch

LETTER OF THE DAY: I FANTASISE I FANCY MUM

The Mirror 28 January 2004

Dear Miriam,

MY mother is 43, still very attractive, with a fantastic body and I've always thought I'd really fancy her if she wasn't who she is.

I'm 25 and still live at home with her. There's only ever been the two of us so we're very close.

But now I've started to have obsessive fantasies about having sex with her. To be honest, what I'd really like to do is tell her how I feel about her and hope she feels the same.

Should I tell her? Or should I do nothing and hope these feelings I have for her just go away? Would there be any consequences if she felt the same?

1. The text above was submitted to the problem page of a newspaper. Dr Miriam Stoppard provided an answer based on Freud's ideas. Write a possible answer which includes all of the following:
   a) The name of the conflict that this man is still facing. [1 mark]
   b) The stage at which this conflict is normally resolved. [1 mark]
   c) An outline of the key events and feelings during this conflict. [1 mark]
   d) One reason why this individual may have failed to resolve the conflict. [1 mark]

JESSIE DRAMA IS A KATASTROPHE

The Mirror 27 March 2007 (edited)

HAS anyone missed Jessie Wallace – or Kat from EastEnders as she is forever destined to be known? ...

A Class Apart was Ms Wallace's first appearance on the BBC since leaving the soap ... Jessie ... played Candy, a gorblimey Cockernee single mum from a council estate fighting to get her unnaturally gifted son Kyle into a decent school ...headmaster Anthony offered Kyle a scholarship, betting that he could transform the boy – who spent his nights joy-riding and standing on motorway bridges gobbing into convertibles – into the winner of the Michaelmas Poetry Competition ...

Both of them went on a 'journey' and, of course, she taught him more about Life than he could teach Kyle. (Thanks to her, Anthony went from being an anal-retentive arse who wouldn't step on the immaculate grass quadrant to someone prepared to jump around on a bouncy castle.) ...

1. Describe the characteristics of an 'anal-retentive' personality. [3 marks]
2. Outline how Anthony could have developed an anal personality according to Freud's theory. [3 marks]

Starter: gender

See PowerPoint 4-11: *Psychodynamic approach to gender.*

This slide show illustrates some sterotypical and some counter-stereotypical situations. Each image has a question on the notes page of the slide show.

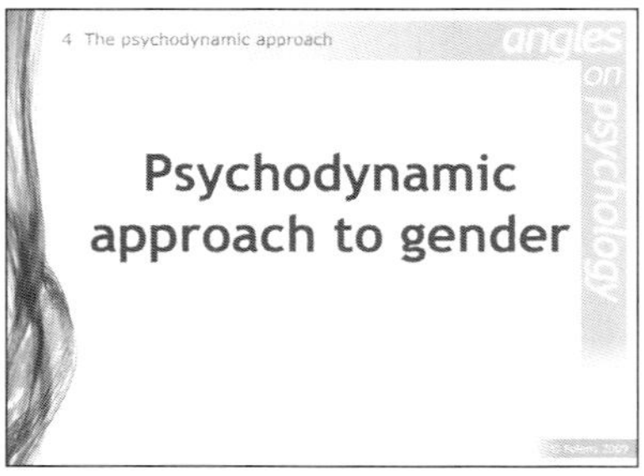

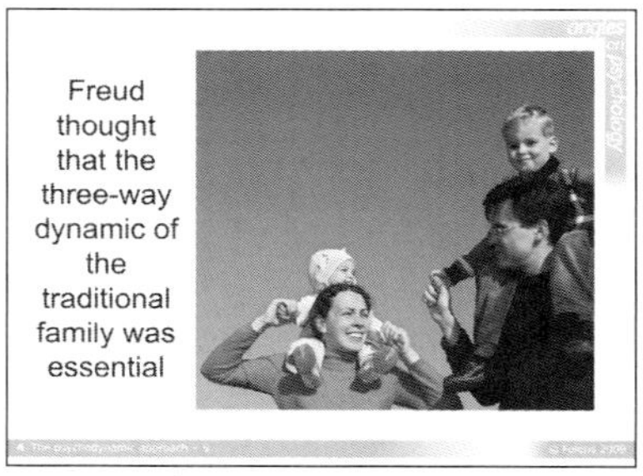

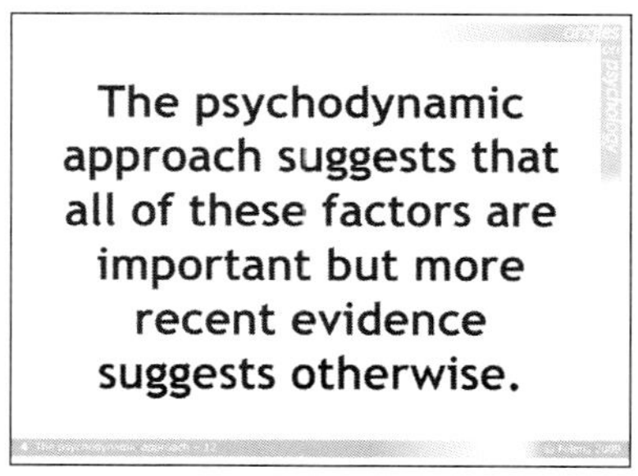

Gender and the superego

Jo and Dario were looking for a difference in superego development between girls and boys as predicted by Freud's theory. They expected younger children to be similar in the effect that guilt had on their behaviour as their superegos would be poorly developed. They thought that older children, who had entered the latency stage, would have stronger superegos and experience greater guilt. Freud suggested that the Oedipus complex resulted in boys having a stronger superego than girls.

Using children at a playgroup, Jo and Dario investigated superego strength using a special cage for Jo's hamster. The hamster would run on the wheel but had been trained to go into a box when it heard a very faint click. Inside the box was a secret door that led out into a hidden box behind the cage. The click and opening and closing of the secret door could be activated remotely by Dario.

Jo asked each child separately if he or she would watch the hamster to make sure it didn't escape while she was out of the room. If the child said they didn't want to, they were taken back to the playroom. Dario and Jo also told the children's parents about the study when they dropped their children off at the playschool and only used children whose parents had agreed. The room also contained a television playing a cartoon and some exciting-looking toys. Jo and Dario watched through a net curtain and when the child's attention drifted from the hamster, they opened the secret door so that it would seem to have escaped.

1. Dario and Jo tested two age groups.

   a) Which two age groups should they have tested to see superego development? [2 marks]

   b) What event happens before the latency stage that is critical to the development of the superego? [2 marks]

2. Jo went back into the room and 'caught' the child not looking at the hamster. She said she was disappointed because they hadn't watched her hamster and now it had escaped. She noted if they sounded or looked guilty and whether they apologised or made excuses. Some children didn't seem to care that they had been responsible for the hamster's disappearance; others clearly felt guilty: they seemed distressed and either said they were sorry or tried to wriggle out of being blamed.

   a) The older groups appeared to feel more guilt. What does this suggest about their superegos? [1 mark]

   b) Boys in the older group were no more likely to appear to feel guilty than girls. What does this suggest about superego development? [1 mark]

   c) Describe a problem with the objectivity of the data they were collecting. [2 marks]

3. a) Outline **one** ethical issue raised by this experiment. [1 mark]

   b) Identify and outline the ethical guideline that is relevant to the issue you have identified in (a). [2 marks]

   c) Identify two things that Dario and Jo did that were ethically good. [2 marks]

4. This study compared two groups of children of different ages.

   a) Is this a cross-sectional or longitudinal design? [1 mark]

   b) Describe an alternative way to investigate how the superego develops. [3 marks]

   c) Outline **one** strength and **one** weakness of this alternative design. [4 marks]

Gender

Print this table onto several sheets of different coloured card. Cut up each sheet into a different coloured pack of cards and shuffle each pack. Students working in groups can use the cards to complete the blank table on the next page in the correct order.

Boys	Girls
The focus of organ-pleasure shifts from the anus to the genitals (penis).	Organ-pleasure focus shifts from the anus to the genitals and the girl notices she doesn't have a penis but some other people do.
A boy has an unconscious, instinctive wish to have sex with his mother and wants to stay attached to her.	The girl blames her mother for removing her penis and is angry with her.
The boy becomes aware that he is being excluded from aspects of his parents' lives, such as getting into bed with them.	The girl recognises her father as powerful because he has a penis (penis envy) so wishes to attach to her father.
The boy recognises his father as a powerful rival for his mother's love and has an unconscious wish to kill him.	The girl sees her mother as a rival for her father's affection.
The boy sees that not all children have a penis and fears his father may castrate him for loving his mother (castration anxiety).	In place of the penis as a symbol of social power, the girl unconsciously desires a baby as a symbol of social power.
The boy resolves this conflict by repressing his love for his mother and attaches to his father (identification with the aggressor).	The girl resolves this conflict and satisfies her unconscious wish by repressing her desire for the father and identifying with the mother.
The boy develops a male gender identity through identification so becomes active and dominant with a strong superego.	Having identified with her mother the girl takes on a female gender identity, so is quiet and submissive.

Boys	Girls

Essays

Question 1

Gilbert's parents were very strict. He was brought up with many rules and demands on his behaviour, such as the times at which he woke up and went to sleep and when he used the bathroom. Although that was many years ago, Gilbert still finds that he lives a very regulated life and finds people who are untidy impossible to cope with. Benito was a sickly child and spent a lot of time in hospital during his early months. As an adult, Benito is finding it difficult to settle down in a relationship. Carole and her little brother used to get on well together, playing in the garden and in the bath together at the end of the day. As the children grew older, Carole became quite jealous of her brother but then settled down. At about the same time as her jealousy arose, Carole fell off her bike when she was showing off and hurt herself badly. She was banned from going out to play for weeks. Now, at 26, Carole is a mother of four herself. She was pregnant by the time she was 16 and tends to have physical rather than lasting relationships.

1. Choose **two** of the named people above.
2. Using Freud's theory of psychosexual development, explain why each of these two individuals has grown up as described in the text.
3. To what extent is this an adequate explanation of their personalities?

....

....

....

....

....

....

....

....

....

....

....

....

....

....

....

....

continue overleaf if necessary

Essays *continued*

Question 2

Threes into one do go

Freud said that there are three parts to our personality and certainly, when I try to make a decision, I can feel them fighting. Take yesterday for example. I only wanted to take today off work to go to beach. Part of me seemed to be saying 'Go on, do it, you'll enjoy it'. Another part seemed to be arguing back, saying 'But you have masses to do in the office, you can't possibly not turn up, it's unfair on everyone else'. Then, some other part tries a peace-keeping move: 'Of course you deserve a break, but the day after tomorrow's Saturday, you can go to the beach then and rest all of Sunday too and you'll feel better for not dropping everyone else in it'.

The article above describes the three aspects of the personality according to Freud. Identify each part in the text and describe it. You might like to consider the name of each part of the personality, how it is motivated and what governs its operation.

....

....

....

....

....

....

....

....

....

....

....

....

....

....

....

....

....

....

continue overleaf if necessary

Do dreams have meaning?

Diana dreamt of being a man

Joan Hanger,
The Mirror, 24 May 2004 (edited)

DREAMS can offer the most intimate insights ... which is why millions of us regularly ponder their significance. Princess Diana was no different. But whenever she had a confusing dream there was one woman the Princess could turn to for expert advice in interpreting its meaning. Dream analyst and writer Joan Hanger first met Diana in 1996 ... It was the start of an incredible friendship that lasted until Diana's death in a Paris car crash in August 1997.

From nightmares about being attacked by a dog to dreams featuring her mother, cross-dressing and snakes, they offer a fascinating and unique glimpse into Diana's world. Here ... Joan recounts some of Diana's most significant dreams and explains how the Princess's hopes, fears and desires are revealed through them.

In this dream, Diana saw herself in a man's suit for a secret dinner. She wore a suit, tie, brogues.

She laughed about it to me and remembered that when she woke, she couldn't stop laughing about the dream. But as it was taking place, she didn't like it at all.

I said that she may have had this dream at a time when she needed to show her inner strengths – strengths she didn't know she had ... 'I often have to be someone I know I'm not.'

I told her that clothes are incredible symbols in our dreams – they can show positive signs of the side of ourselves we don't show in our everyday life. In dreams, unusual clothes also show us that we have the power to choose how we express ourselves. 'Seeing yourself dressed as a man points out your internal sense of authority and strength to deal with whatever challenges may come your way.'

Royal secrets – shadows watched Diana

Joan Hanger,
The Mirror, 25 May 2004 (edited)

IN one dream, Diana had been confidently riding a big, grey horse along a winding track. In the distance, she saw a Shetland pony with a large person riding it.

'I felt like trying to catch up with this pair,' said Diana. 'But I couldn't move fast enough and I felt frustrated because I'd been riding so brilliantly until I saw them.'

As she slowly came closer to the pony, she could see that the rider was a woman – with a large derrière. 'It's Camilla Parker Bowles,' Diana said to herself in her dream.

The dream ended with the Princess eventually overtaking the pony – and Camilla studiously avoiding looking at her.

1. Use Freudian ideas about dream interpretation to explain the content of Diana's dreams.
2. Working with a partner, describe one of your dreams for them to interpret. To what extent can we be confident about the credibility of any interpretation?

Creative activities

1 Desperately seeking psychodynamic support

Celebrities with all kinds of mental health problems have sought the help of Priory clinics. Invent a name for a Priory Clinic in your area. Design a leaflet for the clinic that could be placed in doctors' surgeries for people to pick up and read while they are waiting. It should be aimed at people seeking help with their mental health. It should include:

- an explanation of the ways in which mental health issues can arise
- a description of some techniques that may be used in treatment.

2 Psychodynamic soap

Imagine that you are a scriptwriter for a soap on television. Create a character who has been introduced years before, as a child, and who reappears in adulthood. Script two episodes, one from each period. The behaviour of the adult in the later episode must be explainable in Freudian terms on the basis of their experiences in the first episode. Include a justification that would help the actors to understand the unconscious motives of the behaviours they have to portray.

Evidence of practice: a correlational study

Strict parents, stubborn children?

Stubbornness is an anal personality trait. We might expect this to be more common in people with strict parents who imposed restrictions in childhood. Parents can assert authority through telling children off, grounding them, insisting that they attend church, Brownies, Scouts, gymnastics, music lessons and many other commitments. They might have rules about wearing shoes indoors, washing hands before eating, television viewing or access to other privileges.

These ideas could be used to write closed questions or Likert scales on a questionnaire.

Stubborn, intractable people tend to 'dig their heels in' and refuse to budge. Think up some situations that might arise where someone could 'give in' or 'hold their ground'. Alternatively, think of a selection of words that might be used to describe stubborn versus flexible or accommodating people.

In-group, out-group?

If Tajfel & Turner's (1979) ideas about social identity apply to different age groups, then we might expect beliefs about young people to vary with age. For example, young people might feel that they are hard-working, polite and generous whereas older people may not. Furthermore, the more strongly an individual feels that these characteristics apply, the stronger their identification with their group would be. This means we have two possible correlations – one between a person's age and the number of positive attributes they associate with young people and another between how strongly they identify with the 'younger' age group and the number of positive attributes they associate with young people.

The attributes of young people could be measured by counting the number of words such as 'friendly', 'useful' and 'helpful' an individual attributes to young people. Age can be measured in years or groups of years such as 10–15, 15–20, etc. Strength of social identification could be measured by rating statements such as 'I feel youthful', 'I like popular music', 'I think wearing fashionable clothes is important', 'I like to have the latest model mobile'.

Preparation:

1. This investigation is a correlation. You will need to collect a lot of data so try to work in a group. You need to agree on two variables you can measure on rating scales in a self-report.
2. Agree an aim for your group and devise a suitable hypothesis.
3. Decide how you will collect self-report data, e.g. using a questionnaire.
4. What is your target population and what sample size do you want? How you will obtain a sample (by opportunity, volunteer, stratified or random sampling)?
5. Write a few questions using different styles (e.g. word selection, closed questions and Likert scales). Remember the data must be numerical.
6. Think carefully about ethical issues – are you sure that your questions will not embarrass anyone? Check your questions with your teacher.
7. Test your rating scales for reliability. Would you get the same results if you used them twice? If two different individuals score a participant's data, do they come up with the same scores on each variable? If they do the scales have high inter-rater reliability.
8. Collect your data ensuring that it is confidential. Put the data into a table and draw a scattergram with a title and headings on the axes.
9. Analyse your data using a Spearman correlation. Record the correlation coefficient and use a table of critical values to find out whether the correlation is significant. If it is, is it positive or negative? Was this what you predicted? State your conclusion – was your hypothesis correct?
10. Write a summary of the advantages and disadvantages of correlational studies and use examples of your research to illustrate this.

Oral personalities and the Rorschach test

Jacobs *et al.* (1966) were interested in the oral personality characteristics of smokers and non-smokers. They tested orality using Rorschach inkblots. These are a kind of projective test which, like the thematic apperception test, cause people to 'project' their personality into the description of what they see.

(a)

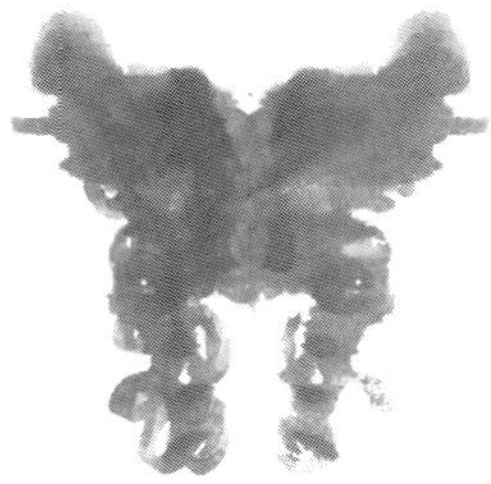

(b)

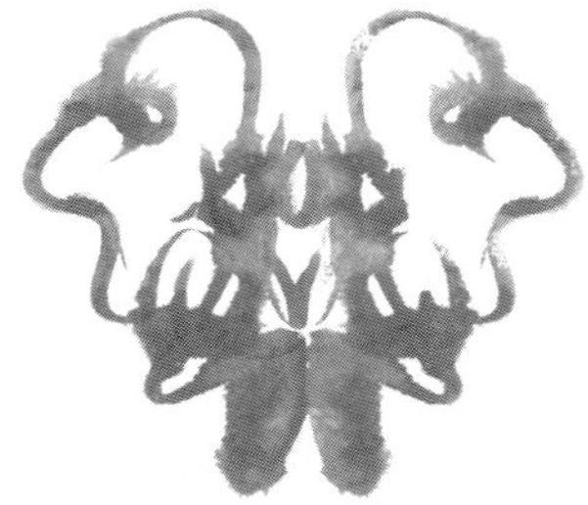

(c)

1. Look at the three inkblots above. Select one of them and suggest how it might be interpreted by:
   a) an individual with an oral personality. [1 mark]
   b) an individual who does not have an oral personality. [1 mark]
2. a) Define subjectivity. [1 mark]
   b) Explain why the answers you have given in questions 1a and b may be subjective. [1 mark]
   c) Explain why the Rorschach test may lack reliability. [1 mark]
3. The study conducted by Jacobs *et al.* was a laboratory experiment. This is unusual as a research method in the psychodynamic approach.
   a) Describe a research method that is more commonly used in the psychodynamic approach. [3 marks]
   b) Explain the advantages of the method you have described in (a) over a laboratory experiment. [3 marks]
   c) Explain the disadvantages of the method you have described in (a) compared with a laboratory experiment. [3 marks]
4. The sample used by Jacobs *et al.* consisted of 134 males, with an average age of 26 years. Seventy-six of these were students and 58 were industrial workers.

   Comment on the generalisibility of the findings from this study. [2 marks]
5. Jacobs *et al.* were also interested in the existence of a relationship between orality and other characteristics such as defiance or recklessness.
   a) What statistical test could they use to look for a link between pairs of characteristics? [1 mark]
   b) If people with more oral personalities were also more reckless, what result would you expect from this test? [1 mark]
   c) If people with more oral personalities were also less defiant, what result would you expect from this test? [1 mark]

Testing with TAT

This is like a Thematic Apperception Test image. How might it be interpreted?

Cramer (2007) provides evidence from both cross-sectional and longitudinal studies on the use of defence mechanisms by adolescents. She used the thematic apperception test (TAT) to measure defence mechanisms.

1. In one part of the study, she investigated over 100 participants at ages 11, 12 and 18. The sample consisted of every third child born in one city during a 17-month period.
   a) Was this a cross-sectional or longitudinal design? [1 mark]
   b) Identify the sampling method used. [1 mark]
   c) Approximately half of the sample was male. Why might this be important? [1 mark]
2. The three defence mechanisms identified were denial, projection and identification.
   a) Cramer tested each researcher's coding of participants' responses to the TAT. She found a correlation of +0.7 for denial, +0.82 for projection and +0.79 for identification. Comment on these correlations and what they show. [2 marks]
   b) Why was it important to conduct these correlations? [2 marks]
3. Cramer tested the samples in other ways, such as for intelligence. She found differences in intelligence between samples she was comparing for use of defence mechanisms. Why could this be a problem? [1 mark]
4. Each participant was tested individually, rather than in groups. Suggest why this was a good idea. [2 marks]
5. a) The coding method used on the TAT had been checked previously by comparing the findings on the TAT with other measures of development such as observations of children, adolescents and adults. The TAT score differentiated between groups as predicted. Did this demonstrate validity or reliability? [1 mark]
   b) i) What is meant by 'objectivity'? [1 mark]
   ii) Explain why the TAT may lack objectivity. [1 mark]
6. Older participants told longer stories. Explain one reason why this could be problematic. [2 marks]
7. Some of the results are presented in the Table below

	Mean score for use of each defence mechanism		
Age (years)	Denial	Projection	Identification
11	0.44	2.41	1.50
12	0.49	2.60	1.93
18	0.76	2.88	2.10

   a) Describe **three** general patterns or trends in these data. [3 marks]
   b) Choose a suitable graph or chart and illustrate the data for 'denial'. [3 marks]
8. State **one** advantage and **one** disadvantage of longitudinal designs. [2 marks]

Stretch and challenge

1. Look at an actual TAT picture here: Source: http://www.chssc.salford.ac.uk/healthSci/psych2000/images/Tat.jpg
2. Suggest some possible interpretations of the picture and what they might mean.

The psychodynamic approach quick quiz

1

a) What is a defence mechanism?

b) What are the stages of psychosexual development according to Freud?

c) What is a correlation?

d) Name two defence mechanisms.

e) What is meant by qualitative data?

f) Define opportunity sampling.

g) What is the key issue for the psychodynamic approach?

h) Name the levels of awareness that Freud suggested we possess.

i) Give an example of a case study in the psychodynamic approach.

j) Identify one study that contradicts an aspect of Freud's theory.

k) State an advantage of correlations.

l) Is the id (it) moral?

m) Give an example of the consequences of fixation at the anal stage.

n) What is a cross-sectional design?

o) Give an example of repression.

p) State a disadvantage of case studies.

2

a) What is a case study?

b) In which psychosexual stage does the Oedipus complex occur?

c) What a longitudinal design?

d) Define fixation.

e) State an advantage of case studies.

f) Describe the Oedipus complex.

g) What are the three aspects of the personality according to Freud?

h) Give an example of the consequences of fixation at the oral stage.

i) Identify one study that supports an aspect of Freud's theory.

j) Name a defence mechanism other than repression.

k) Is the superego (above-I) instinctive?

l) Give an example of an ethical issue in a case study.

m) Which study have you learned in detail other than that of Little Hans?

n) Define random sampling.

o) State a disadvantage of correlations.

p) When does Freud say a child acquires his or her gender identity?

The psychodynamic approach quick quiz

Answers

1

a) What is a defence mechanism? **A mental strategy to protect us from painful, frightening or guilty feelings**

b) What are the stages of psychosexual development according to Freud? **Oral, anal, phallic, latency, genital**

c) What is a correlation? **A relationship between two variables**

d) Name two defence mechanisms. **Any two of e.g.: repression, denial, projection, reaction, regression**

e) What is meant by qualitative data? **Non-numerical, descriptive results**

f) Define opportunity sampling. **Selecting participants according to availablility**

g) What is the key issue for the psychodynamic approach? **Depends on choice, e.g.: therapy, explaining irrational behaviour**

h) Name the levels of awareness that Freud suggested we possess. **Conscious, preconscious, unconscious**

i) Give an example of a case study in the psychodynamic approach. **e.g. Freud (1905) Little Hans**

j) Identify one study that contradicts an aspect of Freud's theory. **e.g. Golombok (2000): children from gay families cannot experience the Oedipus complex but are no different from those in heterosexual families**

k) State an advantage of correlations. **e.g. they can be used when manipulating variables is not practical or not ethical**

l) Is the id (it) moral? **No**

m) Give an example of the consequences of fixation at the anal stage. **Stinginess, stubbornness, orderliness**

n) What is a cross-sectional design? **One in which participants of different ages are compared at the same moment in time to study development with age**

o) Give an example of repression. **e.g. being unable to remember childhood abuse**

p) State a disadvantage of case studies. **A single individual cannot be representative so hard to generalise from findings**

The psychodynamic approach quick quiz

Answers *continued*

2

a) What is a case study? **An in-depth investigation of a single individual using techniques such as interviews and observations**

b) In which psychosexual stage does the Oedipus complex occur? **Phallic stage**

c) What a longitudinal design? **One which participants are followed over a period of time to see changes in development with age**

d) Define fixation. **Focus of the libido on a particular body part during a stage of development. Trauma at this stage can affect the later personality**

e) State an advantage of case studies. **Many different techniques can be used to get fuller, more valid data**

f) Describe the Oedipus complex. **A boy attaches to his mother but sees his father as a dangerous rival so represses his mother-love and attaches to his father, the aggressor**

g) What are the three aspects of the personality according to Freud? **Id, ego, superego/it, I, above-I**

h) Give an example of the consequences of fixation at the oral stage. **Dependence, enjoyment of food and drink, acceptance**

i) Identify one study that supports an aspect of Freud's theory. **e.g. Freud (1905) Little Hans**

j) Name a defence mechanism other than repression. **Denial, projection, reaction, regression**

k) Is the superego (above-I) instinctive? **No**

l) Give an example of an ethical issue in a case study. **Confidentiality**

m) Which study have you learned in detail other than that of Little Hans? **One of: Cramer (1997), Axline (1947) or Bachrach *et al.* (1991)**

n) Define random sampling. **Selecting participants so that each member of a population has an equal chance of being in the sample**

o) State a disadvantage of correlations. **A single correlation cannot allow a causal relationship to be determined**

p) When does Freud say a child acquires his or her gender identity? **In the phallic stage/ when they resolve the Oedipus complex**

Psychodynamic approach test

Centre No.						Paper Reference							Surname	Initial(s)
Candidate No.						6	P	S	0	2	/	1	Signature	

Psychology Advanced Subsidiary

Unit 2: The Psychodynamic Approach

Time: 50 minutes

Instructions to candidates

Answer ALL the questions.

Information for candidates

The total mark for this paper is 40.

Advice to candidates

Quality of written communication will be taken into account in the marking of your response to question 11. This question is indicated with an asterisk (*). Quality of written communication includes clarity of expression, the structure and presentation of ideas, and grammar, punctuation and spelling.

Question number	Leave blank
1	
2	
3	
4	
5	
6	
7	
8	
9	
10	
11	
Total	

SECTION A

Answer ALL questions.
You are advised to spend approximately 7 minutes on this section.

Choose answer A, B, C or D, and put a cross in the box (☒). If you change your mind, put a line through the box (~~☒~~) and then put a cross in another box (☒).

1. According to Freud the preconscious contains:

☐ **A** hidden memories we can never recall
☐ **B** memories we can only sometimes recall
☐ **C** memories that are too unpleasant to recall
☐ **D** no memories at all **(1)**

2. A case study is best defined as:

☐ **A** a way to collect in-depth data from just one person
☐ **B** a way to collect lots of experimental data
☐ **C** an investigation that is conducted over a long time
☐ **D** an investigation that draws causal conclusions **(1)**

3. In Freud's study of Little Hans, black bridles on horses probably represented:

☐ **A** Hans' father's penis
☐ **B** Hans' father's moustache
☐ **C** the harness on the horse that died in the street
☐ **D** the horse's penis **(1)**

4. According to Freud which stage is most important to a child's gender development?

☐ **A** anal
☐ **B** genital
☐ **C** phallic
☐ **D** oral **(1)**

Use this situation to answer the next two questions.

Dave has a blazing row with his teacher and gets sent out. He goes home and argues with his older sister. She asks him if something went wrong at college. He says 'no' and really can't remember there being a problem.

5. Which defence mechanism would explain why Dave argued with his sister?

☐ **A** displacement
☐ **B** reaction
☐ **C** repression
☐ **D** regression **(1)**

6. Which defence mechanism would explain why Dave could not recall what had happened at college?

☐ **A** displacement
☐ **B** reaction
☐ **C** repression
☐ **D** regression **(1)**

(Total 6 marks)

TOTAL FOR SECTION A: 6 MARKS

SECTION B

Answer ALL questions.
You are advised to spend approximately 25 minutes on this section.

7. Three sisters, Verity (age 35), Clair (age 33) and Susan (age 31) have different personality characteristics. Thirty years ago, their house blew up and they had a very troubled time which affected the development of each of them. At the time, Verity was five years old, Clair was three and Susan was one.

(a) In which Freudian psychosexual stage was each girl when the house blew up?
(i) Verity ....
(ii) Clair ....
(iii) Susan .... **(3)**

(b) **(i)** For **two** of the girls, describe what their adult personalities could be like and why.

Name of girl ....

....

....

....

....

Name of girl ....

....

....

....

.... **(4)**

(c) Evaluate Freud's theory of psychosexual development.

....

....

....

....

....

....

....

.... **(4)**
(Total 11 marks)

8. Correlations can be used in psychodynamic psychology.

(a) What is a correlation?

.... **(1)**

(b) Use the scattergraphs below to answer this part of the question.

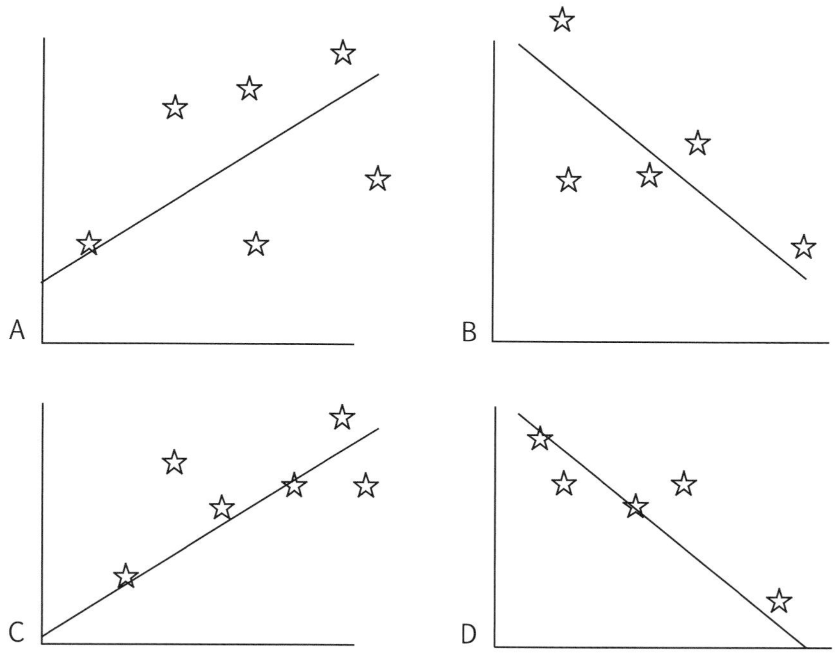

(i) Which diagram shows a strong positive correlation?

.... **(1)**

(ii) Which diagram shows a weak negative correlation?

.... **(1)**

(c) Outline **one** advantage of the correlational method.

....

.... **(1)**

(Total 4 marks)

9. There are many issues that affect the usefulness of the findings of psychological research.

(a) (i) What is meant by 'subjectivity'?

....

.... **(1)**

(ii) What is meant by 'generalisability'?

....

....

....

.... **(2)**

(iii) Identify an example of a study in psychodynamic psychology. You can do this by using the name(s) of the researchers and/or a brief description (there are no marks for this part of the task).
The study I am referring to is: ....

Explain why either subjectivity or generalisability may have been a problem in this study.

....

....

....

.... **(2)**

(Total 5 marks)

TOTAL FOR SECTION B: 20 MARKS

SECTION C

Answer ALL questions.
You are advised to spend approximately 18 minutes on this section.

10. Explain the difference between longitudinal and cross-sectional designs.

....

....

....

.... **(2)**

***11.** You will have learned about one of the following studies from the psychodynamic approach in your course:

Axline (1964): The case study of 'Dibs'
Bachrach *et al.* (1991): How good is psychoanalysis?
Cramer (1997): Personality and defence mechanisms in adolescence

Choose **one** study from the list above.

The study I am evaluating is: ....

Describe and evaluate the study you have chosen.

....

....

....

....

....

....

....

....

....

....

....

....

.... **(12)**

(Total 14 marks)

TOTAL FOR SECTION C: 14 MARKS

TOTAL MARKS FOR PAPER: 40 MARKS

Mark scheme

SECTION A

1. **B** memories we can only sometimes recall **(1)**

2. **A** a way to collect in-depth data from just one person **(1)**

3. **B** Hans' father's moustache **(1)**

4. **C** phallic **(1)**

5. **A** displacement **(1)**

6. **C** repression **(1)**

SECTION B

7. *Three sisters, Verity (age 35), Clair (age 33) and Susan (age 31) have different personality characteristics. Thirty years ago, their house blew up and they had a very troubled time which affected the development of each of them. At the time, Verity was five years old, Clair was three and Susan was one.*

(a) *In which Freudian psychosexual stage was each girl when the house blew up?*
(i) *Verity* **Phallic**
(ii) *Clair* **Anal**
(iii) *Susan* **Oral** **(3)**

(b) (i) *For **two** of the girls, describe what their adult personalities could be like and why.*
(Max 3 for explanation of one adult)

Verity:
Sexual overconfidence (explained);
Sexual underconfidence (explained);
e.g. she might be too scared to date people and have never had a partner;

Clair:
Stubbornness (explained);
Orderliness (explained);
Stinginess (explained);
e.g. she might be really messy at home or at work;

Susan:
Dependent (explained);
Gullible (explained);
e.g. she might be unable to cope living on her own and be very needy with her partner; **(4)**

(c) *Evaluate Freud's theory of psychosexual development.*
Strengths:

Massie & Szajnberg (2002) support the idea that traumatic childhood relationships with parents are related to later mental health problems;

Huprich *et al.* (2004) found a difference between orality in different types of criminals, supporting the idea that oral personalities exist;

O'Neill *et al.* (1992) found a link between anal personality and enjoyment of toilet humour, supporting the idea of the the anal personality;

Maltby & Price (1999) found that anality was linked to political conservatism, supporting the idea of orderliness in anal personalities;

Weaknesses:

Freud's evidence from little Hans can be criticised as his father knew about Freud's ideas giving biased support for the Oedipus complex;

Golombok (2000) found no evidence to support Freud's idea that failure to complete the Oedipus complex, e.g. in non-standard families, causes developmental problems;

Freud's focus on body parts lacks believability – it is unlikely that children are motivated by unconscious sexuality in the way he suggested;

Freud's use of case studies can be criticised as unscientific as they are subjective and of single individuals who are different so the evidence is unlikely to generalise to everyone; **(4)**

8. *Correlations can be used in psychodynamic psychology.*

(a) *What is a correlation?*
A link/relationship between two variables; **(1)**

(b) *Use the scattergraphs below to answer this part of the question.*
(i) *Which diagram shows a strong positive correlation?* **C** **(1)**
(ii) *Which diagram shows a weak negative correlation?* **B** **(1)**

(c) *Outline one advantage of the correlational method.*
It can be used to investigate variables that would be unethical to manipulate;

It can be used to investigate variables that would be impractical to manipulate; **(1)**

9. *There are many issues that affect the usefulness of the findings of psychological research.*

(a) (i) *What is meant by 'subjectivity'?*
The bias of a researcher/analyst when they see a situation only from their own perspective; **(1)**

(ii) *What is meant by 'generalisability'?*
Whether findings can be applied to a wider group than the population/sample tested;

Whether findings can be applied to situations beyond the specific one investigated;

e.g. the causes of one individual's problems might be different from those of other people; **(2)**

(iii) *Identify an example of a study in psychodynamic psychology. You can do this by using the name(s) of the researchers and/or a brief description (there are no marks for this part of the task). Explain why either subjectivity or generalisability may have been a problem in this study.*
Freud's study of Little Hans:

Subjectivity:

Hans' father reported most of the information about his son and their relationship, which might have affected what he wanted to report to Freud;

He also knew about Freud's ideas which might have affected what he thought was important;

Generalisibility:

This was one case so not all children would necessarily respond in the same way as they may have different unconscious fears;

No two individuals will have had exactly the same experiences so the findings might not apply to others;

Cramer:

Subjectivity:

Interpreting participants' stories from TATs depends on the individual researcher's views to an extent;

Classifying identity state could be biased as individual researchers would have opinions about what represented 'dependable/productive';

Generalisibility:

Although the group was mixed in terms of education and parental social class, two-thirds were Caucasian so the findings might not be typical of all ethnic groups;

They were also all from urban areas and differences in factors such as job prospects or role models might make adolescent identity different in rural areas;

Although the focus of the study was on adolescence, all were studied for the last time at exactly the same age (23) and not everyone develops at the same rate: late developers might not be well represented; **(2)**

SECTION C

10. *Explain the difference between longitudinal and cross-sectional designs.*

Longitudinal designs compare the effects of getting older by following the same people as they age;

Whereas cross-sectional designs look at people at different ages at one moment in time; **(2)**

***11.** *You will have learned about one of the following studies from the psychodynamic approach in your course:*

Axline (1964): The case study of 'Dibs'
Bachrach et al. *(1991): How good is psychoanalysis?*
Cramer (1997): Personality and defence mechanisms in adolescence
*Choose **one** study from the list above. Describe and evaluate the study you have chosen.* **(12)**

Level	Mark	Descriptor
		AO1: Knowledge and understanding of psychological concepts. AO2: Application of psychological concepts.
1	0	No content worth of marks.
2	1–3	A brief, simple answer with some relevance to the study but with little reference to methodological detail or evaluation. Answer lacks clarity and/or organisation. Little use of relevant terminology and poor spelling, punctuation and/or grammar.

3	4–6	An answer with simple but largely relevant description which is accurate but limited. Limited clarity and/or organisation. Some use of relevant terminology. Frequent spelling, punctuation and/or grammatical errors. At the top of the band some evaluation is present.
4	7–9	The answer contains both relevant and accurate methodological detail and/or results. Clarity of expression and organisation are competent with some use of relevant terminology. Some spelling, punctuation and/or grammatical errors are likely to be present. At the top of the band both reference to method/results and some evaluation are present.
5	10–12	The answer contains accurate detail of method and results and this is effectively evaluated. Description and evaluation are well balanced. Clarity of expression and organisation are effective and the candidate makes good use of relevant terminology. Few spelling, punctuation or grammatical errors are present.

Indicative content:
Cramer:
(AO1)

- **Cramer (1997);**
- **Investigated whether adolescents in different identity states differed in their use of defence mechanisms;**
- **Participants were rated for their identity state on variables such as being dependable/ productive;**
- **Their use of defence mechanisms/projection/denial was tested using the TAT;**
- **Identity moratorium was positively correlated with denial/projection;**

(AO2)

- **The sample was varied in terms of gender, SEs and occupation so was likely to be representative;**
- **The sample size was 91, which is large for a study of this kind and generalisation from bigger samples is more likely to be valid;**
- **The TAT may not be reliable as different interpretations can be given for the same story so the judgement of defence mechanisms might not be consistent;**
- **So the measurements of defence mechanisms may not be valid either as different conclusions could be reached about what a participant's story meant;**

Resources

See PowerPoint 4-22: *Resources.*

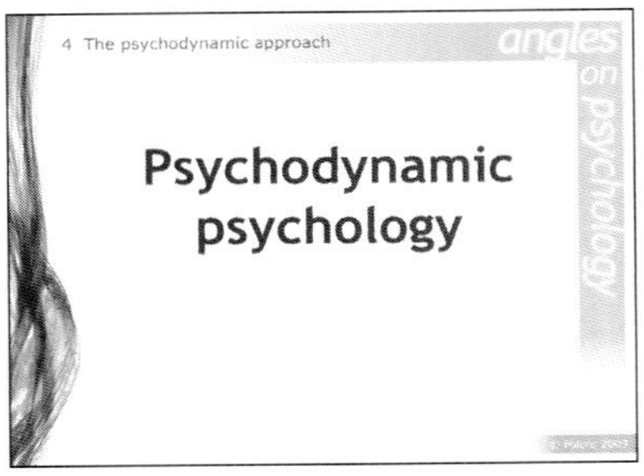

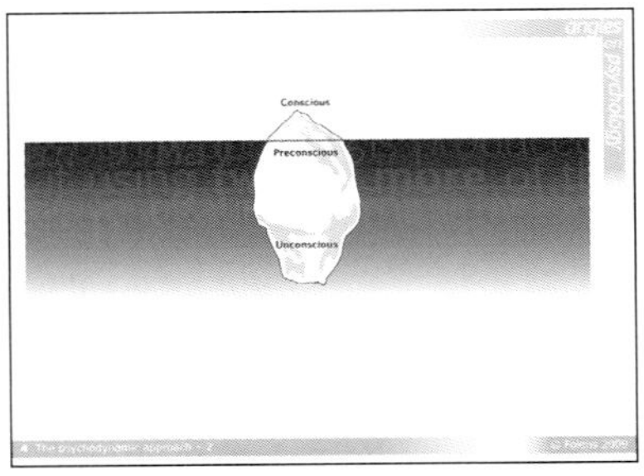

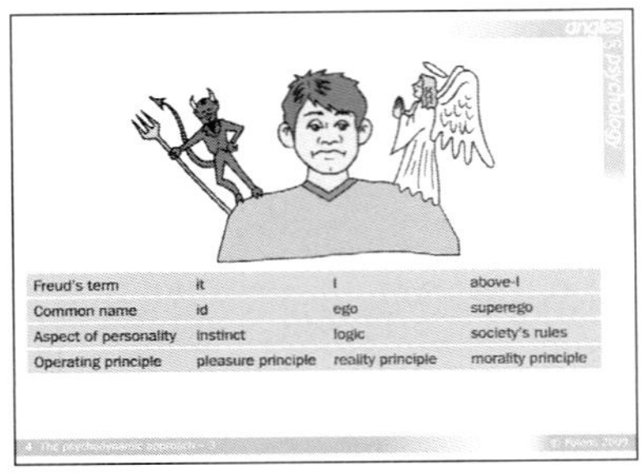

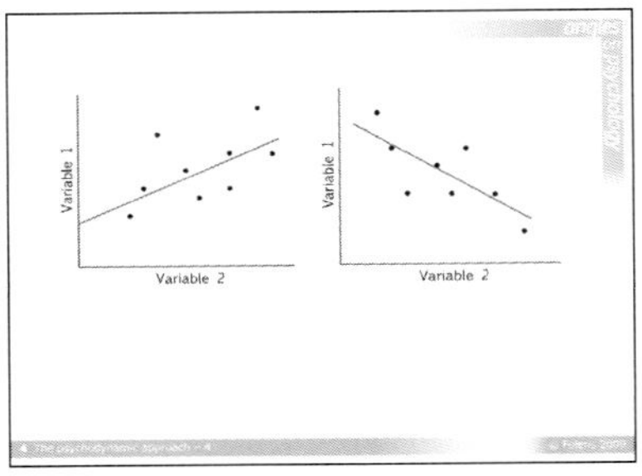

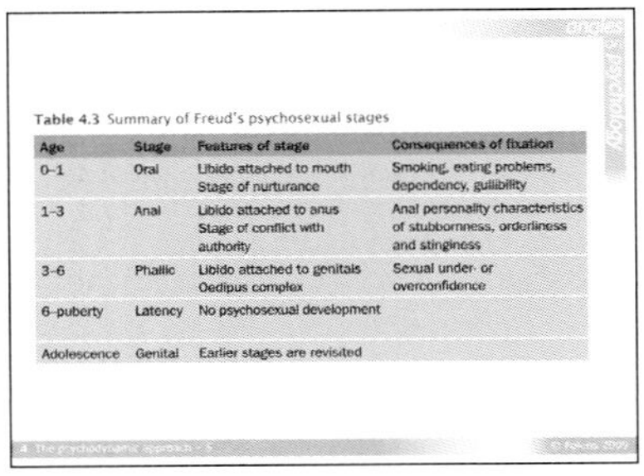

References

Cramer, P. (2007) 'Longitudinal study of defense mechanisms: late childhood to late adolescence'. *Journal of Personality*, 75, 1–24.

Draaisam, D. (2000) *Metaphors of Memory: A History of Ideas About the Mind.* Cambridge: Cambridge University Press.

Jacobs, M.A., Anderson, L.S., Champagne, E., Karush, N., Richman, S.J. & Knapp, P.H. (1966) 'Orality, impulsivity and cigarette smoking in men: further findings in support of a theory'. *Journal of Nervous and Mental Diseases*, 143(3): 207–19.

Teacher's Support Guide

Chapter 5

The biological approach

Activity number	Activity title	Activity/file type
The biological aproach		
5.1	Introduction	ST PP
5.2	Starter: synapse colouring flipbook	ST SC CA
5.3	Genes and the environment	CA
5.4	Twin studies	CE A
5.5	Adoption studies	SAQ
5.6	Starter: biology of gender	ST PP
5.7	Biology of gender	MW A
5.8	Gendered brains	MW SC
5.9	Practical and ethical issues with using animals in psychology	CE A
5.10	Brain scanning: PET and MRI	CE A
5.11	Money (1975)	CE A
5.12	Inferential statistics and the Mann–Whitney test: cloze	CE A
5.13	The nature–nurture debate	SAQ
5.14	Essays: questions 1 and 2	LAQ
5.15	'Smell the roses' scan	ET
5.16	Creative activities 1 and 2	KI
5.17	Evidence of practice: looking and language, left and right	RM
5.18	Lateralisation	RM
5.19	MRI scanning	RM
5.20	The biological approach quiz	QQ A
5.21	The biological approach test	UT A
5.22	Resources	PP
5.23	References	

5.1 Introduction

See PowerPoint 5-1: *Lateralisation and the CNS.*

A short slide show of images, each with a question, illustrating activities that are typically lateralised to the left or right and some spinal reflexes. The answers to the quesitons are on the notes pages of the slide show.

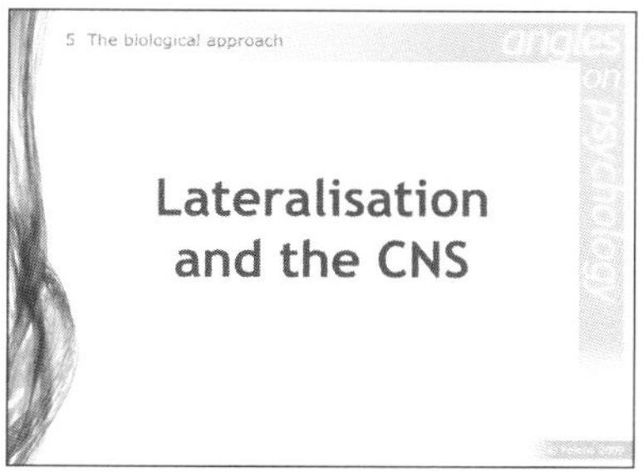

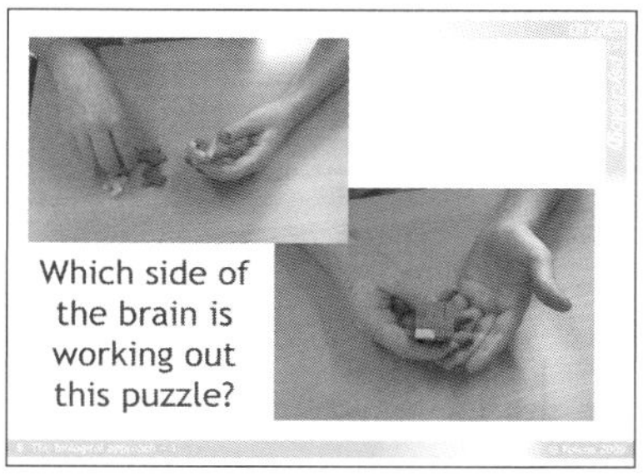

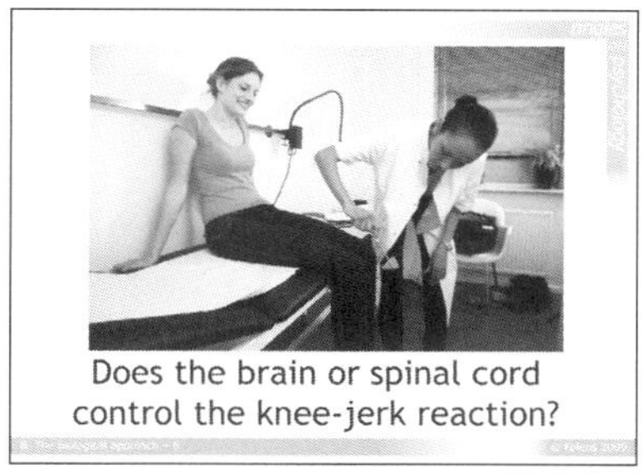

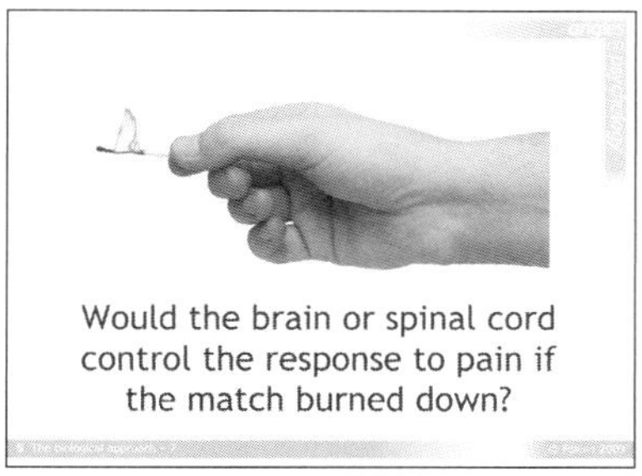

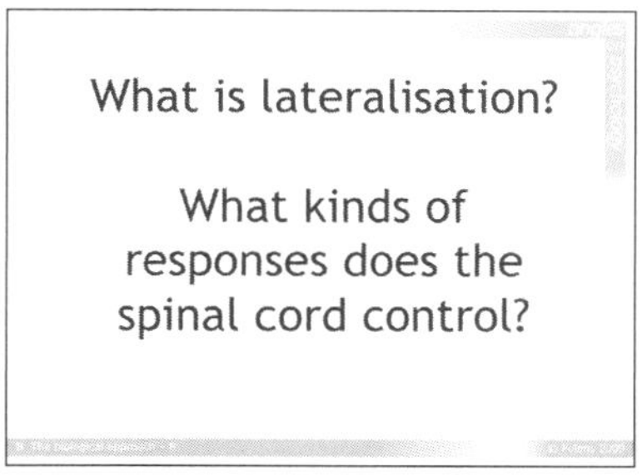

Starter: synapse colouring flipbook

Colour in each of the following a different colour:

- neurotransmitters
- synapse
- receptors
- pre-synaptic neurone
- post-synaptic neurone.

Add labels to the five areas above on the last diagram only.

Write out a numbered sequence describing what is happening in illustrations 1, 10, 11, 13 and 18

Assemble in a booklet and flip the pages.

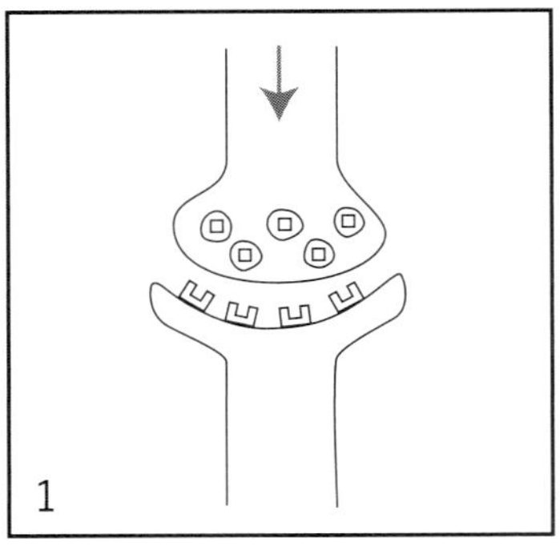

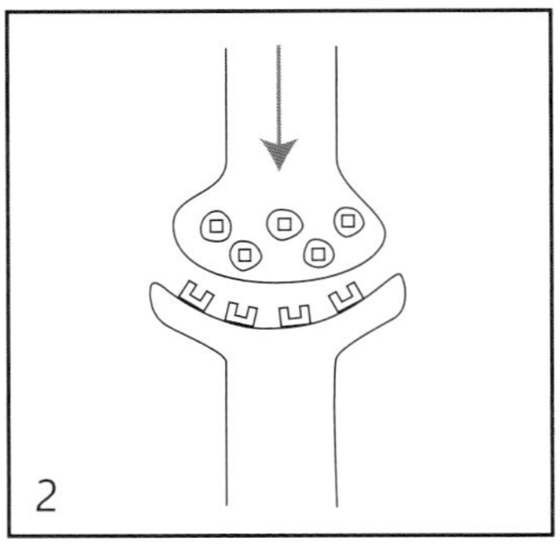

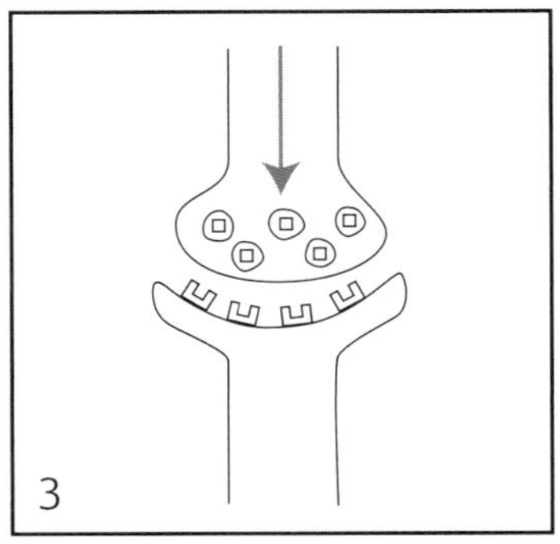

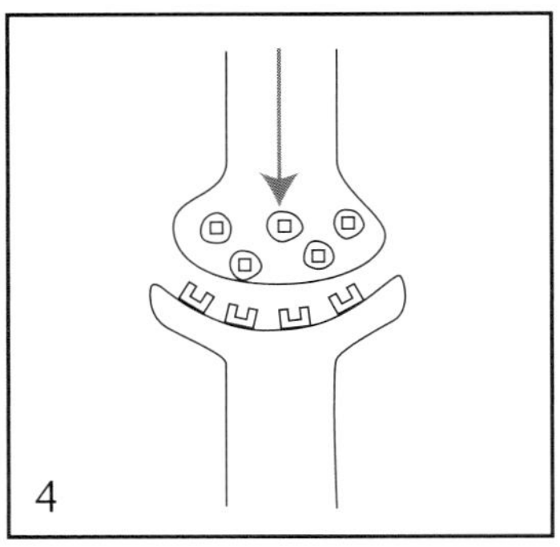

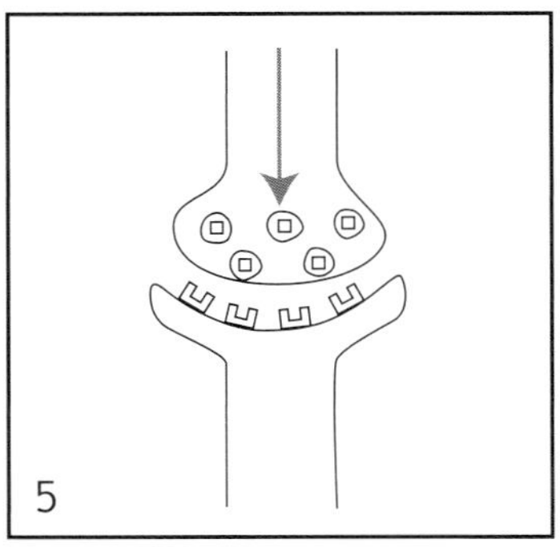

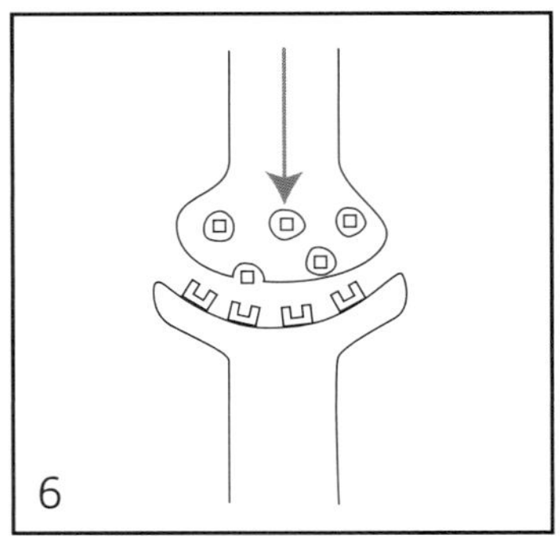

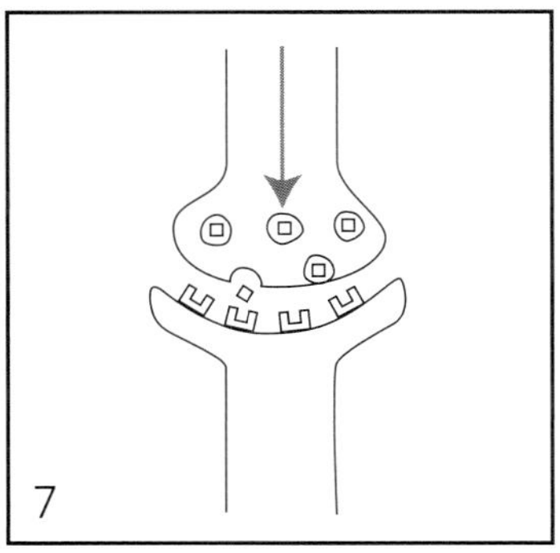

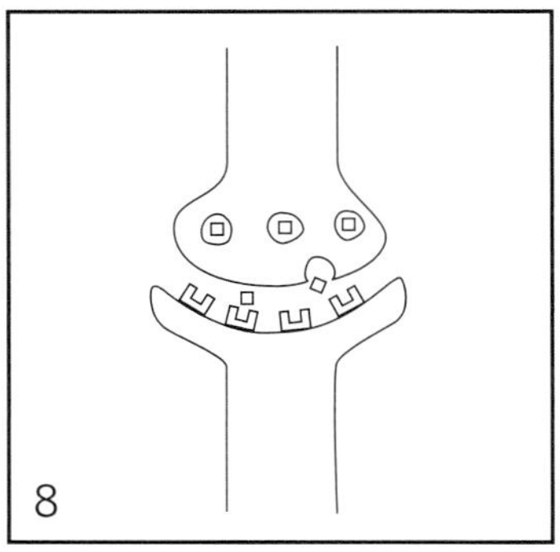

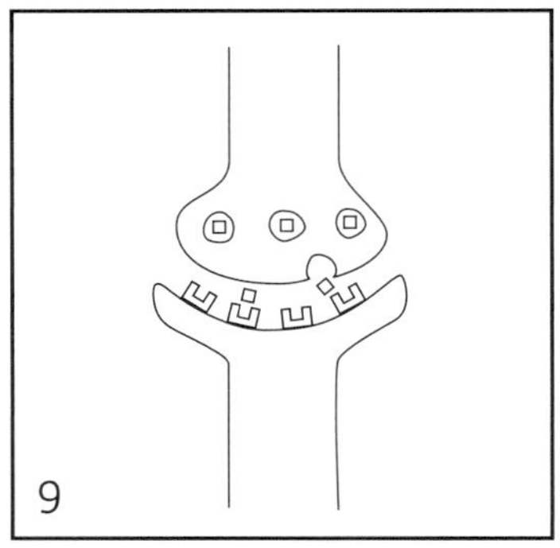

Starter: synapse colouring flipbook *continued*

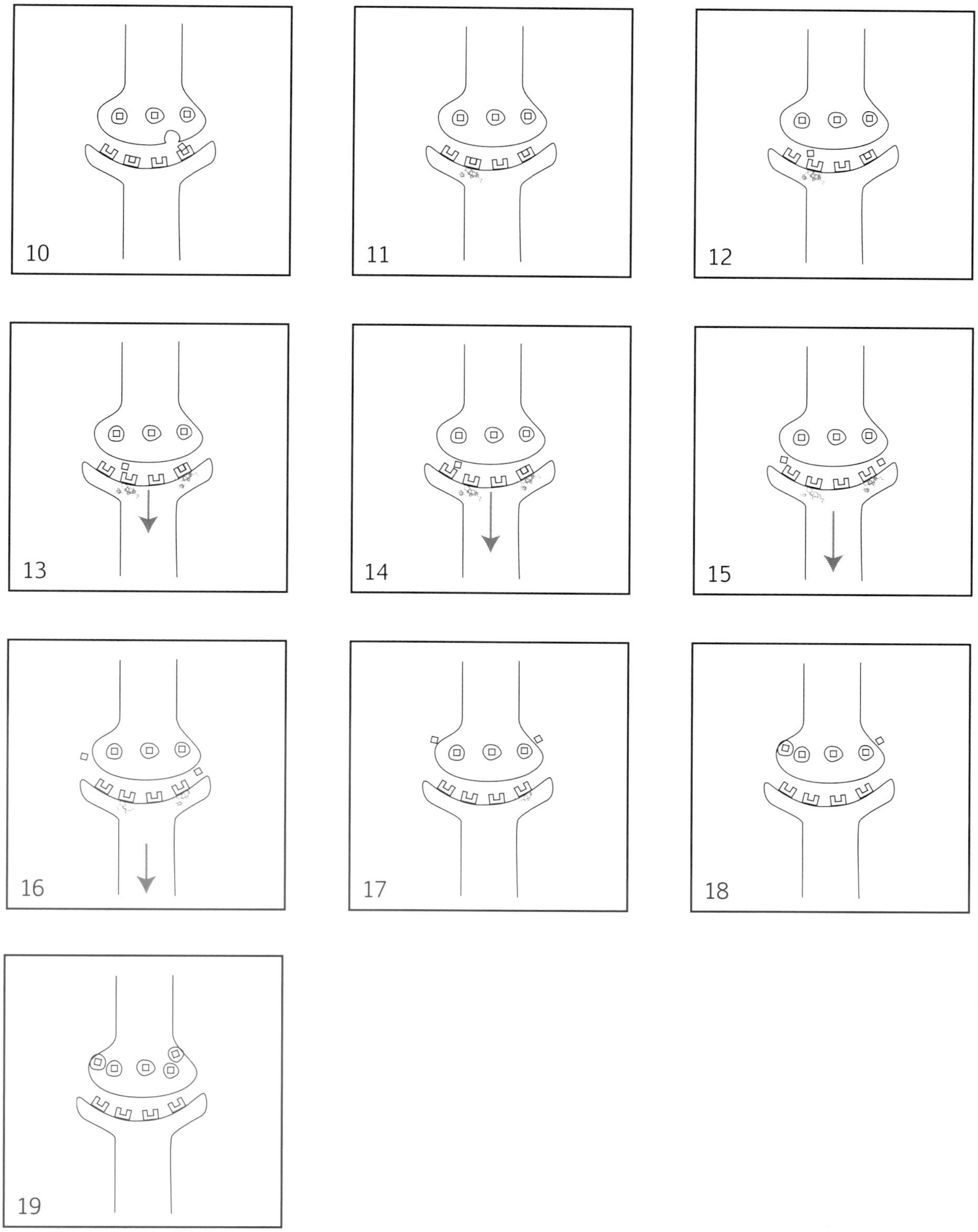

Stretch and Challenge

1. Design a flipbook to show how a spinal reflex happens. You can use page 124, Figure 5.6 of *Angles on Psychology* as a starting point.
2. Use this website to find out about brain structure:

   http://thebrain.mcgill.ca/flash/d/d_06/d_06_cr/d_06_cr_mou/d_06_cr_mou.html

Genes and the environment

Philip and Fred are MZ twins. They both have fiery tempers.

Suggest **two** reasons why.

Sian and Shaun are DZ twins. They both suffer from depression.

Suggest **two** reasons why.

Derek, Dave, Diane and Demetra were all adopted because their mothers have severe schizophrenia. As adults, Derek, Dave and Diane have all been hospitalised at some point with symptoms of psychosis but Demetra has not.

What two things do these results suggest about the cause of schizophrenia?

Like Derek, Dave, Diane and Demetra, four children, William, Wendy, Winston and Willow were also adopted. In each case, their mother was mentally healthy. William, Wendy, Winston and Willow are all mentally healthy as adults.

How do these findings help to understand the findings relating to Derek, Dave, Diane and Demetra about the cause of schizophrenia?

Belinda and Beatrice are old. They are MZ twins but were separated during the war at three years of age. They were in their 60s before they met up. They are very alike in personality.

Suggest why this might be the case.

Gordon has four brothers and a sister. All of them are very shy. Most of their aunts and uncles are shy too.

Think of **two** explanations for this pattern.

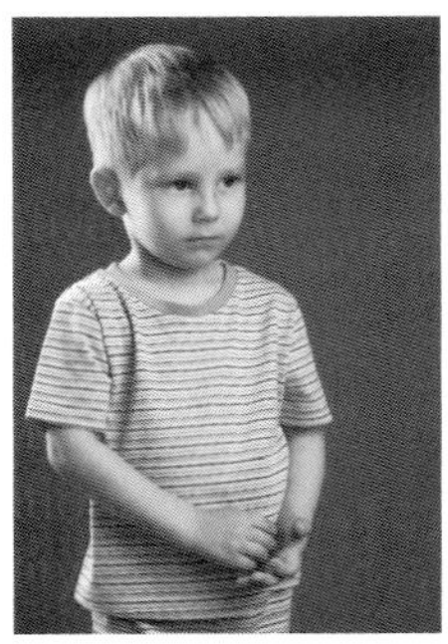

Twin studies

_____________ twins are also called monozygotic twins and share_____________% of their genes. Fraternal twins or _____________ twins share only half of their genetic material on average. For identical twins raised together, any differences that arise during development are likely to be caused by _____________ effects. In non-identical twins such differences could be the result of _____________ differences. However, because identical twins are more likely to be treated in the same way, we cannot be sure that their _____________ is purely genetically caused. One way to be more certain is to study separated twins. Sadly, not all twins are raised together during their development. If monozygotic twins are raised apart, differences that appear between them are likely to be due to their _____________ rather than to their _____________. If those who have been raised in the _____________ family are more alike than those who have grown up apart, this suggests a role for environmental factors.

Gottesman & Shields (1966) studied the incidence of schizophrenia in twins. They investigated the probability of both twins sharing the disorder, that is, their _____________ for this characteristic. When considering just hospitalised cases, they found that in _____________ twins, 42% had schizophrenia if their twin also had the disorder, but in dizygotic twins, only 9% had schizophrenia if their twin did. This tells us that dizygotic twins have a _____________ probability of sharing schizophrenia than monozygotic twins, suggesting that schizophrenia is partly genetically controlled. If schizophrenia was _____________ genetic, all monozygotic twins of sufferers would also have the condition.

It is not only mental illnesses that show this pattern. Loehlin (1992) investigated the personality characteristics of neuroticism and extraversion. The correlation for monozygotic twins reared together was _____________ than for monozygotic twins reared apart. This showed that there is some environmental element in the development of _____________. A similar pattern is seen in concordance for sexual orientation. Looking at non-heterosexual orientation, Kendler *et al.* (2000) found that concordance for monozygotic twins was _____________% and for same-sex dizygotic twins was _____________%. This finding is likely to be reliable as it was based on a sample of _____________ twins.

13.3	entirely	lower
31.6	environmental	monozygotic
100	genes	personality
1588	genetic	same
concordance	greater	similarity
dizygotic	identical	upbringing

Twin studies

Answers

Identical twins are also called monozygotic twins and share **100**% of their genes. Fraternal twins or **dizygotic** twins share only half of their genetic material on average. For identical twins raised together, any differences that arise during development are likely to be caused by **environmental** effects. In non-identical twins such differences could be the result of **genetic** differences. However, because identical twins are more likely to be treated in the same way, we cannot be sure that their **similarity** is purely genetically caused. One way to be more certain is to study separated twins. Sadly, not all twins are raised together during their development. If monozygotic twins are raised apart, differences that appear between them are likely to be due to their **upbringing** rather than to their **genes**. If those who have been raised in the **same** family are more alike than those who have grown up apart, this suggests a role for environmental factors.

Gottesman & Shields (1966) studied the incidence of schizophrenia in twins. They investigated the probability of both twins sharing the disorder, that is, their **concordance** for this characteristic. When considering just hospitalised cases, they found that in **monozygotic** twins, 42% had schizophrenia if their twin also had the disorder, but in dizygotic twins, only 9% had schizophrenia if their twin did. This tells us that dizygotic twins have a **lower** probability of sharing schizophrenia than monozygotic twins, suggesting that schizophrenia is partly genetically controlled. If schizophrenia was **entirely** genetic, all monozygotic twins of sufferers would also have the condition.

It is not only mental illnesses that show this pattern. Loehlin (1992) investigated the personality characteristics of neuroticism and extraversion. The correlation for monozygotic twins reared together was **greater** than for monozygotic twins reared apart. This showed that there is some environmental element in the development of **personality**. A similar pattern is seen in concordance for sexual orientation. Looking at non-heterosexual orientation, Kendler *et al.* (2000) found that concordance for monozygotic twins was **31.6**% and for same-sex dizygotic twins was **13.3**%. This finding is likely to be reliable as it was based on a sample of **1588** twins.

Identical	upbringing	entirely
100	genes	greater
dizygotic	same	personality
environmental	concordance	31.6
genetic	monozygotic	13.3
similarity	lower	1588

Adoption studies

Adoption studies have been used to investigate the heritability of a range of psychological variables, such as personality and mental health. Daniels & Plomin (1985) investigated shyness using an adoption study. One hundred and fifty-two adopted and 150 non-adopted infants and their parents (including the biological mothers) were rated for relevant variables such as shyness and sociability. They found that shyness and low sociability in infants and their biological mothers were positively correlated when the infants were not adopted. They also found positive correlations for shyness and low sociability between infants and biological mothers when the infants were adopted.

Roth & Finley (1998) reviewed evidence relating to the heritability of antisocial personality disorder, which is more prevalent in adoptees than non-adoptees. They found that adopted children who already have a biological risk (that is, have at least one biological parent with a background of criminality or antisocial personality disorder) are more likely to have antisocial personality disorder themselves. Adopted children without such a risk factor are typically unlikely to develop the disorder in the adoptive environment. However, the combination of adoption and genetic risk makes antisocial personality disorder quite common in adoptees. This risk was increased if the adoptive parents also had a history of criminal behaviour.

Roth and Finley (1998) identified several problems with adoption studies:

- Most adoption studies consider biological information only from the mother not the father.
- The existence of criminal behaviour is used as evidence of antisocial behaviour disorder although this may not necessarily be the case.
- The absence of a criminal record does not necessarily confirm the absence of antisocial behaviour disorder.
- Although the adoptive family environment is often better in terms of stability, education and health (factors which tend to reduce criminality), adopted-away children are often placed in family environments which are similar to their biological ones.

1. a) i) What relationship did Daniels & Plomin (1985) find between shyness in non-adopted infants and their biological mothers?
   ii) Suggest **two** reasons for this finding.
   b) i) What relationship did Daniels & Plomin (1985) find between shyness in adopted infants and their biological mothers?
   ii) Suggest **one** reason for this finding.
   c) Taking Daniels & Plomin's evidence from both adopted and non-adopted infants, what can you conclude about the heritability of shyness?
2. a) What did Roth & Finley (1998) conclude about children with a family history of antisocial personality disorder or criminality?
   b) What did Roth & Finley (1998) conclude about children who were adopted into a family with a history of criminality?
   c) What can you conclude about the influence of the process of adoption itself on antisocial personality disorder?
   d) i) What set of circumstances would produce the greatest chance of a child developing antisocial personality disorder?
   ii) Is it inevitable that a child in this situation will develop antisocial personality disorder?
3. Outline why each of the issues raised by Roth & Finley (1998) in the bullet points above is potentially problematic.

Starter: biology of gender

See PowerPoint 5-6: *Biology of gender.*

This slide show contains charts and images to illustrate the biological control of gender development.

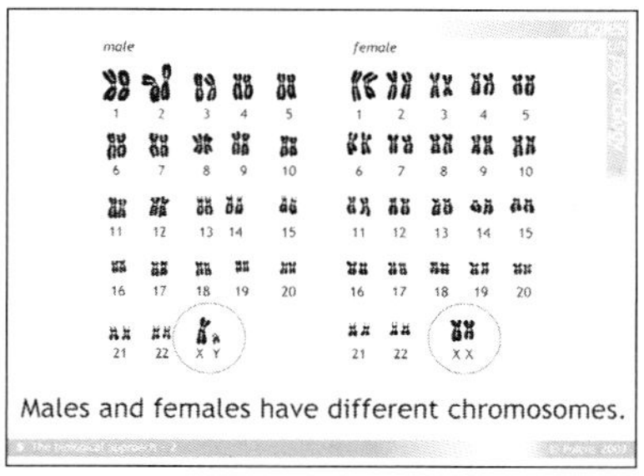

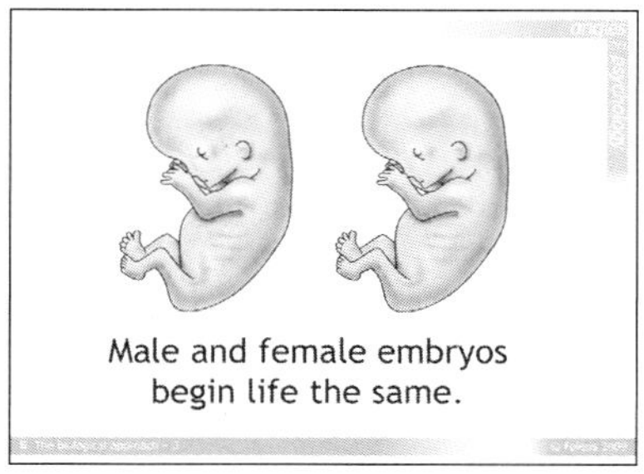

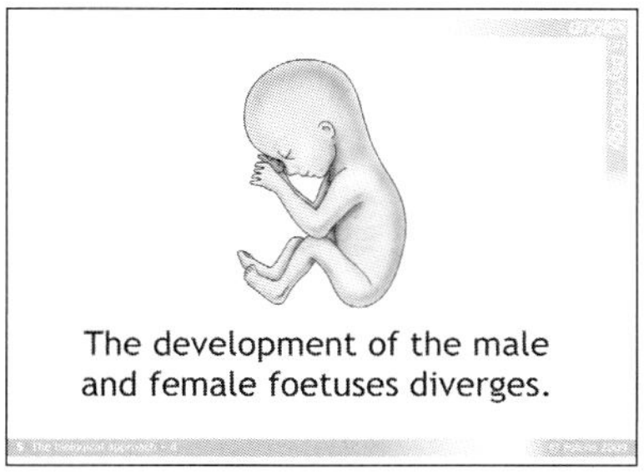

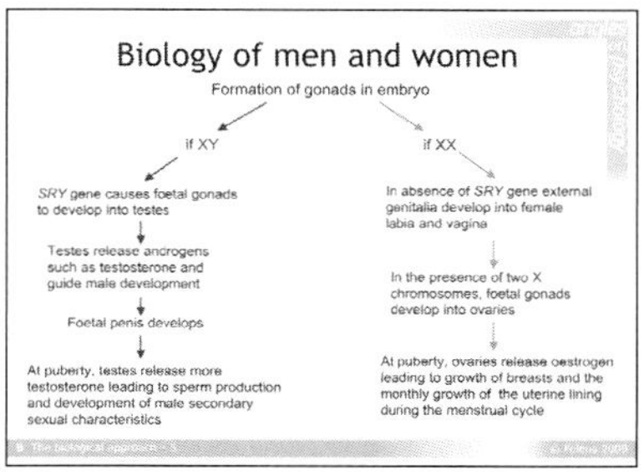

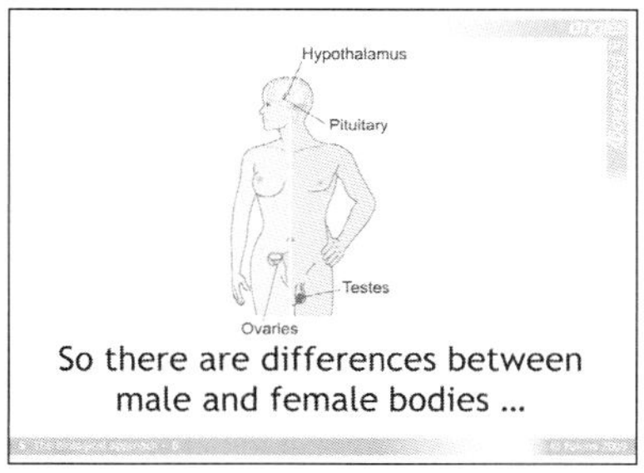

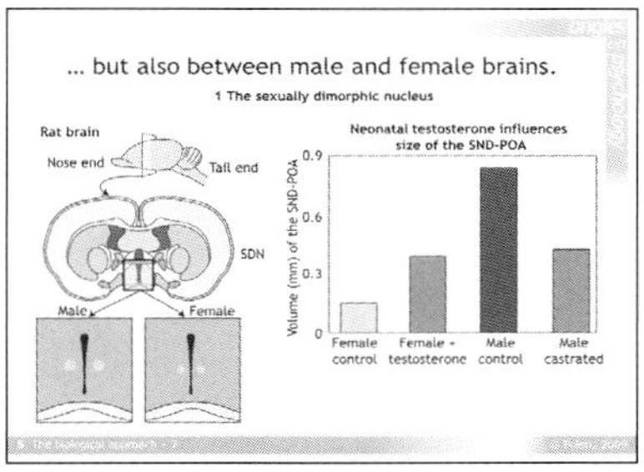

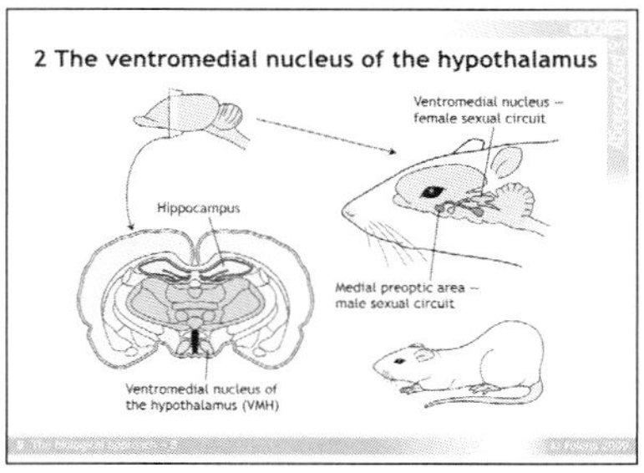

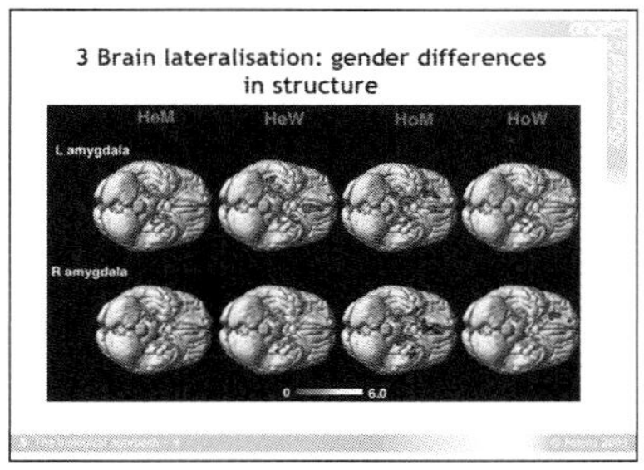

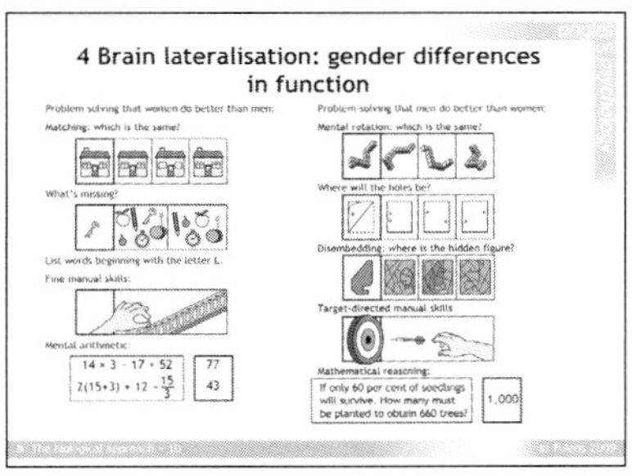

Biology of gender

Term
Phenotype
Turner's syndrome
SRY gene
Oestrogen
Androgen insensitivity syndrome
Testosterone
Sex chromosomes
Genotype

Definition
A hormone responsible for the onset of sperm production in pubescent males
The key factor in foetal development that triggers the development from female into male
The physical, psychological and behavioural characteristics of an individual
A disorder in which the testes of a genetically male foetus remain inside the body and the external genitalia appear female
The initial determining factor in the development of a foetus into a male or female
The genes an individual has for a particular characteristic
A hormone responsible for the growth of breast tissue in pubescent females
A disorder in which the individual's sex chromosomes consist of a single X

Biology of gender

Term	Definition
Phenotype	A hormone responsible for the onset of sperm production in pubescent males
Turner's syndrome	The key factor in foetal development that triggers the development from female into male
SRY gene	The physical, psychological and behavioural characteristics of an individual
Oestrogen	A disorder in which the testes of a genetically male foetus remain inside the body and the external genitalia appear female
Androgen insensitivity syndrome	The initial determining factor in the development of a foetus into a male or female
Testosterone	The genes an individual has for a particular characteristic
Sex chromosomes	A hormone responsible for the growth of breast tissue in pubescent females
Genotype	A disorder in which the individual's sex chromosomes consist of a single X

5.8 Gendered brains

media watch

Revealed: how scent of a woman attracts lesbians

The Guardian 9 May 2006

Sex pheromones, the chemicals some scientists believe waft off the body to help attract sexual partners, are processed differently in the brain depending on our sexuality.

Using a brain scanning technique called positron emission tomography, scientists found that a potent chemical lurking in male sweat causes a rush of electrical activity in the brains of straight women and gay men, while lesbians and straight men treat it like any other common odour.

Ivanka Savic, a neuroscientist at the Stockholm Brain Institute who led the study, said the finding suggested specific brain circuits were engaged when we were exposed to chemicals we found sexually stimulating. She added that the scans did not reveal whether sexual behaviour was learned or hard-wired in our brains at birth.

In the study, three groups of 12 volunteers, including lesbians, heterosexual women and straight men, were asked to sniff a variety of odours. They included odourless air, four common scents and a chemical, known as androstadienone (AND) that is ten times more abundant in male than female sweat and is suspected of acting as a male pheromone.

After smelling the odours, the volunteers were given brain scans that revealed which regions of their brains had the greatest increase in blood flow, a measure of how much they had been stimulated. The scans showed that after sniffing AND, a region of the brain called the anterior hypothalamus lit up in heterosexual women and gay men.

The brain scans of lesbian women and straight men showed a marked difference after sniffing the male sweat chemical, however. Brain scans revealed activity increasing in parts of the brain called the piriform cortex and amygdala, which are believed to light up when the brain processes any odour.

The researchers also found that lesbians and heterosexual men responded in the same way to a potential female pheromone called EST. Brain scans showed that clusters of neurons lit up in the brains of both groups when they smelled the odour, which were not activated in heterosexual women.

'This is the first study to show that these chemicals can activate specific brain circuits,' Dr Savic said. The study appears today in the journal *Proceedings of the National Academy of Sciences*.

1. a) Describe how a positron emission tomography (PET) scan works.
   b) Briefly outline how a PET scan is analysed or used to understand brain function.
2. a) The studies described compared **four** groups of participants. List them.
   b) Describe an ethical issue the researchers could have encountered in obtaining their samples.
   c) Describe how this issue could have affected the results.
3. The article reports that Savic says 'the scans did not reveal whether sexual behaviour was learned or hard-wired in our brains at birth'.
   a) Explain what is meant by this statement.
   b) i) Describe John Money's (1975) study.
      ii) Explain how Money's study provided evidence relating to both alternatives presented in Savic's statement.
      iii) Outline **two** strengths and **two** criticisms of Money's study.

Stretch and challenge

1. What might be the implications of this research for the marketing of fragrances to heterosexual and homosexual markets?
2. The report above actually combines the findings of two studies reported by Savic and colleagues. Look at the full text of both online and see how the study developed:

- http://www.pnas.org/content/102/20/7356.full.pdf+html
- http://www.pnas.org/content/103/21/8269.full.pdf+html

Practical and ethical issues with using animals in psychology

Laboratory animals such as rats are similar to humans in terms of _____________ so we can use them as _____________ for human development and behaviour. For example, they are useful for investigating the role of hormones on _____________ development, testing the processes of learning and understanding some aspects of mental _____________. It is possible to conduct research on animals that could not be performed on humans, such as experiments on pregnant female rats, newborn animals that have their ovaries or testes _____________ or are treated with _____________ replacements. These studies help us to understand the influence of early hormone levels on later sexual behaviour. Such laboratory experiments are good because they are well _____________, have comparison or control groups and the sexual behaviours of animals can be clearly _____________ and easily recorded. These features help to ensure that the findings are valid and reliable.

Studies conducted on animals are often highly invasive and can cause _____________ and distress. Guidelines for research with animals state that such trauma should be _____________. The design of studies and choice of statistical test should be optimised so that the _____________ possible number of animals can be used. Researchers responsible for studies that cause suffering are monitored and must ensure that their animals are maintained with _____________ discomfort, for example providing appropriate food, _____________ and social companions. In order to justify the suffering caused to animals, research should be of the _____________ possible quality and of certain benefit.

Are the findings of animal experiments relevant to humans? It should be possible to _____________ from animals such as rats to humans because we have a shared _____________ history so our hormonal and _____________ systems, which are important in the biological determination of sex and other physical and psychological characteristics, are very similar; for instance, we have the same endocrine glands that release similar hormones. It therefore seems likely that the biological processes controlling development and behaviour are _____________.

In some ways, the biological systems of humans and animals are _____________. For example, although all female mammals have a biological cycle that affects their breeding capacity, most do not have menstrual cycles and few other species are sexually _____________ when they are not sexually receptive. Human and animal _____________ are also different. The cortex in humans (outer layer) is much _____________ in relation to our size than in other animals. In some respects, therefore, generalisation from animals to humans is highly _____________ but in other ways it is not.

Stretch and challenge

Look for examples of investigations using animals. Which different approaches use animal studies? Find one example of each. Which approaches conduct the most invasive research?

Look up the views of Peter Singer (1975) and Jeffrey Gray (1991) and compare them.

active	defined	illnesses	nervous
biology	different	larger	pain
brains	evolutionary	lowest	removed
caging	generalise	minimised	sexual
controlled	highest	minimum	the same
credible	hormone	models	

Practical and ethical issues with using animals in psychology

Answers

Laboratory animals such as rats are similar to humans in terms of **biology** so we can use them as **models** for human development and behaviour. For example, they are useful for investigating the role of hormones on **sexual** development, testing the processes of learning and understanding some aspects of mental **illnesses**. It is possible to conduct research on animals that could not be performed on humans, such as experiments on pregnant female rats, newborn animals that have their ovaries or testes **removed** or are treated with **hormone** replacements. These studies help us to understand the influence of early hormone levels on later sexual behaviour. Such laboratory experiments are good because they are well **controlled**, have comparison or control groups and the sexual behaviours of animals can be clearly **defined** and easily recorded. These features help to ensure that the findings are valid and reliable.

Studies can be conducted on animals are often highly invasive and can cause **pain** and distress. Guidelines for research with animals state that such trauma should be **minimised**. The design of studies and choice of statistical test should be optimised so that the **lowest** possible number of animals can be used. Researchers responsible for studies that cause suffering are monitored and must ensure that their animals are maintained with **minimum** discomfort, for example providing appropriate food, **caging** and social companions. In order to justify the suffering caused to animals, research should be of the **highest** possible quality and of certain benefit.

Are the findings of animal experiments relevant to humans? It should be possible to **generalise** from animals such as rats to humans because we have a shared **evolutionary** history so our hormonal and **nervous** systems, which are important in the biological determination of sex and other physical and psychological characteristics, are very similar; for instance we have the same endocrine glands that release the similar hormones. It therefore seems likely that the biological processes controlling development and behaviour are **the same**.

In some ways, the biological systems of humans and animals are **different**. For example, although all female mammals have a biological cycle that affects their breeding capacity, most do not have menstrual cycles and few other species are sexually **active** when they are not sexually receptive. Human and animal **brains** are also different. The cortex in humans (outer layer) is much **larger** in relation to our size than in other animals. In some respects, therefore, generalisation from animals to humans is highly **credible** but in other ways it is not.

biology	pain	nervous
models	minimised	the same
sexual	lowest	different
illnesses	minimum	active
removed	caging	brains
hormone	highest	larger
controlled	generalise	credible
defined	evolutionary	

Brain scanning: PET and MRI

MRI can be used as a ____________ or functional technique, the latter being called ____________. The participant lies on a narrow bed which slides into a ____________ tube inside the scanner. They must keep very ____________ so that the images are clear. It is ____________ inside the scanner but the participant can communicate with the researcher through a headset. A standard MRI scan produces ____________ images which look like photographs of slices through the brain. MRI scanning uses a strong ____________ field which affects some atoms. Protons (positively charged particles) in hydrogen atoms in water behave like ____________ needles. The scanner's electromagnet causes the protons to 'point' in the ____________ direction. When radio waves are passed through the head the protons return to their original positions and this is detected by the scanner. Parts of the brain with more hydrogen atoms appear ____________; those with fewer hydrogen atoms look darker. In fMRI, a similar technique is used but the chemical responding to the magnetic field is haemoglobin – the oxygen-carrying molecule in the blood. As ____________ is needed for brain activity more and less active brain areas look different.

PET scans record brain activity by measuring the breakdown of a radioactive ____________. This is a chemical such as water or glucose that is used up during brain activity. The tracer is ____________ into the participant's bloodstream and reaches the brain about 1 minute later. During the next ten to fifteen minutes the tracer ____________ and releases minute amounts of radioactivity (initially in the form of ____________) which are detected by the scanner. The scanner is a ____________-shaped ring around the participant's head which detects gamma rays that are produced when the positrons being produced collide with electrons. The location of radioactive decay indicates activity levels in ____________ brain areas. Different amounts of brain activity appear on the scan as different ____________.

In both fMRI and PET the participant is typically scanned in two conditions. One set of scans is taken when they are inactive, or engaged in a control task, as a ____________. Another set is made when they are performing the experimental task. The difference between them indicates which parts of the brain are used in that activity. The participant ____________ each task so that the scans can be averaged.

baseline	fMRI	positrons
breaks down	injected	repeats
colours	magnetic	same
compass	narrow	still
detailed	noisy	structural
different	oxygen	tracer
doughnut	paler	

Brain scanning: PET and MRI *continued*

Positron emission tomography (PET) can be used to investigate memory. Piolino *et al.* (2004) scanned participants recalling autobiographical memories (i.e. episodic memories about their own lives). The memories were either recent (up to a year) or remote (five to ten years). The PET scans showed that both kinds of memories activated a range of brain areas, especially on the left side of the brain. However, recalling recent memories largely involved part of the left prefrontal cortex whereas the remote memories activated an area of the parietal cortex on both sides of the brain. They also found that the hippocampus was activated during recall - although this activation was mainly on the right regardless of the age of the memory. Greater activity in the hippocampus was found, however, when remote memories were retrieved compared with recent ones. When debriefed, participants were also asked about autonoetic consciousness; that is, their 'feeling of remembering' and the vividness of the mental image. Participants reported both stronger autonoetic consciousness and more vivid mental imagery for recent memories compared with remote ones.

Gilboa *et al.* (2004) also compared recent and remote memories. They used functional magnetic resonance imaging (fMRI) to record brain activity and family photographs to provide context for recall. These were obtained by confederates without the participants' involvement. Photographs of people unknown to the participants were used as control stimuli. In the debrief, they were asked whether they had ever seen the photographs or whether they had not seen them in many years. The participants were nine adults aged 38–58 years (mean 51). Gilboa *et al.* identified activation in different areas of the brain from Piloini *et al.* Areas in the occipital and parietal lobes were activated when recalling both recent and remote memories. One area of the cortex (the retrosplenial cortex, in the temporal lobe) was activated only by recall of recent memories. They found that hippocampal activation depended on the vividness of the memory rather than its age, so vivid memories were associated with greater hippocampal activity. However, remote memories were particularly linked to activation of one region of the hippocampus (the rostrocaudal axis) whilst recent memories mainly activated the anterior (front) part of the hippocampus.

1. Use one of these studies and suggest a plan for the next stage of an investigation which the researchers could pursue and explain why this would be useful and interesting.

Brain scanning: PET and MRI

Answers

MRI can be used as a **structural** or functional technique, the latter being called **fMRI**. The participant lies on a narrow bed which slides into a **narrow** tube inside the scanner. They must keep very **still** so that the images are clear. It is **noisy** inside the scanner but the participant can communicate with the researcher through a headset. A standard MRI scan produces **detailed** images which look like photographs of slices through the brain. MRI scanning uses a strong **magnetic** field which affects some atoms. Protons (positively charged particles) in hydrogen atoms in water behave like **compass** needles. The scanner's electromagnet causes the protons to 'point' in the **same** direction. When radio waves are passed through the head the protons return to their original positions and this is detected by the scanner. Parts of the brain with more hydrogen atoms appear **paler**; those with fewer hydrogen atoms look darker. In fMRI, a similar technique is used but the chemical responding to the magnetic field is haemoglobin – the oxygen-carrying molecule in the blood. As **oxygen** is needed for brain activity more and less active brain areas look different.

PET scans record brain activity by measuring the breakdown of a radioactive **tracer**. This is a chemical such as water or glucose that is used up during brain activity. The tracer is **injected** into the participant's bloodstream and reaches the brain about 1 minute later. During the next ten to fifteen minutes the tracer **breaks down** and releases minute amounts of radioactivity (initially in the form of **positrons**) which are detected by the scanner. The scanner is a **doughnut**-shaped ring around the participant's head which detects gamma rays that are produced when the positrons being produced collide with electrons. The location of radioactive decay indicates activity levels in **different** brain areas. Different amounts of brain activity appear on the scan as different **colours**.

In both fMRI and PET the participant is typically scanned in two conditions. One set of scans is taken when they are inactive, or engaged in a control task, as a **baseline**. Another set is made when they are performing the experimental task. The difference between them indicates which parts of the brain are used in that activity. The participant **repeats** each task so that the scans can be averaged.

structural	compass	positrons
fMRI	same	doughnut
narrow	paler	different
still	oxygen	colours
noisy	tracer	baseline
detailed	injected	repeats
magnetic	breaks down	

Money (1975)

John Money investigated whether gender identity could be ____________ or is biologically fixed. He had successfully gender-reassigned children born with ____________ genitalia so was interested in finding out whether children are 'gender ____________' at birth.

Money followed up 45 males after gender-reassignment treatment. One of these was an identical (____________) twin. This provided a ____________ – a biologically identical boy who did not have gender-reassignment treatment. At ____________ months of age a circumcision operation on one boy, Bruce, damaged his ____________ so badly that it could not be repaired. Dr Money suggested surgically changing his external genitalia from male to female. Aged just under ____________ years, Bruce was castrated, had a ____________ created, received ____________ treatment and was raised as a girl called Brenda. The family treated her differently from her brother Brian, for example her hair was kept ____________ and tied with ribbons, she was dressed in clothes such as pink trousers and ____________ blouses, she wore jewellery and was given ____________ to play with. She also received further reconstructive surgery and hormone treatment to give her a ____________ appearance.

Brenda was regularly seen by Dr Money. He reported that, at aged ____________, Brenda had a female ____________ and predicted that in ____________ she would have a female sexual life. There was also evidence of gender role ____________ and social learning. For example, he reported that the mother and father often showed affection for one another and sometimes, when Brenda's brother came into the house, she would imitate this and give him a ____________. Similarly, ____________ helped her mother in the house, doing cleaning and tidying the kitchen (which was encouraged) whereas ____________ did not. Differences were also reported in choice of toys: Brenda wanted dolls, dolls' houses and ____________ whilst Brain asked for toy ____________, garages and petrol pumps. Further differences were seen in ____________ plans. When asked what they wanted to be when they grew up, Brenda said teacher or doctor whereas Brian chose policeman or fireman.

Money also reported some ____________ behaviours but explained them as the result of ____________ her brother. These included being stubborn, very energetic and ____________ among a group of girls.

Money's evidence suggested that gender ____________ through surgery, hormone treatment and rearing experiences was possible. He claimed that Brenda had a female gender identity. If so, this would imply that gender identity is ____________ at birth, i.e. that, in psychological terms, we are ____________ 'gender neutral'. However, subsequent evidence from 'Brenda' suggests that this was not the case.

Diamond & Sigmundson (1997) report that Brenda ____________ her treatment as a girl. During her childhood, she found both her ____________ and the expectations of others ____________ to cope with. This worsened as she grew older. When she was finally told about her early life she chose to revert to a ____________ identity through further surgery. Evidence from the adult 'David Reimer' suggests that the conclusion drawn by Money (1975) was incorrect and that, in the case of an individual without ambiguous genitalia, gender identity is ____________ determined.

Bruce Reimer as a young adult

Money (1975) *continued*

adulthood	feelings	oestrogen
ambiguous	female	penis
biologically	frilly	prams
born	future	reassignment
Brenda	gender identity	rejected
Brian	hug	seven
cars	imitating	stereotyping
changed	long	tomboyish
control	male	two
difficult	monozygotic	undifferentiated
dolls	neutral	vagina
dominant	nine	

Money (1975)

Answers

John Money investigated whether gender identity could be **changed** or is biologically fixed. He had successfully gender-reassigned children born with **ambiguous** genitalia so was interested in finding out whether children are 'gender **neutral**' at birth.

Money followed up 45 males after gender reassignment treatment. One of these was an identical (**monozygotic**) twin. This provided a **control** – a biologically identical boy who did not have gender-reassignment treatment. At **seven** months of age a circumcision operation on one boy, Bruce, damaged his **penis** so badly that it could not be repaired. Dr Money suggested surgically changing his external genitalia from male to female. Aged just under **two** years, Bruce was castrated, had a **vagina** created, received **oestrogen** treatment and was raised as a girl called Brenda. The family treated her differently from her brother Brian, for example her hair was kept **long** and tied with ribbons, she was dressed in clothes such as pink trousers and **frilly** blouses, she wore jewellery and was given **dolls** to play with. She also received further reconstructive surgery and hormone treatment to give her a **female** appearance.

Brenda was regularly seen by Dr Money. He reported that, at aged **nine**, Brenda had a female **gender identity** and predicted that in **adulthood** she would have a female sexual life. There was also evidence of gender role **stereotyping** and social learning. For example, he reported that the mother and father often showed affection for one another and sometimes, when Brenda's brother came into the house, she would imitate this and give him a **hug**. Similarly, **Brenda** helped her mother in the house, doing cleaning and tidying the kitchen (which was encouraged) whereas **Brian** did not. Differences were also reported in choice of toys: Brenda wanted dolls, dolls' houses and **prams** whilst Brain asked for toy **cars**, garages and petrol pumps. Further differences were seen in **future** plans. When asked what they wanted to be when they grew up, Brenda said teacher or doctor whereas Brian chose policeman or fireman.

Money also reported some **tomboyish** behaviours but explained them as the result of **imitating** her brother. These included being stubborn, very energetic and **dominant** among a group of girls.

Money's evidence suggested that gender **reassignment** through surgery, hormone treatment and rearing experiences was possible. He claimed that Brenda had a female gender identity. If so, this would imply that gender identity is **undifferentiated** at birth, i.e. that, in psychological terms, we are **born** 'gender neutral'. However, subsequent evidence from 'Brenda' suggests that this was not the case.

Diamond & Sigmundson (1997) report that Brenda **rejected** her treatment as a girl. During her childhood, she found both her **feelings** and the expectations of others **difficult** to cope with. This worsened as she grew older. When she was finally told about her early life she chose to revert to a **male** identity through further surgery. Evidence from the adult 'David Reimer' suggests that the conclusion drawn by Money (1975) was incorrect and that, in the case of an individual without ambiguous genitalia, gender identity is **biologically** determined.

Money (1975)

Answers *continued*

changed	dolls	tomboyish
ambiguous	female	imitating
neutral	nine	dominant
monozygotic	gender identity	reassignment
control	adulthood	undifferentiated
seven	stereotyping	born
penis	hug	rejected
two	Brenda	feelings
vagina	Brian	difficult
oestrogen	prams	male
long	cars	biologically
frilly	future	

Inferential statistics and the Mann–Whitney test

Inferential statistics tests include the Spearman test, a test of ____________ and the Mann–Whitney test, a test of ____________. In statistical testing we aim to reject the ____________ hypothesis by showing that it is unlikely that the pattern in our data could have arisen by ____________. The possibility we choose for this degree of chance is called the ____________. In psychological studies this is generally set at ____________%. This means that, if the test says our results are significant, we can be ____________% sure that the pattern of results could not have arisen by chance. This indicates how ____________ we are about the pattern in our results and is expressed as a ____________. So a 5% level of risk is written as $p \leq$ ____________.

As there is a possibility that the conclusion could be wrong it is sometimes important to be more certain. The significance level can be made ____________ stringent, e.g. accepting only a ____________% probability that the ____________ between conditions could have arisen by chance. This is expressed as $p \leq$ ____________.

The Mann–Whitney test finds out whether or not a difference in results could have arisen by chance or is due to the ____________. It is used when the research method is a/an ____________, the design is ____________ and the ____________ is ____________, interval or ratio. It cannot be used with ____________ data or for a ____________ design.

To conduct a Mann–Whitney test you need to know:

- whether the ____________ hypothesis is directional or non-directional (for a directional hypothesis a ____________-tailed test is used, for a non-directional hypothesis, a ____________-tailed test is used)
- the significance level
- how many ____________ there were in each level of the IV (n_1 and n_2).

The Mann-Whitney test produces a number called the ____________ value which is given the symbol 'U'. To decide whether there is a significant difference between the levels of the IV, this is compared with a value from a table called the ____________ value. For the Mann-Whitney test to be significant, the observed value must be smaller than or equal to the critical value. If not, then the difference is ____________ and the null hypothesis must be accepted.

Imagine an experiment in which the observed value is 4. There were 7 participants in one condition and 5 in the other. The alternative hypothesis was one tailed and the significance level required was $p \leq 0.05$.

The observed value of U = ____________ is ____________ than ____________ (the critical value), so we can conclude that there is a ____________ difference between the conditions. We can therefore ____________ the null hypothesis and ____________ the alternative hypothesis.

Table of critical values for Mann–Whitney U
One-tailed tests at $p \leq 0.05$ and two-tailed tests at $p \leq 0.1$

$n_1 \rightarrow$ / $n_2 \downarrow$	3	4	5	6	7
3	0	0	1	2	2
4	0	1	2	3	4
5	1	2	4	5	6
6	2	3	5	7	8

Inferential statistics and the Mann–Whitney test *continued*

0.01
0.05
1
4
5
6
95
accept
alternative
chance
confident
correlation
critical
difference
differences
experiment
independent groups
independent variable
less
level of measurement
ordinal
more
nominal
non-significant
null
observed
one
participants
probability
reject
repeated measures
significance level
significant
two

Inferential statistics and the Mann–Whitney test

Answers

Inferential statistics tests include the Spearman test, a test of **correlation** and the Mann–Whitney test, a test of **differences**. In statistical testing we aim to reject the **null** hypothesis by showing that it is unlikely that the pattern in our data could have arisen by **chance**. The possibility we choose for this degree of chance is called the **significance level**. In psychological studies this is generally set at **5%**. This means that, if the test says our results are significant, we can be **95%** sure that the pattern of results could not have arisen by chance. This indicates how **confident** we are about the pattern in our results and is expressed as a **probability**. So a 5% level of risk is written as $p \leq$ **0.05**.

As there is a possibility that the conclusion could be wrong it is sometimes important to be more certain. The significance level can be made **more** stringent, e.g. accepting only a **1%** probability that the **difference** between conditions could have arisen by chance. This is expressed as $p \leq$**0.01**.

The Mann–Whitney test finds out whether or not a difference in results could have arisen by chance or is due to the **independent variable**. It is used when the research method is a/an **experiment**, the design is **independent groups** and the **level of measurement** is **ordinal**, interval or ratio. It cannot be used with **nominal** data or for a **repeated measures** design.

To conduct a Mann–Whitney test you need to know:

- whether the **alternative** hypothesis is directional or non-directional (for a directional hypothesis a **one**-tailed test is used, for a non-directional hypothesis, a **two**-tailed test is used)
- the significance level
- how many **participants** there were in each level of the IV (n_1 and n_2).

The Mann-Whitney test produces a number called the **observed** value which is given the symbol 'U'. To decide whether there is a significant difference between the levels of the IV, this is compared with a value from a table called the **critical** value. For the Mann–Whitney test to be significant, the observed value must be smaller than or equal to the critical value. If not, then the difference is **non-significant** and the null hypothesis must be accepted.

Imagine an experiment in which the observed value is 4. There were 7 participants in one condition and 5 in the other. The alternative hypothesis was one-tailed and the significance level required was $p \leq 0.05$.

The observed value of U = **4** is **less** than **6** (the critical value), so we can conclude that there is a **significant** difference between the conditions. We can therefore **reject** the null hypothesis and **accept** the alternative hypothesis.

Table of critical values for Mann–Whitney U
One-tailed tests at $p \leq 0.05$ and two-tailed tests at $p \leq 0.1$

$n_1 \rightarrow$ / $n_2 \downarrow$	**3**	**4**	**5**	**6**	**7**
3	0	0	1	2	2
4	0	1	2	3	4
5	1	2	4	5	**6**
6	2	3	5	7	8

Inferential statistics and the Mann–Whitney test

Answers *continued*

correlation
differences
null
chance
significance level
5
95
confident
probability
0.05
more
1

difference
0.01
independent variable
experiment
independent groups
level of measurement
ordinal
nominal
repeated measures
alternative
one
two

participants
observed
critical
non-significant
4
less
6
significant
reject
accept

The nature–nurture debate

Could one twin boy grow up as a girl?

1. The nature–nurture debate refers to the relative importance of genes and the environment in the development of characteristics.
   a) Which side of the debate refers to:
      i) the influence of genes?
      ii) the influence of the environment?
   b) Suggest **three** different psychological factors that could be important to development in a child's environment.
2. Money (1975) provided evidence for the nature–nurture debate in his investigation of gender reassignment.
   a) Money reported that, at nine years old, the gender-reassigned twin made stereotypically female choices of toys and clothes. Which side of the debate does this support?
   b) Money also reported that the gender-reassigned twin displayed some stereotypically male behaviours, such as trying to urinate standing up and being very dominant. Which side of the debate does this aspect of the findings support?
   c) In later life, the gender-reassigned twin reported that she fought with the male twin for toys like guns, that she was teased for being masculine at school and told her parents that she felt like a boy. Which side of the debate does this support?
3. A genetic condition can cause XY babies to lack the hormone dihydrotestosterone. They appear to be female so are reared as girls and are happy with their female gender identity. When they reach puberty and hormones again affect development, these individuals turn slowly into boys. Once this transition is complete, they are happy with their male gender identity. How does this evidence contribute to the nature–nurture debate?
4. Although we refer to the nature–nurture debate most psychological characteristics are controlled by a mixture of the two influences.
   a) Some people can roll their tongues and others can't. This ability is influenced by a single gene. In general, people with at least one dominant allele (with the genotype TT or Tt) can tongue roll. Those with a pair of recessive alleles (tt) cannot. What would this suggest about where 'tongue rolling' lies on the nature–nurture spectrum?
   b) For many years it was assumed that this ability was fixed for life. However, it *is* possible to get better at it. What does this tell you about the influence of nature and nurture?
5. Monozygotic twins (MZs) are genetically identical – they share 100% of their genes. Dizygotic twins (DZs) are only as similar as ordinary brothers and sisters.
   a) Is it possible to have different sex:
      i) monozygotic twins?
      ii) dizygotic twins?
   b) Explain your answers to parts a) i) and a) ii).
   c) In terms of some personality factors, such as extraversion, and mental illnesses such as schizophrenia, monozygotic twins are more similar than dizygotic twins.
      i) Does this support the nature or nurture side of the debate? Explain your answer.
      ii) Even MZs are not always identical in such characteristics. What does this tell you about the influence of nature and nurture on extraversion and schizophrenia?
   d) Because monozygotic twins tend to look more alike that dizygotic twins, people tend to treat them in the same way, whereas they don't necessarily with dizygotic twins. How might this affect conclusions to studies based on the differences between MZs and DZs?

Essays

Question 1

Wanted a girl, gave birth to a boy?

Advertisements for an illegal private hospital have been appearing on the internet. They say that if you wanted a child of one sex and gave birth to a child of the other, they can guarantee to change your child's gender.

Describe and evaluate psychological evidence relating to this claim.

continue overleaf if necessary

Essays

Question 2

As part of your course you will have studied a key issue in the biological approach.

Describe this key issue and explain it using **two or more** of the concepts listed below:

- the central nervous system
- neurones
- synapses
- receptors
- neurotransmitters
- genes
- hormones
- brain lateralisation.

....

....

....

....

....

....

....

....

....

....

....

....

....

....

....

....

....

....

continue overleaf if necessary

'Smell the roses' scan

Walla, P., Hufnagl, B., Lehrner, J., Mayer, D., Lindinger, G., Imhof, H., Deeke, L. and Lang, W. (2003) 'Olfaction and face encoding in humans: a magnetoencephalographic study'. *Cognitive Brain Research*, 15: 105-15.

Aim: To investigate the effect of smell on forgetting using magnetoencephalography (MEG) (an imaging technique that can record brief changes in brain activity).

Procedure: Participants were shown faces and asked to make judgements that resulted in either deep processing (by judging likeability) or shallow processing (by judging hair length). Some faces were presented simultaneously with a smell of roses. During this processing, the participants' brains were being scanned. The participants were later asked to recognise the faces they had seen before amongst others they had not.

Findings: Participants were worse at identifying those faces that had initially been associated with the smell. The MEG records also revealed a difference. The brief brain activity associated with the initial processing of the faces was reduced when the faces were presented with the smell.

1. The study above is one example of psychologists using a different brain scanning technique from PET or MRI. How could you explain the effect they found in terms of the levels of processing model?
2. Use the internet to find out about a range of different uses and other brain scanning methods. You could begin with some of these:

Detecting fairness

- http://www.medicalnewstoday.com/articles/104922.php – Reaction to fairness in the brain akin to reaction to money and chocolate
- http://www.futurepundit.com/archives/005142.html – Brain scans show reactions to fairness and unfairness
- http://www.physorg.com/news127571850.html – Are humans hardwired for fairness?

Putting feelings into words

http://www.scn.ucla.edu/pdf/AL(2007).pdf – (free full text article)

Social status

http://www.medicalnewstoday.com/articles/105200.php – Brain scans hint at 'hard-wiring' for hierarchy

Racism

http://www.eurekalert.org/pub_releases/2003-11/dc-iia111303.php – Interracial interactions are cognitively demanding

Alcoholism

http://www.bnl.gov/bnlweb/pubaf/pr/PR_display.asp?prID=06-97 – Study offers clues to brain's protective mechanisms against alcoholism

Eating and learning:

- http://www.inspirationline.com/Brainteaser/dessert.htm – Why do we always have room for dessert?
- http://www.hhmi.org/bulletin/pdf/spring2004/Thought.pdf – Food for thought
- http://faculty.washington.edu/chudler/train.html – Training ourselves

Creative activities

1 Scan plan

You are a psychology student at university and have been invited to assist on a collaborative project between the Psychology Department and the Radiology Department of the university hospital. They want you to help in providing patients with accessible information about their brain scanning technique. Design a leaflet providing information about whether MRI and PET scans will illustrate structure or function of the brain, how detailed information from the scan will be, how the scanner works and what will happen during the scan.

Include information about a new type of scan, such as BOLD or SPECT and evaluate it compared with methods such as PET and MRI.

2 Diet drug

Imagine you are a psychologist who works alongside a large family medical practice. Many of the patients with weight problems have seen articles like the one opposite in their newspapers. Although they are keen to be prescribed the drug by their GPs, they are concerned because they don't like the idea of 'messing with their brains' just to get thin.

Design a poster which includes diagrams and text that explains how neurones work, and how drugs such as Acomplia can influence their functioning.

New anti-fat pill

Acomplia is a wonder drug for fat people. It contains a drug called a cannabinoid-1 receptor antagonist. These drugs block receptors in the brain and reduce your appetite.

It works by switching off the same brain circuits that make people hungry when they smoke cannabis. So it stops you getting hungry.

Evidence of practice: an experiment

Looking and language

Most people look right when they answer language-related questions and left when they answer questions about spatial relationships. You can investigate this with questions that test spatial and language-related ability and observe participants' direction of gaze. As there are differences between the language processing of men and women, you might predict a difference between them on this task. Here are some example questions:

1. State three synonyms for 'fast'.
2. How many sides does a give-way sign have?
3. Which word has more letters, 'girl' or 'boy'?
4. What is the meaning of the word 'greedy'?
5. Name a town on the south coast of England.
6. In which direction does the Queen face on a penny coin?
7. Name a word that means the opposite of 'happy'.
8. If you are going north, and take three left turns followed by one right turn, in which direction are you now heading?

Left, right; language and writing

Natsopoulos *et al.* (1998) and Tankle, Heilman (1983) found differences between left- and right-handers in terms of language ability and mirror writing respectively. Although right-handed children were found to be better at language in general, left-handed participants were better at mirror writing than right-handers.

Preparation:

1. Choose who you are working with.
2. Decide on a topic on which to conduct an experiment with an independent groups design (for example, but not necessarily, based on one of the ideas above).
3. Agree an aim for your group and devise a suitable hypothesis.
4. Plan your procedure and consider what variables you will need to control.
5. Decide on your independent variable and how it will be operationalised.
6. Decide on your dependent variable and how it will be operationalised. Decide whether you will be collecting data using an ordinal, interval or ratio level of measurement.
7. What is your target population and what sample size do you want? How will you obtain a sample? Is this choice likely to give you results that are generalisable?
8. Are you going to allocate participants randomly to conditions? Why/why not?
9. Ensure that your tests or measures and experimental situation are ethical.
10. Produce or find any stimulus material or apparatus that you need and obtain permission if required. Do you need to randomise the order of presentation of stimuli? Decide where and when you will conduct your experiment and who will do which jobs.

Evidence of practice: looking and language, left and right *continued*

11. Collect the data for your experiment and enter them into a raw data table.
12. Analyse your data using descriptive statistics: find at least one measure of central tendency and at least one measure of dispersion (e.g. the range), then plot a graph. Make sure that you have a title and column and row headings on your table and a title and axes labels on your graph.
13. Analyse your data using inferential statistics: conduct a Mann–Whitney test on one aspect of your data. Write out:

    a) the observed value

    b) your two group sizes

    c) whether your hypothesis is directional or non-directional

    d) the level of significance you are using.

    Find the critical value from a table and write it down. Compare the critical value with your observed value and draw a conclusion in relation to your hypothesis.
14. Comment on your method and conclusions in terms of:

    a) validity

    b) reliability

    c) credibility

    d) generalisability.

Lateralisation

Most people are right-handed, some are left-handed and others are mixed-handers, i.e. they use the right hand for some actions and the left for others. Amunts *et al.* (2000) investigated whether this behavioural difference related to a difference in brain lateralisation. They used an MRI scan to investigate the 'hand region' of the motor cortex in males and females. One measure was the depth of the central sulcus, a 'valley' that runs vertically behind the motor cortex. They found that in males, the central sulcus on the left hemisphere was deepest for right-handers, shallowest for left-handers, with mixed-handers being between the two. Sixty-two per cent of the left-handers had a deeper central sulcus on the right, although this difference was not significant. There was no difference in the depth of the central sulcus on the left and right hemispheres in females.

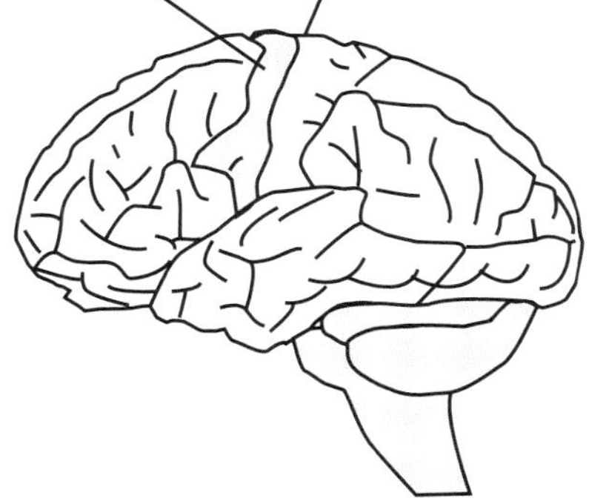

1. a) Describe **one** finding from Amunts *et al.* that illustrates lateralisation.
   b) Describe **one** finding from Amunts *et al.* that illustrates an absence of lateralisation.
2. a) Outline the magnetic resonance imaging (MRI) technique.
   b) This investigation was a laboratory experiment.
      i) Identify **one** independent variable.
      ii) Identify **one** dependent variable.
   c) Describe **one** advantage and **one** disadvantage of the laboratory experiment as a research method in the biological approach.
3. a) Amunts *et al.* could have used the Mann–Whitney test to analyse some of their results. Explain why they would have chosen the Mann–Whitney test, referring to their study in your answer.
   b) In the absence of previous research in this area, would Amunts *et al.* have used a significance level of $p \leq 0.05$ or $p \leq 0.01$?
   c) With regard to language, women show less lateralisation than men. They might therefore have predicted a similar pattern for handedness.
      i) Write a suitable directional hypothesis for this prediction.
      ii) When testing this prediction, would a one-tailed or a two-tailed test be used?

MRI scanning

Human decision-making can be investigated using functional magnetic resonance imaging (fMRI). Knutson *et al.* (2007) used this to study people making shopping decisions. They showed participants pictures of goods such as Belgian chocolates which they could buy with $20 they had been given. They first looked at an item to see if they wanted it (the 'product' phase), then saw how much it cost (the 'price' phase) and then had to decide whether or not to buy it (the 'choice' phase). They were scanned during each four-second phase. In the product phase, greater liking was associated with activation of a brain region called the nucleus accumbens. In the price phase, very high prices increased activity in a region called the insula and decreased activity in part of the prefrontal cortex. The relative activity levels in these three areas predicted purchasing decisions.

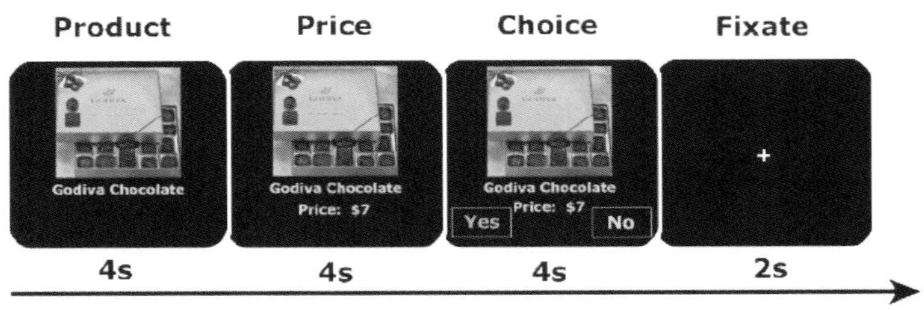

1. Describe how **either** MRI or fMRI scanning works.
2. Data from six of the participants were excluded because the participant moved his or her head more than 2 mm while being scanned. Why did this matter?
3. When choosing to buy the product, or not, the participants selected either 'yes' or 'no', which appeared randomly on the left- or right-hand side of the screen. Why was it important that the position of the response on the screen varied randomly?
4. At the end of each task the participant had two seconds to focus on a cross before the next item appeared. Why was this an important part of the procedure?
5. There were 80 different products. Half of the participants saw one set of 40 products first, followed by the others. The remaining participants saw the two sets in reverse order.
   a) What is this technique called?
   b) Give **one** reason why it might have been used in this study.
6. All of the participants were right-handed. Why might this have been important?
7. Of the 26 participants, 12 were female. Both the men and women purchased about 30% of the products presented. Why were roughly equal numbers of each gender chosen?
8. This study measured several variables which showed correlations.
   a) One was the anticipation of gain or benefit because the participant liked the item.
      i) In which brain area was activity seen during this phase?
      ii) How did the seen activation relate to desire for the item?
   b) In the price phase, **two** correlations were identified. Describe both of them.
9. When presented with the same item twice, participants tended to make the same decision (to buy it or not) as they had done before. This was tested using a correlation which gave an observed value of $r = 0.83$, significant at $p \leq 0.001$. Eighty-seven per cent of items bought on the first viewing were also bought the second time they were seen and 95% of decisions not to buy were the same the second time.
   a) Does this suggest the measure was valid or reliable?
   b) Were participants more consistent in decisions to 'buy' or 'not buy'?
   c) Which statistical test could have been used for this correlation? Justify your answer.

The biological approach quiz

1

a) Name three brain areas.

b) What is a synapse?

c) Give one advantage of using animals in experiments.

d) Define brain lateralisation.

e) Name one neurotransmitter.

f) Does an embryo start off life male or female?

g) Describe a PET scan.

h) Give one example of a twin study.

i) Name the levels of measurement.

j) What sex chromosomes do males and females have?

k) Is the Mann–Whitney test used for correlations or experiments?

l) Identify one study that illustrated gender differences in brain activity.

m) Give an example of a figure used for 'significance level'.

n) Name three glands that are important in sexual development.

o) State one piece of evidence that contradicts the nature argument in gender development.

p) Describe the key issue for the biological approach.

2

a) What are the two parts of the CNS?

b) Name three brain lobes.

c) What is meant by the 'nature–nurture debate'?

d) What is a receptor?

e) What is meant by MZ and DZ twins?

f) Give one disadvantage of using animals in experiments.

g) Which hemisphere is used for language?

h) Describe an MRI scan.

i) Name the main male and female hormones.

j) Give one example of an adoption study.

k) Identify one study that supports the nature argument in gender development.

l) Is the Mann–Whitney test used for repeated measures or independent groups designs?

m) What are serotonin and dopamine?

n) Identify one difference in structure between male and female brains.

o) Which two studies must you know in detail for the biological approach?

p) What was the topic for the practical exercise for the biological approach?

The biological approach quiz

Answers

1

a) Name three brain areas. **e.g. cortex, hippocampus, hypothalamus, amygdala, SDN, POA, (not lobes)**

b) What is a synapse? **The gap between neurones, crossed by a chemical messenger**

c) Give one advantage of using animals in experiments. **More control can be exercised than over humans/deprivation or surgical procedures can be used which would be unethical on humans**

d) Define brain lateralisation. **Differences between left and right hemispheres**

e) Name one neurotransmitter. **e.g. serotonin, dopamine, noradrenaline, GABA**

f) Does an embryo start off life male or female? **Female**

g) Describe a PET scan. **Brain scan using radioactive chemicals (tracers) which are injected and detected as they breakdown when used by brain activity**

h) Give one example of a twin study. **e.g. Gottesman & Shields (1966), Gottesman (1991), Loehlin (1992), Bailey & Pillard (1991), Bailey *et al.* (2000), Kendler *et al.* (2000)**

i) Name the levels of measurement. **Nominal, ordinal, interval, ratio**

j) What sex chromosomes do males and females have? **Male = XY, Female = XX**

k) Is the Mann–Whitney test used for correlations or experiments? **Experiments**

l) Identify one study that illustrated gender differences in brain activity. **e.g. Kulynych *et al.* (1992), Shaywitz *et al.* (1995), Rossell *et al.* (2002), Jaeger *et al.* (1998)**

m) Give an example of a figure used for 'significance level'. **e.g. $p \leq 0.05$, $p \leq 0.01$**

n) Name three glands that are important in sexual development. **e.g. ovaries, testes, pituitary gland**

o) State one piece of evidence that contradicts the nature argument in gender development. **Voyer (1996) suggests there is a publication bias – that more studies that find brain differences between the genders get published than ones that don't**

p) Describe the key issue for the biological approach. **e.g. mental health/sexual orientation and the nature-nurture debate**

The biological approach quiz

Answers *continued*

2

a) What are the two parts of the CNS? **Brain and spinal cord**

b) Name three brain lobes. **Three of: frontal, parietal, temporal, occipital**

c) What is meant by the 'nature–nurture debate'? **The argument over which the extent to which a characteristic is controlled by genes (nature) or the environment (nurture)**

d) What is a receptor? **An area on the post-synaptic membrane of a neurone which responds to neurotransmitters (so can help to generate the next nerve impulse)**

e) What is meant by MZ and DZ twins? **MZ = monozygotic = identical twins, DZ = dizygotic = non-identical twins**

f) Give one disadvantage of using animals in experiments. **Simpler brains therefore cannot be sure that they are good models for human responses**

g) Which hemisphere is used for language? **Left (mainly)**

h) Describe an MRI scan. **An (electro)magnetic field affects (protons in) water which move/respond like needles on a compass. When they move back to their original positions they affect the emission of radio waves, which is detected by the scanner**

i) Name the main male and female hormones. **Male = testosterone, female = oestrogen**

j) Give one example of an adoption study. **Heston (1966)**

k) Identify one study that supports the nature argument in gender development. **Diamond & Sigmundson (1997)**

l) Is the Mann–Whitney test used for repeated measures or independent groups designs? **Independent groups**

m) What are serotonin and dopamine? **Neurotransmitters**

n) Identify one difference in structure between male and female brains. **e.g. males have a longer left temporal plane than right, females are about equal/males' language functions are more lateralised (to the left)**

o) Which two studies must you know in detail for the biological approach? **Money (1975) and one of: Gottesman & Shields (1966)/Raine *et al.* (1997) or De Bellis *et al.* (2001)**

p) What was the topic for the practical exercise for the biological approach? **This will depend on your chosen topic, e.g. language or gender**

Biological approach test

Centre No.						Paper Reference							Surname	Initial(s)
Candidate No.						6	P	S	0	2	/	1	Signature	

Psychology Advanced Subsidiary

Unit 2: The Biological Approach

Time: 50 minutes

Instructions to candidates

Answer ALL the questions.

Information for candidates

The total mark for this paper is 40.

Advice to candidates

Quality of written communication will be taken into account in the marking of your response to question 10. This question is indicated with an asterisk (*). Quality of written communication includes clarity of expression, the structure and presentation of ideas, and grammar, punctuation and spelling.

Question number	Leave blank
1	
2	
3	
4	
5	
6	
7	
8	
9	
10	
11	
Total	

SECTION A

Answer ALL questions.
You are advised to spend approximately 7 minutes on this section.

Choose answer A, B, C, D or E, and put a cross in the box (☒). If you change your mind, put a line through the box (~~☒~~) and then put a cross in another box (☒).

1. Which of the following are brain scanning techniques?

☐ **A** PET
☐ **B** RAT
☐ **C** MRI
☐ **D** A and C above **(1)**

2. Animal studies are credible because animals:

☐ **A** have smaller, simpler brains than humans
☐ **B** are protected by law
☐ **C** and humans have evolved with similar brains
☐ **D** can bite the researcher if they are in pain **(1)**

3. Hormones are important in gender development. Which statement below is **incorrect**:

☐ **A** both men and women produce testosterone and oestrogen
☐ **B** testosterone causes a foetus to become male
☐ **C** oestrogen causes a foetus to become female
☐ **D** oestrogen causes the development of secondary sexual characteristics in females **(1)**

4. Which statement below is **not** true of the central nervous system?

☐ **A** it is made up of the brain and spinal cord
☐ **B** it can be divided into sections including the autonomic and peripheral nervous systems
☐ **C** it is essential to all human reactions
☐ **D** it is made up only of sensory and motor neurones **(1)**

5. Which **two** of the following are parts of the brain?

☐ **A** hypothalamus
☐ **B** pituitary
☐ **C** cortex
☐ **D** androgen
☐ **E** SRY **(2)**

(Total 6 marks)

TOTAL FOR SECTION A: 6 MARKS

SECTION B

Answer ALL questions.
You are advised to spend approximately 25 minutes on this section.

6. **(a)** One way to study the influence of biology on behaviour is through scanning methods. Outline how a PET (positron emission tomography) scan works.

....

....

....

....

....

.... **(3)**

(b) Another way to study the influence of biology on behaviour is to use adoption studies. Explain how they are conducted and what they show.

....

....

....

....

....

....

....

.... **(3)**

(c) Outline one way that twins can be used to show the influence of biology on behaviour.

....

....

....

.... **(1)**

(Total 7 marks)

7. Money (1975) investigated a case of a boy whose penis was severed in a circumcision accident and was raised as a girl.

(a) Why was this a particularly interesting and useful case compared with the other gender-reassignment cases studied by Money (1975)?

....

.... **(1)**

(b) What biological treatment did the child receive to help in the gender-reassignment process?

....

....

....

.... **(2)**

(c) What did the child's family do to help in the gender-reassignment process?

....

.... **(1)**

(d) (i) What is meant by the 'nature–nurture debate'?

....

.... **(1)**

(ii) Ultimately, how successful was the gender reassignment and what does this tell us about the nature–nurture debate?

....

....

....

.... **(2)**

(Total 7 marks)

8. As part of the requirements for the Biological Psychology part of your course you will have conducted an experiment.

Write the aim or hypothesis of your experiment here: ....

(a) (i) What sampling method did you use?

....

.... **(1)**

(ii) Comment on the validity, reliability or generalisibility of your findings in relation to your sample.

....

....

....

.... **(2)**

(b) (i) Describe the apparatus, materials or stimuli that you used.

....

....

.... **(1)**

(ii) Comment on the validity, reliability or generalisibility of your findings in relation to your apparatus, materials or stimuli.

....

....

....

....

.... **(2)**

(Total 6 marks)

TOTAL FOR SECTION B: 20 MARKS

SECTION C

Answer ALL questions.
You are advised to spend approximately 18 minutes on this section.

9. Describe the structure and function of a synapse. You may use a diagram to help you.

....

....

....

....

....

....

.... **(4)**

***10.** Katrin and her mum and dad live in a small, very isolated village. All the other children are boys. Katrin's mum is worried that this will affect Katrin's gender development as she never socialises with any little girls and she is already a 'tomboy'. Apply your understanding of the concepts and ideas from the biological approach to explain whether she is likely to be affected in the long term.

....

....

....

....

....

....

....

....

....

....

....

....

.... **(10)**

TOTAL FOR SECTION C: 14 MARKS

TOTAL MARKS FOR PAPER: 40 MARKS

Mark scheme

SECTION A

1. **D** A and C above (i.e. PET and MRI) **(1)**

2. **C** and humans have evolved with similar brains **(1)**

3. **C** oestrogen causes a foetus to become female **(1)**

4. **D** it is made up only of sensory and motor neurones **(1)**

5. **A** hypothalamus and **C** cortex **(2)**

SECTION B

6. **(a)** *One way to study the influence of biology on behaviour is through scanning methods. Outline how a PET (positron emission tomography) scan works.*

The participant is injected with a (radioactive) tracer; such as glucose (^{11}C)/oxygen (^{15}O) that is used by respiring/active brain cells;

So radioactive particles are emitted when the tracer molecules are used up (in the brain); These are detected by a scanner around the head; which detects radioactivity in the form of positrons;

More radioactivity is released in brain areas that are more active, which shows up on the scan as different colours (white/red/yellow); (3)

(b) *Another way to study the influence of biology on behaviour is to use adoption studies. Explain how they are conducted and what they show.*

A group of children who have been adopted are assessed later in life on certain characteristics;

This is compared with the characteristics of their adoptive parents and their biological parents;

If the adopted children are more like their adoptive parents then nurture/the environment is important to the development of that characteristic;

If the adopted children are more like their biological parents then nature/genes are important to the development of that characteristic; (3)

(c) *Outline one way that twins can be used to show the influence of biology on behaviour.*

Identical/MZ twins can be compared with DZ twins to see if they are more similar;

Separated identical/MZ twins can be compared to see if they are less similar than MZ twins raised together; (1)

7. *Money (1975) investigated a case of a boy whose penis was severed in a circumcision accident and was raised as a girl.*

(a) *Why was this a particularly interesting and useful case compared with the other gender-reassignment cases studied by Money (1975)?*

Because the boy had an identical twin brother who was not sex-reassigned (to act as a control); (1)

(b) *What biological treatment did the child receive to help in the gender reassignment process?*

Hormone treatment with oestrogen to produce breast development;

Surgery to construct female genitalia/a vagina; (2)

(c) *What did the child's family do to help in the gender-reassignment process?*
Dressed Brenda in girls' clothes;

Gave her girls' toys;

Let her hair grow long;

Positively reinforced her for being feminine; (1)

(d) (i) *What is meant by the 'nature–nurture debate'?*
The argument over the extent to which characteristics are controlled by genes (nature) or the environment (nurture); (1)

(ii) *Ultimately, how successful was the gender reassignment and what does this tell us about the nature–nurture debate?*
It was unsuccessful as David Reimer had felt like a boy all along;

When he found out about his childhood he had treatment to return to a male appearance; (2)

8. *As part of the requirements for the Biological Psychology part of your course you will have conducted an experiment. Write the aim or hypothesis of your experiment here:*

(a) (i) *What sampling method did you use?*
One of: opportunity/random/stratified/volunteer

(ii) *Comment on the validity, reliability or generalisibility of your findings in relation to your sample* **e.g. findings from opportunity samples are unlikely to be generalisable because the diversity of the sample is likely to be limited (look for an illustration of how it was limited);**

Findings from opportunity samples may be unreliable because the sample is taken at a particular time or location and the individuals available over time or location may be substantially different (look for an illustration of how);

Findings from volunteer samples are unlikely to be generalisable because such samples tend to consist of similar people e.g. ones who have more time or are better educated (look for an illustration of how it was limited); (1)

(b) (i) *Describe the apparatus, materials or stimuli that you used.*
e.g. word lists, pictures, tests; (1)

(ii) *Comment on the validity, reliability or generalisibility of your findings in relation to your apparatus, materials or stimuli.*
e.g. lack of validity due to bias in materials (look for why);

Lack of reliability because different members of the group collected different sets of data;

Lack of generalisability because materials could only be used with certain participants (e.g. older children); (2)

SECTION C

9. *Describe the structure and function of a synapse. You may use a diagram to help you.*

Diagram max. 2 points – do not allow same marking points for written part of answer;

Neurotransmitters are released (from the pre-synaptic membrane) in response to a nerve impulse;

Neurotransmitters diffuse/travel across synapse (to post-synaptic membrane);

and attach to receptor site (which are specific to different neurotransmitters);

This affects the post-synaptic neurone and when sufficient neurotransmitters have attached a new nerve impulse is generated;

The neurotransmitters are recycled into the pre-synaptic membrane/neurone; (4)

***10.** *Katrin and her mum and dad live in a small, very isolated village. All the other children are boys. Katrin's mum is worried that this will affect Katrin's gender development as she never socialises with any little girls and she is already a 'tomboy'. Apply your understanding of the concepts and ideas from the biological approach to explain whether she is likely to be affected in the long term.* **(10)**

Level	Mark	Descriptor
		AO1: Knowledge and understanding of psychological concepts AO2: Application of psychological concepts.
1	0	No content worth of marks.
2	1–2	A brief, simple answer with some relevance to the gender development but with little reference to the influence of biology or evaluation. Answer lacks clarity and/or organisation. Little use of relevant terminology and poor spelling, punctuation and/or grammar.
3	3–5	An answer with simple but largely relevant description which is accurate but limited. Limited clarity and/or organisation. Some use of relevant terminology. Frequent spelling, punctuation and/or grammatical errors. At the top of the band some accurate reference to either the biology of gender development or evaluation is present.
4	6–8	The answer contains both relevant and accurate evidence and has some effective application of ideas to Katrin's gender development. Clarity of expression and organisation are competent with some use of relevant terminology. Some spelling, punctuation and/or grammatical errors are likely to be present. At the top of the band both reference to Katrin's gender development and some evaluation are present.
5	9–10	The answer contains accurate evidence (from studies and/or theories) and this is effectively applied to Katrin's gender development. Description and evaluation are well balanced. Clarity of expression and organisation are effective and the candidate makes good use of relevant terminology. Few spelling, punctuation or grammatical errors are present.

Indicative content:

- **Gender development is controlled by sex chromosomes, and Katrin is a girl with XX; (AO1)**
- **This will become more apparent at puberty when oestrogen is released from the ovaries and this begins to affect her development more; (AO1)**
- **She will develop breasts etc. so look more female which will help to change her gender identity; (AO2)**
- **When the boys go through puberty they will release testosterone which will make them different from her, e.g. developing deep voices; (AO1)**
- **This will also help to make them seem different; (AO2)**
- **Even when attempts are made to control gender identity biologically after birth through hormones, surgery and family environment, they are unsuccessful (like Money, 1975); (AO2)**
- **So Katrin is unlikely to develop a male gender identity just because of her environment; (AO2)**
- **The only way to change gender after birth is to implant the SRY gene and this did not happen to Katrin; (AO1)**
- **She will have developed a female brain which is different from a male brain, e.g. in the size of the SDN; (AO1)**

Resources

See PowerPoint 5-22: *Resources.*

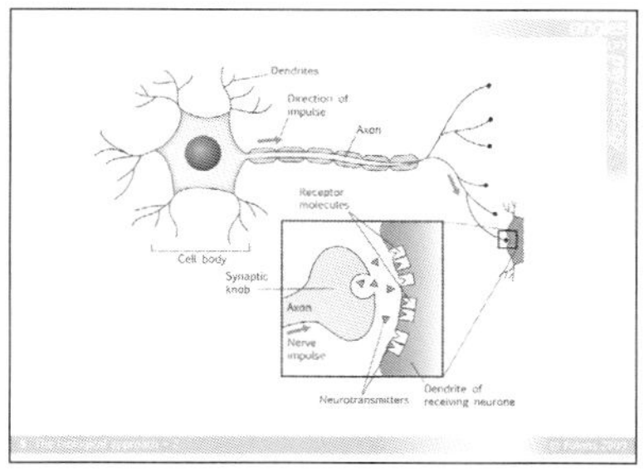

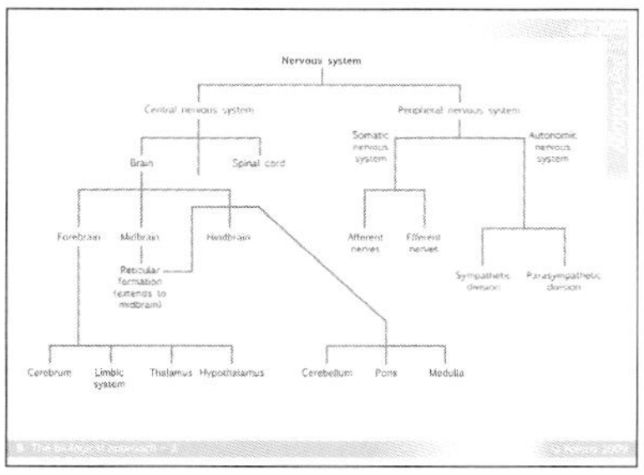

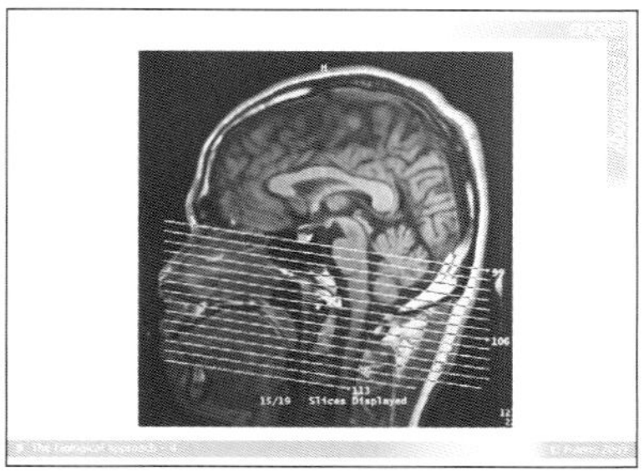

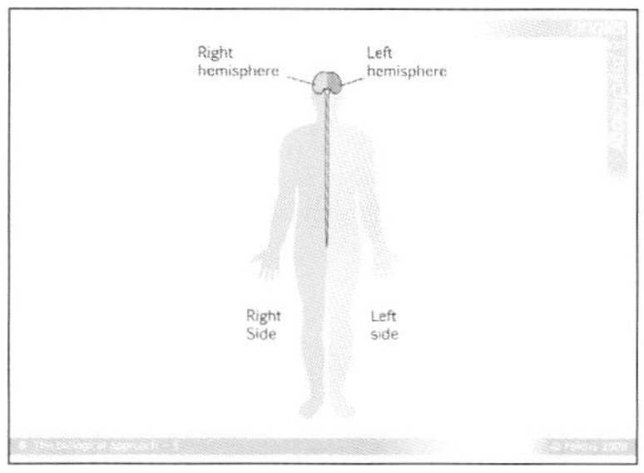

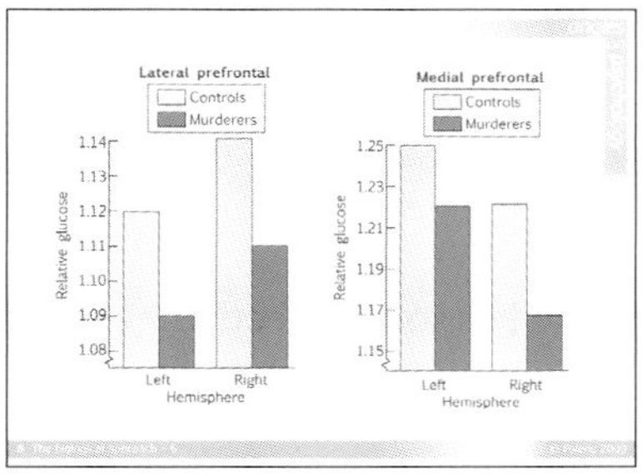

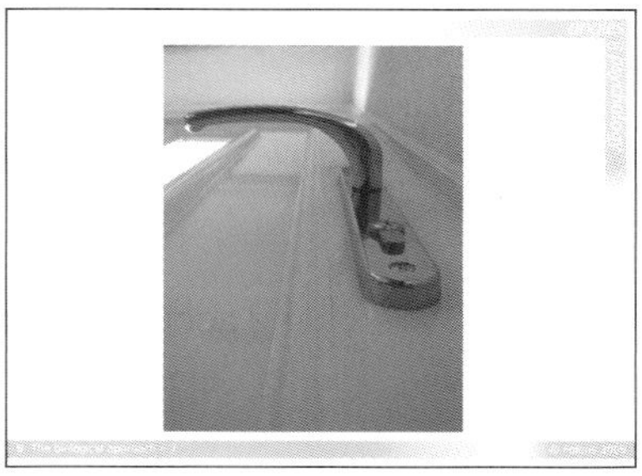

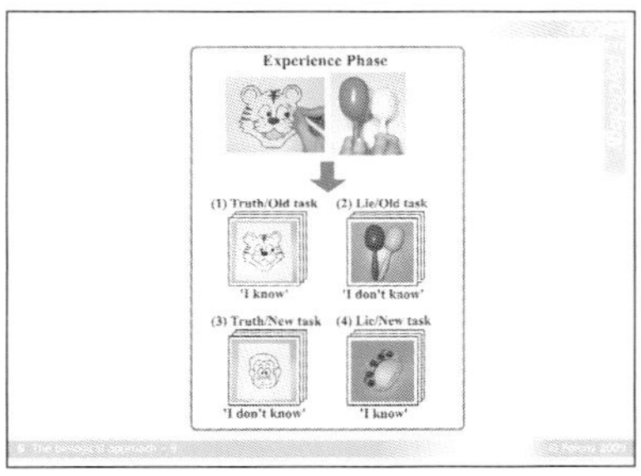

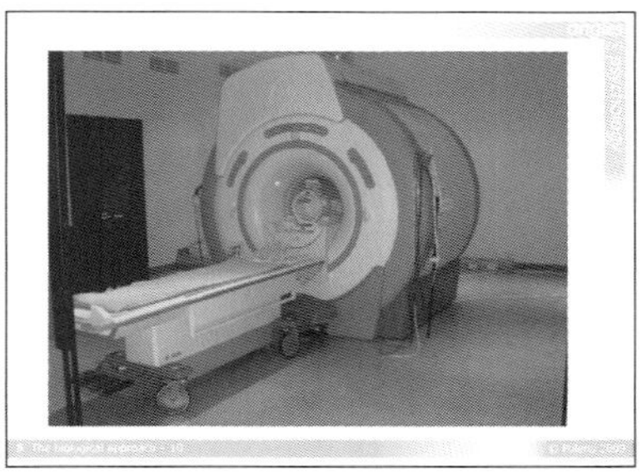

Table 5.2 Concordance for schizophrenia in twins of schizophrenics

	MZ		DZ	
Grade	N	%	N	%
1	10	42	3	9
1 and 2	13	54	6	18
1, 2 and 3	19	79	15	45
Normal	5	21	18	55
Total	24	100	33	100

	mean volume (cm^3)	
structure	males	females
cerebral volume	1344.53	1188.50
grey matter	850.75	767.96
white matter	493.79	420.34
corpus callosum	8.04	7.69

Table of critical values for Mann-Whitney U:
one-tailed tests at $p \leq 0.05$
and two-tailed tests at $p \leq 0.1$

n_1 → / n_2 ↓	3	4	5	6
3	0	0	1	2
4	0	1	2	3
5	1	2	4	5
6	2	3	5	7

Time taken to make 20 plurals of pseudonouns (in seconds)

Participant no. →	Group no. ↓	1	2	3	4	5	6	7	8	9	10	Mean
Males	A	104	121	77	64	98	151	129	196	87	73	
Females	B	51	65	76	56	83	94	53	61	59	72	

Table of critical values for Mann-Whitney *U*:
one-tailed tests at $p \leq 0.025$ and two-tailed tests at $p \leq 0.05$

n_1 → / n_2 ↓	2	3	4	5	6	7	8	9	10	11	12
8	0	2	4	6	8	10	13	15	17	19	22
9	0	2	4	7	10	12	15	17	20	23	26
10	0	3	5	8	11	14	17	20	23	26	29
11	0	3	6	9	13	16	19	23	26	30	33

References

Amunts, K., Jancke, L., Mohlberg, H., Steinmetz, H. & Zilles, K. (2000) 'Interhemispheric asymmetry of the human motor cortex related to handedness and gender'. *Neuropsychologia,* 38(3): 304–12.

Daniels, D. & Plomin, R. (1985) 'Origins of individual differences in infant shyness'. *Developmental Psychology*, 21(1): 118–21

Gilboa, A., Winocur, G., Grady, C.L., Hevenor. S.J. & Moscovitch. M. (2004) 'Remembering our past: functional neuroanatomy of recollection of recent and very remote personal events'. *Cerebral Cortex*, 14(11): 1214–25.

Knutson, B., Rick, S., Wimmer, G.E., Prelec, D. & Loewenstein, G. (2007) 'Neural predictors of purchases'. *Neuron,* 53: 147–56.

Natsopoulos, D., Kiosseoglou, G., Xeromeritou, A. & Alevriadou, A. (1998) 'Do the hands talk on mind's behalf? Differences in language ability between left- and right-handed children'. *Brain and Language*, 64(2): 182–214.

Roth, W.E. & Finley, G.E. (1998) 'Adoption and Antisocial Personality: Genetic and Environmental Factors Associated with Antisocial Outcomes'. *Child and Adolescent Social Work Journal*, 15(2): 133–49.

Tankle, R.S. & Heilman, K.M. (1983) 'Mirror writing in right-handers and in left-handers'. *Brain and Language*, 19(1): 115–23.

Chapter 6

The learning approach

Activity number	Activity title	Activity/file type
The learning approach		
6.1	Introduction to classical conditioning	ST CA TN prep
6.2	Classical conditioning	MW SAQ A
6.3	Guessing goldfish	WM MW A
6.4	Garry's garden games	SAQ
6.5	Surfing with Sashi	SAQ SC
6.6	Goldfish pass memory test	MW SC
6.7	Classical and operant conditioning	CE A
6.8	Bandura, Ross & Ross (1961)	CE A
6.9	Observations	CE A
6.10	Social learning theory	CE A
6.11	Two approaches to therapy	CE A
6.12	Gender and learning	MW SC
6.13	Choosing a statistical test	SAQ A
6.14	Essays: questions 1 and 2	LAQ
6.15	Gender stereotypes: girls play 'house', boys play 'spaceship'	ET
6.16	Creative activities 1 and 2	KI
6.17	Evidence of practice: observing gender	RM
6.18	Gender in journals	RM
6.19	Brave boys?	RM
6.20	The learning approach quick quiz	QQ A
6.21	The learning approach test	AT A
6.22	Resources	PP
6.23	References	

Introduction to classical conditioning

Preparation

You need to obtain a large selection of empty chocolate wrappers and boxes. They need to have been empty for a while to lose their smell. If you have the will power and budget, you could purchase a range of confectionary, separate it from its wrappers and keep it for students to consume afterwards! Alternatively, you could get a different class to save them up for you in advance. Ideally, they should appear still to contain food, hence boxes are better.

Teacher notes

Like Pavlov's dogs, students and teachers have probably been classically conditioned to salivate. Chocolate always comes in a characteristic wrapper – that is often in sight as we eat. As a consequence, sweet wrappers become powerful conditioned stimuli (CSs) for salivation. Whenever we eat chocolate (the unconditioned stimulus), we see the wrapper (the CS) first. So, although initially wrappers are neutral stimuli, they rapidly become capable of eliciting the conditioned resonse (CR) of salivation. This occurs because the chocolate, which causes the unconditioned response of salivation, is always paired with a wrapper. The pairing may be *trace* (see the wrapper, open it, throw it away and then eat the chocolate) or *forward* (see the wrapper, open it and start eating the chocolate, with the wrapper still covering part or the bar, or still in view).

When you are ready to demonstrate the effect, start teaching; then arrange the wrappers in highly visible places. Continue to teach until you can see students swallowing! Stop and ask them why they are salivating. Finally, ask them to identify the UCS, CS, UCR and CR.

Students (and teachers!) will readily salivate to the sight of the wrappers. If you have not yet taught the theory, students are likely to respond that they are salivating because they are anticipating or preparing for food. You can counter this by asking them whether babies respond in the same way to the sight of sweet wrappers and, if not, how the response is acquired. Students are likely to observe that the noise of sweets being unwrapped is also a highly effective CS.

Classical conditioning

1. Match up the following terms:

Term
Conditioned response
Extinction
Unconditioned stimulus
Spontaneous recovery
Conditioned stimulus
Unconditioned response

Definition
A trigger for a behaviour that produces a response only after repeated pairing with another stimulus
The reappearance of a previously lost conditioned response when the conditioned stimulus is later reintroduced
A behaviour such as a reflex which naturally occurs when a particular trigger is present
A behaviour that occurs when a particular trigger with which it has been repeatedly paired is present
A trigger for a behaviour that naturally produces a response
The disappearance of a response when the conditioned stimulus is repeated many times without the unconditioned stimulus

2. Identify the UCS, UCR, CS and CR in the following examples:

   a) A woman on holiday from a busy job treats herself to exotic fruits like mango and pineapple every morning for breakfast. Slowly, over the week, she relaxes. When she returns to work she finds she's immediately just as busy as before and is soon overwhelmed. On the way home she stops at the shops, something she usually finds stressful, but within minutes of being in the fruit and veg aisle she feels very calm.

   b) A Dachshund dog is frequently taken to the pub by his owner and tries to mount the landlord's Alsatian puppy. When the Dachshund's owner throws a party and his house smells of beer, the dog gets excited and mounts the guests' legs.

   c) A horse rider who regularly leads her horse always stops and takes the call if her mobile phone rings but never has the phone on when she is riding. One day, when she is riding, she passes a walker whose phone goes off. Her horse halts and won't budge until the walker has finished his call.

Classical conditioning *continued*

1.

Term
Conditioned response
Extinction
Unconditioned stimulus
Spontaneous recovery
Conditioned stimulus
Unconditioned response

Definition
A trigger for a behaviour that produces a response only after repeated pairing with another stimulus
The reappearance of a previously lost conditioned response when the conditioned stimulus is later reintroduced
A behaviour such as a reflex which naturally occurs when a particular trigger is present
A behaviour that occurs when a particular trigger with which it has been repeatedly paired is present
A trigger for a behaviour that naturally produces a response
The disappearance of a response when the conditioned stimulus is repeated many times without the unconditioned stimulus

2. a) A woman on holiday from a busy job treats herself to exotic fruits like mango and pineapple (**UCS**) every morning for breakfast. Slowly, over the week, she relaxes (**UCR**). When she returns to work she finds she's immediately just as busy as before and is soon overwhelmed. On the way home she stops at the shops, something she usually finds stressful, but within minutes of being in the fruit and veg aisle (**CS**) she feels very calm (**CR**).

   b) A Dachshund dog is frequently taken to the pub (**UCS**) by his owner and tries to mount the landlord's Alsatian puppy (**UCR**). When the Dachshund's owner throws a party and his house smells of beer (**CS**), the dog gets excited and mounts the guests' legs (**CR**).

   c) A horse rider who regularly leads her horse always stops her horse (**UCR**) and takes the call if her mobile phone rings (**UCS**) but never has the phone on when she is riding. One day, when she is riding, she passes a walker whose phone goes off (**CS**). Her horse halts and won't budge (**CR**) until the walker has finished his call.

Guessing goldfish

1. Match up the following terms:

Term
Negative reinforcement
Positive reinforcement
Primary reinforcer
Secondary reinforcer

Definition
A consequence that affects the frequency of a behaviour because it has become associated with another source of reward
A consequence that affects the frequency of a behaviour because it is important to survival
A consequence that increases the frequency of a behaviour because it is nice when it happens
A consequence that increases the frequency of a behaviour because it is nice when it stops

2.

media watch Guessing Goldfish

Send your pet problems to our resident veterinary surgeon, Vet Victoria

Dear Vet Victoria,

We have had Sunlight, our goldfish, for about 20 years. My son won it at the fair when he was about 7 – he left home long ago, leaving us to look after Sunlight.

The fish is still going strong and eats like a horse, well, a shark at least. It has a funny habit of attracting my attention if I'm tardy. If I'm late with its food in the morning it swims up and down, wiggles about and goes 'plop' at the surface of the water. Sunlight also eats from my fingers.

a) One explanation for this goldfish's behaviour would be that it is superstitious. What is meant by superstitious behaviour in the context of the learning approach? [1 mark]

b) Fish are usually reluctant to be fed by hand. How could you deliberately teach a goldfish to be fed from the hand? [3 marks]

c) If the family owner stopped responding to the goldfish swimming up and down, wiggling and going 'plop' what would happen to this behaviour? [3 marks]

Guessing goldfish

Answers

Term
Negative reinforcement
Positive reinforcement
Primary reinforcer
Secondary reinforcer

Definition
A consequence that increases the frequency of a behaviour because it is nice when it stops
A consequence that increases the frequency of a behaviour because it is nice when it happens
A consequence that affects the frequency of a behaviour because it is important to survival
A consequence that affects the frequency of a behaviour because it has become associated with another source of reward

Garry's garden games

Garry wants to teach the squirrels in his garden to come into the house through an open window. He has set up a series of bird tables along the lawn, the last one being right beside the kitchen window. The squirrels already come to feed at the farthest bird table and will happily run along a wire so Garry has put pieces of rope between each bird table. Garry hopes to use the principles of operant conditioning to achieve his aim.

1. Garry plans to use food to reward the squirrels for jumping onto the bird tables. What term is used to describe rewards such as this? [1 mark]
2. In order for the squirrels to learn to run along the whole length of each rope, Garry plans to reinforce successive approximations to the behaviour he desires. Suggest how he could achieve this. [1 mark]
3. If the squirrels fall off the rope they might startle themselves and be distressed. In terms of learning processes, what effect will this have on the likelihood of them running along the rope again, and why? [2 marks]
4. Once one squirrel has learned the task of running along the ropes to the kitchen window, Garry may find that other squirrels find their way into his kitchen more quickly. What theory could account for this and how would this happen? [4 marks]
5. If Garry went on holiday and the kitchen window was always closed so the squirrels couldn't get to the food, what would happen to their behaviour and why? [2 marks]

Surfing with Sashi

a) Sashi has been surfing the net for a project at school. A search has given her a list of hundreds of possible sites about castles. It doesn't really matter what information she finds provided that she gets something different. At the end of each page of ten she jots something down and gives herself a break.

b) When Sashi was planning a meal for friends she looked through thousands of recipes online and just occasionally found a decent one.

c) Sashi knows that there has been a problem with the server recently and sometimes it takes five minutes to connect. She sets it up and goes to make a cup of tea but, after a couple of minutes, she keeps pressing a key every few seconds to remove the screen saver so that she can see whether it's connected yet.

d) There is a particular site about cats that Sashi wants to see but there's always an error message so she keeps on and on trying, until she accesses it.

1. What term is used to refer to schedules of reinforcement in which a reinforcer is not received every time an individual performs a response? [1 mark]
2. Different reinforcement schedules are operating in each of the situations described above. Identify each schedule of reinforcement in each of a)–d) above. [4 marks]
3. The response rate and speed of extinction differ between the different schedules of reinforcement and with continuous reinforcement.
   a) What is meant by the term 'extinction'? [1 mark]
   b) Describe the way in which the response rate and speed of extinction differ between one named schedule and continuous reinforcement. [2 marks]

Stretch and challenge

1. As a student, reinforcement is important to your progress. It can come from many sources such as yourself, your teachers, your peers and your family.
   a) Make a list of all the reinforcers you can think of that you as a student are exposed to.
   b) Identify whether each one is a positive or a negative reinforcer.
   c) Try to decide whether any of those reinforcers have a particular reinforcement schedule – for example you may have regular feedback about your homework, or termly reports.

Goldfish pass memory test

media watch

Goldfish pass memory test

Mark Henderson, Science correspondent
The Times 11 October 2003

It is time for the scales to fall from our eyes: scientists have claimed not only that goldfish have a memory span of up to three months, but that they can also tell the time.

The fish, previously believed to have a memory of just a few seconds, can distinguish between different times of day and can also be taught to follow a routine, according to research.

Scientists at Plymouth University have successfully trained the fish to collect food at particular times of day, showing the popular notion of the three-second memory to be very fishy indeed.

The findings add to a growing body of evidence that fish are much more sentient and intelligent than had generally been assumed.

Recent research has suggested that fish feel pain when they are caught on a hook, can be manuplative and socially aware, have long memories and are able to recognise their shoal-mates.

The research, led by Phil Gee of Plymouth University, has added a sophisticated body clock to the piscine intellect. In his experiment goldfish were placed in a bowl in which they were fed only when they pressed a lever. The fish rapidly learnt that pressing the lever produced a food reward.

Once they had been trained in this way, the researchers set up the lever to work for just one hour a day. The fish soon became wise to this, and learnt to press the lever at the same time every day to feed.

'The fish worked out that if they hit the lever around that time, they would get some food,' Dr Gee said. 'Their activity around the lever increased enormously just before the set hour when their food was dispensed.

'But then if no food came out, they stopped pressing the lever when the hour was up. It shows they are probably able to adapt to changes in their cicumstances, like any other small animals and birds.'

The study could have implications for fish farming, Dr Gee said. He suggests that it should be possible to train trout and salmon to swim to feeding stations to certain signals, making it easier for farmers to monitor and harvest their stock.

1. Which theory of learning could explain the ability of the fish to learn to press the lever for food? [1 mark]
2. a) What schedule of reinforcement was being used when the food was only available for part of each day? [1 mark]

   b) Was the response of the fish typical of animals on this schedule? [1 mark]
3. What term describes the effect demonstrated by the fish when the researchers altered the mechanism so that it no longer dispensed food? [1 mark]
4. If a fish farmer wanted to train his trout to swim into a quarantine pool so that they could be isolated if they became unwell, how could it be done? [3 marks]

Goldfish pass memory test *continued*

Stretch and Challenge

Find out about Marion Stamp Dawkins' work on animal welfare online. For example:

- http://www.newscientist.com/article/mg14119094.100-the-emotional-chicken-why-did-the-chicken-cross-the-roadbecause-it-cared-about-something-on-the-other-side-according-to-researcherslooking-for-signs-of-consciousness-in-animals-.html
  (1994) 'The emotional chicken: Why did the chicken cross the road? Because it cared about something on the other side, according to researchers looking for signs of consciousness in animals'. Gail Vines, *New Scientist*, 22 January
- http://www.animal-rights-library.com/texts-m/stampdawkins01.htm
  Look particularly at the section on 'Asking the animals'. Identify examples of reinforcers. How does the work describe help to assess and improve the ethical treatment of animals?
  Stamp Dawkins, M. (1985) 'The scientific basis for assessing suffering in animals'. In P. Singer (ed), *In Defense of Animals*. New York: Basil Blackwell, pp. 27–40.

One study conducted by Stamp Dawkins investigated various potential positive reinforcers for chickens by finding out which conditions they would avoid or move into when they had to squeeze through a narrow gap. Try to find out about this research using appropriate terms in an internet search.

You might also like to read her book: Stamp Dawkins, M. (1993) *Through Our Eyes Only?: The Search for Animal Consciousness*. Oxford: Oxford University Press.

Classical and operant conditioning

There are some basic concepts that apply to learned behaviours in general. When an animal or person responds to an object or individual in their environment, that trigger for behaviour is called a ____________. Some stimuli naturally produce effects on animals and other stimuli can acquire that property through ____________. The behaviour that is produced in response to a stimulus is called a ____________. Psychologists began investigating learning by looking at the relationship between the two; this is sometimes called ____________ psychology. Later, psychologists became interested in the processes occurring in between, i.e. ____________.

____________ occurs when two stimuli, one of which already elicits a response, are paired together. The stimulus that naturally produces a response is called the ____________. The behaviour it elicits is called the ____________. The stimulus it is paired with, which initially does not produce the response in question, is called the ____________. After several pairings, an association is built up between the two stimuli. As a consequence, the new stimulus, now known as the ____________, will also elicit the behaviour in question, now called the ____________. For example, I could condition my rabbit to twitch its nose (____________) by pairing nice-smelling dandelion leaves (____________), which always make its nose twitch, with the sound of me clicking my fingers (____________). After weeks of repeatedly clicking my fingers when I feed her dandelion leaves, she will start to twitch her nose (____________) whenever I click my fingers (____________). However, if I keep clicking my fingers without giving her any dandelion leaves, eventually she will ____________ twitching her nose. This is an example of ____________. If I stopped clicking and giving her dandelion leaves altogether for a while, then started clicking again, she would twitch her nose again. This is called ____________.

____________ occurs when a behaviour is either reinforced or punished. Positive or negative reinforcement will ____________ the frequency of a behaviour that it follows whereas punishment will ____________ the frequency of behaviours. In ____________ the reinforcer is pleasant when it is given whereas in ____________ the reinforcer is pleasant when it stops. The effects of punishment are always ____________. This may be giving something ____________ or taking away something ____________. For example, I may train my dog to walk to heel by giving him a treat when he stays close to me – this is ____________ reinforcement. I could train my neighbour's cat to stay out of the flower beds by spraying him with water every time he sits near the flowers – this is an example of ____________. If Bob has a headache, he takes painkillers and the headache goes away, so he is more likely to take painkillers the next time he has a headache. This is an example of ____________ reinforcement.

Reinforcers such as food, sex and reduction of pain are naturally rewarding; they are called ____________ reinforcers. Another example is ____________. Other reinforcers gain the property of rewarding behaviour only because they have been associated with another consequence that is pleasant. These are called ____________ reinforcers. For example, money is reinforcing because it can buy us things that satisfy our needs such as clothing or heating to keep us warm. Another example is ____________.

Classical and operant conditioning *continued*

classical conditioning
cognition
conditioned response
conditioned stimulus
CR
CS
decrease
extinction
increase
learning
merit marks
nasty
negative
negative reinforcement
neutral stimulus
nice
NS
operant conditioning
positive
positive reinforcement
primary
punishment
response
secondary
social companionship
spontaneous recovery
S–R
stimulus
stop
UCR
UCS
unconditioned response
unconditioned stimulus
unpleasant

Classical and operant conditioning

Answers

There are some basic concepts that apply to learned behaviours in general. When an animal or person responds to an object or individual in their environment, that trigger for behaviour is called a **stimulus**. Some stimuli naturally produce effects on animals and other stimuli can acquire that property through **learning**. The behaviour that is produced in response to a stimulus is called a **response**. Psychologists began investigating learning by looking at the relationship between the two; this is sometimes called **S–R** psychology. Later, psychologists became interested in the processes occurring in between, i.e. **cognition**.

Classical conditioning occurs when two stimuli, one of which already elicits a response, are paired together. The stimulus that naturally produces a response is called the **unconditioned stimulus**. The behaviour it elicits is called the **unconditioned response**. The stimulus it is paired with, which initially does not produce the response in question, is called the **neutral stimulus**. After several pairings, an association is built up between the two stimuli. As a consequence, the new stimulus, now known as the **conditioned stimulus**, will also elicit the behaviour in question, now called the **conditioned response**. For example, I could condition my rabbit to twitch its nose (**UCR**) by pairing nice-smelling dandelion leaves (**UCS**), which always make its nose twitch, with the sound of me clicking my fingers (**NS**). After weeks of repeatedly clicking my fingers when I feed her dandelion leaves, she will start to twitch her nose (**CR**) whenever I click my fingers (**CS**). However, if I keep clicking my fingers without giving her any dandelion leaves, eventually she will **stop** twitching her nose. This is an example of **extinction**. If I stopped clicking and giving her dandelion leaves altogether for a while, then started clicking again, she would twitch her nose again. This is called **spontaneous recovery**.

Operant conditioning occurs when a behaviour is either reinforced or punished. Positive or negative reinforcement will **increase** the frequency of a behaviour that it follows whereas punishment will **decrease** the frequency of behaviours. In **positive reinforcement** the reinforcer is pleasant when it is given whereas in **negative reinforcement** the reinforcer is pleasant when it stops. The effects of punishment are always **unpleasant**. This may be giving something **nasty** or taking away something **nice**. For example, I may train my dog to walk to heel by giving him a treat when he stays close to me – this is **positive** reinforcement. I could train my neighbour's cat to stay out of the flower beds by spraying him with water every time he sits near the flowers – this is an example of **punishment**. If Bob has a headache, he takes painkillers and the headache goes away, so he is more likely to take painkillers the next time he has a headache. This is an example of **negative** reinforcement.

Reinforcers such as food, sex and reduction of pain are naturally rewarding; they are called **primary** reinforcers. Another example is **social companionship**. Other reinforcers gain the property of rewarding behaviour only because they have been associated with another consequence that is pleasant. These are called **secondary** reinforcers. For example, money is reinforcing because it can buy us things that satisfy our needs such as clothing or heating to keep us warm. Another example is **merit marks**.

Classical and operant conditioning

Answers *continued*

stimulus
learning
response
S–R
cognition
classical conditioning
unconditioned stimulus
unconditioned response
neutral stimulus
conditioned stimulus
conditioned response
UCR
UCS
NS
CR
CS
stop
extinction
spontaneous recovery
operant conditioning
increase
decrease
positive reinforcement
negative reinforcement
unpleasant
nasty
nice
positive
punishment
negative
primary
social companionship
secondary
merit marks

Bandura, Ross & Ross (1961)

Bandura, Ross & Ross (1961) were interested in the way children learned aggression through the imitation of aggressive ____________. They also wanted to see whether children were ____________ likely to imitate same-sex models. They tested groups of children aged between ____________ and ____________ years. There were 36 of each sex. Some children saw adult ____________ and others, in the ____________ group, did not. The children in these groups were ____________ for aggressiveness, based on their behaviour at nursery school, which was rated by an experimenter and their teacher, both of whom knew the children well. The participants were scored on variables such as aggression towards objects and to other children. Approximately two-thirds of the children were rated by both the experimenter and the teacher. They had high inter-observer ____________, with a correlation of $r =$ ____________.

Each child was taken individually into a playroom by an experimenter and was shown how to play with stickers and potato prints. The experimenter then escorted the model into the opposite corner of the room and explained that they had other toys to play with.

Half of the children saw models of the same sex as themselves; for the other half the model was the opposite sex. The model was always seen playing with a ____________. In the non-aggressive condition this lasted for ____________ minute(s); in the aggressive condition they saw this for only ____________ minute(s) after which the model attacked a ____________. The model's behaviour included ____________, such as punching and kicking and ____________, such as saying 'kick him' and 'pow'.

To ____________ the possibility of the children demonstrating any aggression they had learned, they were frustrated by being taken to a room with nice toys such as a ____________ and a doll with a wardrobe but then being told that the toys were for other children. The child was then taken to another room containing a Bobo doll and a ____________ as well as other toys such as a tea set, bears and farm animals. The child's behaviour was then ____________ for ____________ minute(s) by another experimenter through a one-way mirror. In half of the sessions, two experimenters scored the child's behaviour simultaneously. Their inter-observer reliability was high, with a ____________ of at about $r = 0.9$.

The children could have left at any time, i.e. they had a ____________. However, an experimenter remained inconspicuously in the room, busying themselves with paperwork away from the child, to reduce the likelihood they would refuse to remain alone or would leave before the session had finished.

The children who were exposed to aggressive models imitated their exact behaviours. They were significantly more aggressive – both physically and verbally – than those children who did not observe an aggressive role model. This effect was greater for ____________ than ____________ although girls were more likely to imitate ____________, and boys ____________, aggression. Boys were also more likely to imitate a ____________ model as were girls, although ____________ so.

The findings show that ____________ and imitation can account for the learning of specific acts without ____________ of either the model or ____________. The results also show that observers are more likely to ____________ same-sex models.

Bandura, Ross & Ross (1961) *continued*

0.89	girls	physical
1	imitate	physical aggression
3	increase	reinforcement
6	less	reliability
10	mallet	right to withdraw
20	matched	role models
Bobo doll	models	same-sex
boys	more	toy building set
control	observation	verbal
correlation	observed	verbal aggression
fire engine	observer	

Bandura, Ross & Ross (1961)

Answers

Bandura, Ross & Ross (1961) were interested in the way children learned aggression through the imitation of aggressive **models**. They also wanted to see whether children were **more** likely to imitate same-sex models. They tested groups of children aged between **3** and **6** years. There were 36 of each sex. Some children saw adult **role models** and others, in the **control** group, did not. The children in these groups were **matched** for aggressiveness, based on their behaviour at nursery school, which was rated by an experimenter and their teacher both of whom knew the children well. The participants were scored on variables such as aggression towards objects and to other children. Approximately two-thirds of the children were rated by both the experimenter and the teacher. They had high inter-observer **reliability**, with a correlation of r = **0.89**.

Each child was taken individually into a playroom by an experimenter and was shown how to play with stickers and potato prints. The experimenter then escorted the model into the opposite corner of the room and explained that they had other toys to play with.

Half of the children saw models of the same sex as themselves; for the other half the model was the opposite sex. The model was always seen playing with a **toy building set**. In the non-aggressive condition this lasted for **10** minutes; in the aggressive condition they saw this for only **1** minute after which the model attacked a **Bobo doll**. The model's behaviour included **physical aggression**, such as punching and kicking and **verbal aggression**, such as saying 'kick him' and 'pow'.

To **increase** the possibility of the children demonstrating any aggression they had learned, they were frustrated by being taken to a room with nice toys such as a **fire engine** and a doll with a wardrobe but then being told that the toys were for other children. The child was then taken to another room containing a Bobo doll and a **mallet** as well as other toys such as a tea set, bears and farm animals. The child's behaviour was then **observed** for **20** minutes by another experimenter through a one-way mirror. In half of the sessions, two experimenters scored the child's behaviour simultaneously. Their inter-observer reliability was high, with a **correlation** of at about r = 0.9.

The children could have left at any time, i.e. they had a **right to withdraw**. However, an experimenter remained inconspicuously in the room, busying themselves with paperwork away from the child, to reduce the likelihood they would refuse to remain alone or would leave before the session had finished.

The children who were exposed to aggressive models imitated their exact behaviours. They were significantly more aggressive – both physically and verbally – than those children who did not observe an aggressive role model. This effect was greater for **boys** than **girls** although girls were more likely to imitate **verbal**, and boys **physical**, aggression. Boys were also more likely to imitate a **same-sex** model as were girls, although **less** so.

The findings show that **observation** and imitation can account for the learning of specific acts without **reinforcement** of either the model or **observer**. The results also show that observers are **more** likely to **imitate** same-sex models.

Bandura, Ross & Ross (1961)

Answers *continued*

models	1	boys
more	Bobo doll	girls
3	physical aggression	verbal
6	verbal aggression	physical
role models	increase	same-sex
control	fire engine	less
matched	mallet	observation
reliability	observed	reinforcement
0.89	20	observer
toy building set	correlation	imitate
10	right to withdraw	

Observations

Observational studies involve watching the behaviour of people or animals. An observation may be used as a research method in itself, or observations can be used to measure the ____________ variable in an ____________. In a ____________ observation, the setting for the study is typical for the activity being observed. Children's aggression or play, for example, could be observed in a ____________. As the individual is familiar with the situation, and it is appropriate for that behaviour, it is likely that the data produced will be ____________. In a contrived or controlled observation, the setting is manipulated by the researcher and may be ____________ i.e. not where the behaviour being observed would normally occur; for example, if people are observed sleeping in a sleep laboratory. In naturalistic observations, the behaviour is likely to be representative of real life so it is ____________ valid. However, a disadvantage is that it is difficult to control ____________ variables compared with a laboratory setting.

A ____________ observer is included within the social activities of the group being observed. He or she is therefore aware of the ____________ in which behaviours occur. For example they are likely to notice subtle emotional changes demonstrated by participants. A disadvantage, however, is that the observer may become very involved in the context and lose the ability to be ____________ about what they see. Also, their mere ____________ may change the participants' behaviour so the data are ____________ valid. The observer can avoid some of these problems by being non-participant. By watching without being part of the social context, they are less likely to be ____________. However, they will also be less ____________ of the context in which behaviours arise.

In a ____________ observation, the participants are unaware of the observer's presence or role. This can be done using a one-way mirror or hidden video recorder. However, this raises ethical issues about ____________ and the ____________. An ____________ observer's presence is obvious to the participants, such as if they are holding a clipboard. This can lead to different problems such as ____________ – if the participants guess what the observers are looking for, this can change their behaviour. If the observer is ____________ this is less likely to be a problem.

A researcher may collect qualitative or quantitative data in an observation. Detailed, descriptive observations such as of a single child's response to a fear-inducing situation would produce ____________ data. In contrast, a researcher might plan to ____________ observed actions in a small number of behavioural categories. This would generate ____________ data. If more than one observer is recording data in a study it is important that they have agreed on the ____________ for behavioural categories. This helps to ensure that inter-observer ____________ is high and helps to avoid observer bias which could happen if they had different expectations.

artificial
aware
consent
context
covert
demand characteristics

dependent
experiment
extraneous
familiar
less
more
naturalistic

objective
operational definitions
overt
participant
playground
presence

qualitative
quantitative
reliability
right to withdraw
subjective
tally
valid

Observations

Answers

Observational studies involve watching the behaviour of people or animals. An observation may be used as a research method in itself, or observations can be used to measure the **dependent** variable in an **experiment**. In a **naturalistic** observation, the setting for the study is typical for the activity being observed. Children's aggression or play, for example, could be observed in a **playground**. As the individual is familiar with the situation, and it is appropriate for that behaviour, it is likely that the data produced will be **valid**. In a contrived or controlled observation, the setting is manipulated by the researcher and may be **artificial** i.e. not where the behaviour being observed would normally occur; for example, if people are observed sleeping in a sleep laboratory. In naturalistic observations, the behaviour is likely to be representative of real life so it is **more** valid. However, a disadvantage is that it is difficult to control **extraneous** variables compared with a laboratory setting.

A **participant** observer is included within the social activities of the group being observed. He or she is therefore aware of the **context** in which behaviours occur. For example they are likely to notice subtle emotional changes demonstrated by participants. A disadvantage, however, is that the observer may become very involved in the context and lose the ability to be **objective** about what they see. Also, their mere **presence** may change the participants' behaviour so the data are **less** valid. The observer can avoid some of these problems by being non-participant. By watching without being part of the social context, they are less likely to be **subjective**. However, they will also be less **aware** of the context in which behaviours arise.

In a **covert** observation, the participants are unaware of the observer's presence or role. This can be done using a one-way mirror or hidden video recorder. However, this raises ethical issues about **consent** and the **right to withdraw**. An **overt** observer's presence is obvious to the participants, such as if they are holding a clipboard. This can lead to different problems such as **demand characteristics** – if the participants guess what the observers are looking for, this can change their behaviour. If the observer is **familiar** this is less likely to be a problem.

A researcher may collect qualitative or quantitative data in an observation. Detailed, descriptive observations such as of a single child's response to a fear-inducing situation would produce **qualitative** data. In contrast, a researcher might plan to **tally** observed actions in a small number of behavioural categories. This would generate **quantitative** data. If more than one observer is recording data in a study it is important that they have agreed on the **operational definitions** for behavioural categories. This helps to ensure that inter-observer **reliability** is high and helps to avoid observer bias which could happen if they had different expectations.

dependent	extraneous	aware	familiar
experiment	participant	covert	qualitative
naturalistic	context	consent	tally
playground	objective	right to withdraw	quantitative
valid	presence	overt	operational definitions
artificial	less	demand characteristics	reliability
more	subjective		

Social learning theory

Social learning theory says that we tend to copy the behaviour of other people called _____________, so we learn by _____________ then _____________ their behaviour. This was demonstrated by Bandura *et al.* (1961) who studied the social learning of _____________. In their study, children observed an adult playing aggressively or non-aggressively with an inflatable _____________. Those children who watched an aggressive model were _____________ likely to be aggressive to the doll later.

Bandura (1977) suggested that for social learning to occur the observer must:

- pay _____________ to the model; that is, be aware of their behaviour
- be able to _____________ what they have seen, e.g. be able to store and recall what the model did
- be capable of _____________ what they have seen, e.g. have the physical strength or ability
- be _____________ to produce the behaviour they have seen; that is, have a reason such as an external reward or inner drive to perform the behaviour.

Behaviours learned through classical or operant conditioning must be _____________ during the conditioning process. In contrast, new behaviours acquired through social learning do _____________ have to have been performed by the learner. As Bandura says, they do, however, need motivation. _____________ motivation may be generated by the model and this can explain why there are _____________ in the effectiveness of models. Some characteristics of a _____________ make imitation more likely. These include being similar to ourselves, e.g. in terms of _____________ and sex; being _____________ or attractive; and being high in _____________, such as sportsmen and women. For example, Bandura *et al.* (1961) found that boys were more likely to copy _____________ models, and girls were more likely to copy _____________ ones. However, as status also matters, _____________ are more likely to copy the behaviour of _____________ than vice versa. This is because stereotypically male characteristics such as being _____________ or dominant are valued more by society than stereotypically female ones such as being _____________ or submissive. Some characteristics of the _____________ matter too: an individual with high self-esteem is _____________ likely to imitate others than one with low self-esteem.

External sources of motivation also matter such as the _____________ of the behaviour for the model. _____________ is more likely when the model is seen to be rewarded for their behaviour. This is called _____________. For example, in another study Bandura (1965) found that children were more likely to imitate aggression if the model was seen being _____________ than if the model was _____________. This illustrates the importance of _____________ factors in social learning – an aspect that is missing from classical or operant conditioning explanations. The learner must understand the consequences for the model indicating that there are cognitive processes between the _____________ of seeing the model and the _____________ of imitating the behaviour.

The learning of _____________ behaviours can readily be explained in this way. Although children will see models of both sexes, they will be selectively reinforced when they imitate _____________ behaviours, for example by their _____________ or their parents. Children are also exposed to biased sources of models. For example Evans & Davies (2000) found that the characters in _____________ were stereotypical. Males were more aggressive and competitive whereas females were more emotionally expressive and passive. Milburn *et al.* (2001) also found stereotypical representations of males and females in _____________, with males being shown as more active and less nurturing than females.

Social learning theory *continued*

age	imitating	punished
aggression	imitation	remember
attention	internal	repeated
Bobo doll	less	reproducing
boys	likeable	response
brave	male	rewarded
children's books	model	role models
clip art	more	safe
cognitive	motivated	same-sex
consequences	not	sex-typed
differences	observer	status
female	observing	stimulus
girls	peers	vicarious reinforcement

Social learning theory

Answers

Social learning theory says that we tend to copy the behaviour of other people called **role models**, so we learn by **observing** then **imitating** their behaviour. This was demonstrated by Bandura *et al.* (1961) who studied the social learning of **aggression**. In their study, children observed an adult playing aggressively or non-aggressively with an inflatable **Bobo doll**. Those children who watched an aggressive model were **more** likely to be aggressive to the doll later.

Bandura (1977) suggested that for social learning to occur the observer must:

- pay **attention** to the model; that is, be aware of their behaviour
- be able to **remember** what they have seen e.g. be able to store and recall what the model did
- be capable of **reproducing** what they have seen, e.g. have the physical strength or ability
- be **motivated** to produce the behaviour they have seen; that is, have a reason such as an external reward or inner drive to perform the behaviour.

Behaviours learned through classical or operant conditioning must be **repeated** during the conditioning process. In contrast, new behaviours acquired through social learning do **not** have to have been performed by the learner. As Bandura says, they do however need motivation. **Internal** motivation may be generated by the model and this can explain why there are **differences** in the effectiveness of models. Some characteristics of a **model** make imitation more likely. These include being similar to ourselves, e.g. in terms of **age** and sex; being **likeable** or attractive; and being high in **status**, such as sportsmen and women. For example, Bandura *et al.* (1961) found that boys were more likely to copy **male** models, and girls were more likely to copy **female** ones. However, as status also matters, **girls** are more likely to copy the behaviour of **boys** than vice versa. This is because stereotypically male characteristics such as being **brave** or dominant are valued more by society than stereotypically female ones such as being **safe** or submissive. Some characteristics of the **observer** matter too: an individual with high self-esteem is **less** likely to imitate others than one with low self-esteem.

External sources of motivation also matter such as the **consequences** of the behaviour for the model. **Imitation** is more likely when the model is seen to be rewarded for their behaviour. This is called **vicarious reinforcement**. For example, in another study Bandura (1965) found that children were more likely to imitate aggression if the model was seen being **rewarded** than if the model was **punished**. This illustrates the importance of **cognitive** factors in social learning – an aspect that is missing from classical or operant conditioning explanations. The learner must understand the consequences for the model indicating that there are cognitive processes between the **stimulus** of seeing the model and the **response** of imitating the behaviour.

The learning of **sex-typed** behaviours can readily be explained in this way. Although children will see models of both sexes, they will be selectively reinforced when they imitate **same-sex** behaviours, for example by their **peers** or their parents. Children are also exposed to biased sources of models. For example Evans & Davies (2000) found that the characters in **children's books** were stereotypical. Males were more aggressive and competitive whereas females were more emotionally expressive and passive. Milburn *et al.* (2001) also found stereotypical representations of males and females in **clip art**, with males being shown as more active and less nurturing than females.

Social learning theory

Answers *continued*

role models	differences	consequences
observing	model	imitation
imitating	age	vicarious reinforcement
aggression	likeable	rewarded
Bobo doll	status	punished
more	male	cognitive
attention	female	stimulus
remember	girls	response
reproducing	boys	sex-typed
motivated	brave	same-sex
repeated	safe	peers
not	observer	children's books
Internal	less	clip art

Two approaches to therapy

Aversion therapy uses _____________ conditioning. It aims to _____________ undesirable behaviours such as drinking alcohol in alcoholics. Before treatment an _____________ produces an unpleasant, i.e. _____________, effect. This is the unconditioned response. During treatment this unpleasant response becomes associated with the stimulus to be avoided, which becomes the _____________.Through repeated pairings of the unconditioned stimulus (_____________) and conditioned stimulus (_____________) an association is built up which causes the client's behaviour to change. This is because the undesirable habit (e.g. drinking) becomes linked to the unpleasant effect (the conditioned response).

Duker & Seys (2000) used aversion therapy to reduce _____________ behaviours such as vomiting in children with learning difficulties. Electric shocks were administered by remote control to the child's foot or hand:

UCS (mild electric shock) → UCR (pain)

UCS (_____________) + NS (_____________) → UCR (pain)

CS (vomiting) → CR (unpleasant expectation of _____________)

As the CR of anticipated pain is aversive the individual _____________ vomiting.

Weinrott *et al.* (1997) treated sex offenders by playing them a tape of a sexual crime (CS) that elicited deviant arousal. They then saw a video showing the negative consequences of sex offences (UCS) which produced a reduction in sexual arousal (_____________). After treatment, the offenders showed less arousal in deviant situations (_____________). However, aversion therapy has also been misused, such as in attempts to 'cure' _____________. There is also a risk that the patient may revert to their previous maladaptive behaviour if the new response undergoes _____________. For example, some of the children treated by Duker & Seys (2000) resumed their harmful behaviours.

A token economy is based on _____________ conditioning, using _____________ reinforcement and _____________ to change individuals' behaviours. In institutions such as _____________, schools or prisons desired responses are rewarded with _____________ (e.g. stickers). These are _____________ reinforcers – they are rewarding because they have been linked to a _____________ reinforcer. The tokens are _____________ and exchanged for privileges or goods like luxury foods. Tokens allow good behaviour, such as being quiet in class or sociable in a hospital, to be reinforced _____________, increasing the likelihood that it will be repeated.

Petry *et al.* (2006) used a token economy with _____________ as tokens to help alcoholics to abstain and Sindelar *et al.* (2007) used the same technique with cocaine abusers. Both programmes were successful and reasonably cost-effective. In general, a token economy is fairly _____________ because staff do not have to be highly trained. However, they do have to be ready to give a token for every appropriate behaviour which can be difficult and _____________. Also, there may be other factors, such as the opinions or actions of other pupils or prisoners, that are more _____________ reinforcers.

A token economy is _____________ distressing than aversion therapy so is _____________ ethical. However, as the institution decides which behaviours should be reinforced there may be _____________ issues if there are differences of opinion about what is 'good behaviour'. Token economies can also lead to institutionalisation if individuals are dependent on the rewards, making _____________ difficult. Finally, neither technique explores nor resolves the underlying _____________ of problem behaviours; they only reduce the negative behaviours.

Two approaches to therapy *continued*

aversive	ethical	positive	shock
cause	extinction	powerful	UCS
cheap	homosexuals	primary	stops
classical	immediately	prize draw entries	time-consuming
conditioned stimulus	less	rehabilitation	tokens
CR	mental hospitals	saved up	UCR
CS	more	secondary	unconditioned stimulus
eliminate	operant	self-harming	vomiting
	pain	shaping	

Two approaches to therapy

Answers

Aversion therapy uses **classical** conditioning. It aims to **eliminate** undesirable behaviours such as drinking alcohol in alcoholics. Before treatment an **unconditioned stimulus** produces an unpleasant, i.e. **aversive**, effect. This is the unconditioned response. During treatment this unpleasant response becomes associated with the stimulus to be avoided, which becomes the **conditioned stimulus**. Through repeated pairings of the unconditioned stimulus (**UCS**) and conditioned stimulus (**CS**) an association is built up which causes the client's behaviour to change. This is because the undesirable habit (e.g. drinking) becomes linked to the unpleasant effect (the conditioned response).

Duker & Seys (2000) used aversion therapy to reduce **self-harming** behaviours such as vomiting in children with learning difficulties. Electric shocks were administered by remote control to the child's foot or hand:

UCS (mild electric shock) → UCR (pain)

UCS (**shock**) + NS (**vomiting**)→ UCR (pain)

CS (vomiting) → CR (unpleasant expectation of **pain**)

As the CR of anticipated pain is aversive the individual **stops** vomiting.

Weinrott *et al.* (1997) treated sex offenders by playing them a tape of a sexual crime (CS) that elicited deviant arousal. They then saw a video showing the negative consequences of sex offences (UCS) which produced a reduction in sexual arousal (**UCR**). After treatment, the offenders showed less arousal in deviant situations (**CR**). However, aversion therapy has also been misused, such as in attempts to 'cure' **homosexuals**. There is also a risk that the patient may revert to their previous maladaptive behaviour if the new response undergoes **extinction**. For example, some of the children treated by Duker & Seys (2000) resumed their harmful behaviours.

A token economy is based on **operant** conditioning, using **positive** reinforcement and **shaping** to change individuals' behaviours. In institutions such as **mental hospitals**, schools or prisons desired responses are rewarded with **tokens** (e.g. stickers). These are **secondary** reinforcers – they are rewarding because they have been linked to a **primary** reinforcer. The tokens are **saved up** and exchanged for privileges or goods like luxury foods. Tokens allow good behaviour, such as being quiet in class or sociable in a hospital, to be reinforced **immediately**, increasing the likelihood that it will be repeated.

Petry *et al.* (2006) used a token economy with **prize draw entries** as tokens to help alcoholics to abstain and Sindelar *et al.* (2007) used the same technique with cocaine abusers. Both programmes were successful and reasonably cost-effective. In general, a token economy is fairly **cheap** because staff do not have to be highly trained. However, they do have to be ready to give a token for every appropriate behaviour which can be difficult and **time-consuming**. Also, there may be other factors, such as the opinions or actions of other pupils or prisoners, that are more **powerful** reinforcers.

Two approaches to therapy

Answers *continued*

A token economy is **less** distressing than aversion therapy so is **more** ethical. However, as the institution decides which behaviours should be reinforced there may be **ethical** issues if there are differences of opinion about what is 'good behaviour'. Token economies can also lead to institutionalisation if individuals are dependent on the rewards, making **rehabilitation** difficult. Finally, neither technique explores nor resolves the underlying **cause** of problem behaviours; they only reduce the negative behaviours.

classical
eliminate
unconditioned stimulus
aversive
conditioned stimulus
UCS
CS

self-harming
shock
vomiting
pain
stops
UCR
CR
homosexuals
extinction

operant
positive
shaping
mental hospitals
tokens
secondary
primary
saved up
immediately

prize draw entries
cheap
time-consuming
powerful
less
more
ethical
rehabilitation
cause

Gender and learning

media watch **Media Messes with Men's Minds Too**

Brandon Keim

Psychology Today magazine Sept/Oct 2006

Airbrushed, studio-model fantasies of unattainable physical perfection make women feel worse about their bodies; and they aren't much good for men either.

Psychologists Deborah Schooler and L. Monique Ward analyzed the media habits, self-image and sexual experience of 184 college males. While media consumption doesn't seem to affect satisfaction with body size and shape, guys who take in the most music videos, prime-time TV and men's magazines are much less comfortable with bodily functions, sweat and hair.

As with women, men uncomfortable with their bodies avoid emotional intimacy and take more sexual risks. According to Schooler, 'It's unclear if there's a change in the images men are seeing, in men's body image generally, or if we're now finally asking the right questions.'

1. a) Describe social learning theory.
   b) Using social learning theory, explain how it is possible for 'Airbrushed, studio-model fantasies of unattainable physical perfection [to] make women feel worse about their bodies'.
   c) i) Outline **one** piece of evidence that supports social learning theory.
   ii) Outline **one** piece of evidence that contradicts social learning theory.
2. Schooler & Ward investigated the influence of various forms of media.
   a) What sources of media did they consider?
   b) What characteristics of the participants did they think that the media might affect?
3. Explain how it would be possible for the same media sources to influence men and women differently.

Stretch and challenge

1. Look for details of the original study on the internet. Try to find a full text copy if you can.
2. When you have read about it, try this quiz. It will encourage you to think critically about media reporting of psychological research:
   http://itre.cis.upenn.edu/~myl/languagelog/archives/003649.html
   You will need to click on the link to read the report they are referring to first.

Reference

Schooler, D. & Ward, L.M. (2006) 'Average Joes: men's relationship with media, real bodies and sexuality'. *Psychology of Men and Masculinity*, 7(1): 27–41.

Choosing a statistical test

1. Different statistical tests are used in studies using different research designs:
   - A Spearman test is for studies with ____________ designs.
   - A chi-squared test is for studies using the experimental method, with a/an independent groups design and ____________ data.
   - A Mann–Whitney test is for studies using the experimental method, with a/an ____________ design and ____________ data (it can also be used with equal ____________ data).
2. For each of the studies below:
   a) Decide which test would be appropriate for the design and data described.
   b) Decide whether the findings indicate a positive or a negative correlation if appropriate.
   c) Identify the research being described.

- Researchers assessed women's personalities and their enjoyment of lavatorial jokes. They found a link between the three anal personality characteristics (tidiness, meanness and stubbornness) and the women's sense of humour.
- A researcher measured the identity development of 46 females and 45 males up to age 23 years and their use of defence mechanisms. She found that the more stable an adolescent's identity, the less use they make of defence mechanisms.
- Some researchers measured orality (using Rorschach ink blots) and aggression in sex offenders. They found that there was a high degree of association between oral dependency and aggression in sex murderers. This supports the idea that orality is a valid concept.
- Seventy-six people were followed up from birth to age 30. The researchers found that the poorer an individual's relationship with their parents in childhood, the higher their risk of mental health problems in adulthood.
- Patients with schizophrenia were treated with either the drug chlorpromazine or given a placebo. A record was kept of whether they remained in remission (mentally healthy) or relapsed (showed symptoms of schizophrenia) after treatment.
- Mice were given either anadamine (a cannabinoid neurotransmitter) or caspazepine (which blocks cannabinoid receptors). They recorded whether the mice were active or not and whether they explored or not.
- Each member of monozygotic twin pairs was asked to rate their attitudes, e.g. to taking exercise, eating sweets, listening to loud music. The twins were found to have similar opinions.
- Records of twins' medical histories were examined. The severity of schizophrenia in one twin was found to be closely related to the severity of schizophrenia in the other twin in monozygotic pairs.
- The volume of grey matter in the brains of girls and boys was measured. In both genders the volume of grey matter fell with age (although faster for boys than girls).
- Males and females performed rhyming tasks while having their brains scanned. In males, brain activity was localised to the left hemisphere whereas in females activity was more symmetrical.
- A researcher demonstrated classical conditioning by allowing male rats to mate with females smelling of either lemon or almond. The males later tended to choose to mate with females that smelled the same as the ones they had mated with before.
- A research group testing a token economy with cocaine abusers used payouts of either $70 or $240. By counting the number of drug-free urine samples over a 12-week period, they found that the participants were more likely to abstain when the payouts were bigger.

Choosing a statistical test *continued*

- Children were observed and scored for levels of playful aggression. They were also tested for testosterone levels. A link was found between testosterone levels and aggression in play.
- Children were shown films containing images of nurses and doctors. The number correctly recalling male nurse/male doctor, female nurse/male doctor, male nurse/female doctor and female nurse/female doctor was recorded.
- Children aged six to twelve years were asked about their choices of toys and TV programmes. In girls, toy choices became less stereotyped but their TV viewing became more stereotyped with age.
- TV viewing was measured in seven- to eight-year-olds. They were then followed up in adulthood. The more violent TV they had watchd as children, the more likely they were to have criminal records as adults.
- Children saw either a film of an adult being aggressive or a film of a model doing the same things but dressed up as a cartoon cat. Children imitated more agression if they saw the cartoon version.

Choosing a statistical test

Answers

1. Different statistical tests are used in studies using different research design:
   - A Spearman test is for studies with **correlational** designs.
   - A chi-squared test is for studies using the experimental method, with an independent groups design and **nominal** data.
   - A Mann–Whitney test is for studies using the experimental method, with an **independent groups** design and **ordinal** data (it can also be used with equal **interval** data).
2. For each of the studies below:
   a) Decide which test would be appropriate for the design and data described.
   b) Decide whether the findings indicate a positive or a negative correlation if appropriate.
   c) Identify the research being described.

Description of study	**Test, reasons for choice, type of correlation and reference**
Researchers assessed women's personalities and their enjoyment of lavatorial jokes. They found a link between the three anal personality characteristics (tidiness, meanness and stubbornness) and the women's sense of humour.	**Spearman: correlation (positive)** **O'Neill *et al.* (1992)**
A researcher measured the identity development of 46 females and 45 males up to age 23 years and their use of defence mechanisms. She found that the more stable an adolescent's identity, the less use they make of defence mechanisms.	**Spearman: correlation (positive)** **Cramer (1997)**
Some researchers measured orality (using Rorschach ink blots) and aggression in sex offenders. They found that there was a high degree of association between oral dependency and aggression in sex murderers. This supports the idea that orality is a valid concept.	**Spearman: correlation (positive)** **Huprich *et al.* (2004)**
Seventy-six people were followed up from birth to age 30. The researchers found that the poorer an individual's relationship with their parents in childhood, the higher their risk of mental health problems in adulthood.	**Spearman: correlation (negative)** **Massie & Szajnberg (2002)**
Patients with schizophrenia were treated with either the drug chlorpromazine or given a placebo. A record was kept of whether they remained in remission (mentally healthy) or relapsed (showed symptoms of schizophrenia) after treatment.	**Chi-squared: experiment, nominal data (drug/placebo, relapse/ remission)** **Adams *et al.* (2005)**

Choosing a statistical test

Answers *continued*

Mice were given either anadamine (a cannabinoid neurotransmitter) or caspazepine (which blocks cannabinoid receptors). They recorded whether the mice were active or not and whether they explored or not.	**Chi-squared: experiment, nominal data (anadamine/caspazepine, active/not, explore/not)** **de Lago *et al.* (2004)**
Each member of monozygotic twin pairs was asked to rate their attitudes, e.g. to taking exercise, eating sweets, listening to loud music. The twins were found to have similar opinions.	**Spearman: correlation (positive)** **Olson *et al.* (2001)**
Records of twins' medical histories were examined. The severity of schizophrenia in one twin was found to be closely related to the severity of schizophrenia in the other twin in monozygotic pairs.	**Spearman: correlation (positive)** **Gottesman & Shields (1966)**
The volume of grey matter in the brains of girls and boys was measured. In both genders the volume of grey matter fell with age (although faster for boys than girls).	**Spearman: correlation (negative)** **De Bellis *et al.* (2001)**
Males and females performed rhyming tasks while having their brains scanned. In males, brain activity was localised to the left hemisphere whereas in females activity was more symmetrical.	**Mann–Whitney: experiment, ratio data** **Shaywitz *et al.* (1995)**
A researcher demonstrated classical conditioning by allowing male rats to mate with females smelling of either lemon or almond. The males later tended to choose to mate with females that smelled the same as the ones they had mated with before.	**Chi-squared: nominal, exposure lemon/almond, later choice lemon/almond** **Kippin (2000)**
A research group testing a token economy with cocaine abusers used payouts of either \$70 or \$240. By counting the number of drug-free urine samples over a 12-week period, they found that the participants were more likely to abstain when the payouts were bigger.	**Mann–Whitney: experiment, ratio data** **Sindelar *et al.* (2007)**
Children were observed and scored for levels of playful aggression. They were also tested for testosterone levels. A link was found between testosterone levels and aggression in play.	**Spearman: correlation (positive)** **Ahedo *et al.* (2002)**

Choosing a statistical test

Answers *continued*

Children were shown films containing images of nurses and doctors. The number correctly recalling male nurse/male doctor, female nurse/male doctor, male nurse/female doctor and female nurse/female doctor was recorded	**Chi-squared: nominal, saw male/female nurse/doctor, recalled male/female nurse/doctor** **Cordua *et al.* (1979)**
Children aged six to twelve years were asked about their choices of toys and TV programmes. In girls, their toy choices became less stereotyped but their TV viewing became more stereotyped with age.	**Spearman: correlation (negative, positive)** **Cherney & London (2006)**
TV viewing was measured in seven- to eight-year-olds. They were then followed up in adulthood. The more violent TV they had watched as children, the more likely they were to have criminal records as adults.	**Spearman: correlation (positive)** **Eron & Huesmann (1986)**
Children saw either a film of an adult being aggressive or a film of a model doing the same things but dressed up as a cartoon cat. Children imitated more aggression if they saw the cartoon version.	**Mann–Whitney: ordinal** **Bandura *et al.* (1963)**

Essays

Question 1

> Lucy is a witch at Warthogs School. She is having trouble performing a levitation spell. She has been told what to do but her feather is staying firmly on the bench. She carefully watches the way her fellow witch and wizard friends raise their wands and listens when they recite the spell. When Lucy imitates their actions and voice she succeeds in lifting the feather.

Describe and evaluate a theory that explains Lucy's learning.

continue overleaf if necessary

Essays

Question 2

> Mervin passed his driving test only a month ago but he drives like a maniac, just like his dad.

Using **one or more** learning theories, explain why Mervin might drive so dangerously.

continue overleaf if necessary

Gender stereotypes: girls play 'house', boys play 'spaceship'

Many news articles illustrating the power of gender stereotypes are available on the Internet. Two links are given below. The first describes the extent to which stereotypes still limit the behaviour and beliefs of adolescents. The second considers differences in the play of boys and girls and the extent to which gender stereotypes are evident in their imaginative play.

1. Gender stereotypes still hamper young:
   http://www.guardian.co.uk/uk_news/story/0,3604,370727,00.html

   See how many examples of gender stereotypes you can find. How they might have arisen?

2. Why girls will be girls and boys, er, boys:
   http://www.telegraph.co.uk/news/main.jhtml?xml=/news/2006/12/17/ngender17.xml

   Search for details of Sue Roger's research on the Internet.

   What does it tell us about children's stereotyped behaviour and what are the implications for parents, teachers or toy shops?

Examples of pages with descriptions:

http://www.skillsactive.com/resources/research/CYWU_Research_Complete.pdf

Reference

Rogers, S. & Evans, J. (2006) 'Playing the game: exploring role play from the children's perspective'. *European Early Childhood Education Research Journal*, 14(1): 43–55.

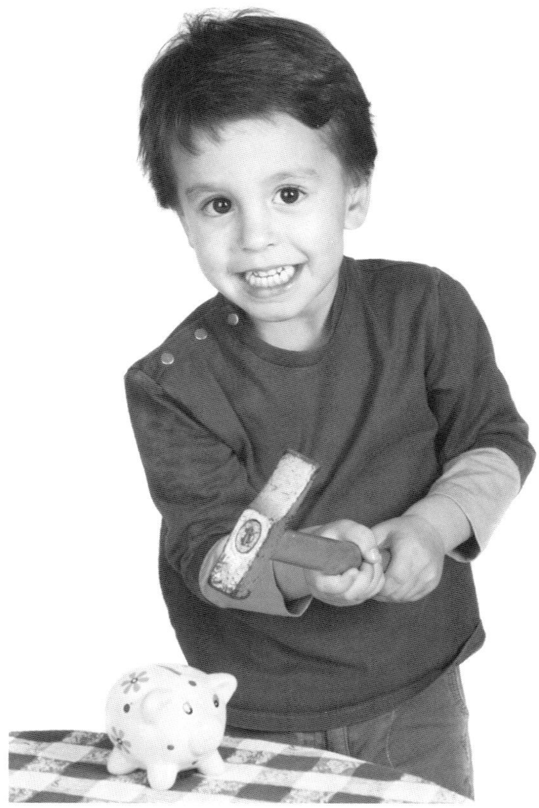

Does it matter that toy shops present toys in a stereotyped way?

Creative activities

1 The 'Mosquito'

Yobs run from buzz box

NEARLY 100 stores and some councils have ordered a machine that repels teenagers from shopfronts. The £500 box – which is called the Mosquito – emits a piercing sound that sends them running for cover. It can usually only be heard by the under 20s – whose hearing is more acute – and has a range of 20 to 30 yards. Some older people can still hear some noise but it is not as high-pitched or annoying for them. A flood of orders has followed a successful trial by Robert Gough after his shop in Barry, South Wales, became plagued by gangs of hoodie yobs. Robert said yesterday: 'Either someone has come along and wiped them off the face of the earth, or it's working'. Sunil Pankhania, 17, who was exposed to the Mosquito in Wembley, North West London, said: 'I can feel it. It hurts. It's like your ears are blocked. It's hurting my teeth'. Pal Shaker Zaman, also 17, added: 'It's like a dog whistle'.

http://www.thesun.co.uk/sol/homepage/news/article191371.ece

Imagine you work for the company that manufactures the 'Mosquito'. Write a press release to explain to potential customers such as restaurant owners how the product works. Base your explanation on learning theory and ensure that you explain all the terms that you use so that they could understand fully.

2 Size zero models

Many organisations are campaigning to have size zero models banned from fashion advertising. This is because of their influence as role models who could potentially increase the incidence of anorexia in young people. Construct two campaign proposals with fully justified arguments, one on behalf of a children's charity, arguing against the use of thin models and the other, on behalf of a fashion house, justifying why such models should be allowed.

Evidence of practice: observing gender

Men, women, animals and humanoids: are they all stereotyped on TV?

Davis (1990) studied stereotyping on TV and found more males than females (by 2:1) and that the males were older than females. The females, however, were four times more likely to be provocatively dressed. Is this still the case?

De Loache *et al.* (1987) explored stereotyping using a children's picture book about bears. When talking through the story, mothers labelled 62% of the animals as male and only 16% as female. Bears were most often labelled as female when there was a big and a little bear together. Is the same discrepancy seen in children's television programmes? Are there any other ways in which gender is distinguished in animals on TV?

Milburn *et al.* (2001) investigated gender stereotyping in clip art. They recorded both human and 'humanoid' images. Similar 'humanoid' images can be found in media sources such as television advertisements. Are they as stereotyped as images of real people?

Duvets, drawing, dolls and dummies

Pomerleau *et al.* (1990) conducted a naturalistic observation in the homes of children aged 5–25 months. They recorded parental choices of clothes, toys and colours (e.g. of dummies and bedding). Boys were found to have more tools, sports equipment and vehicles to play with whereas girls had more fictional characters, drawing toys and dolls. Girls' clothes and dummies were typically pink whereas boys had more blue, red and white clothes and blue dummies. Bedding in girls' rooms was usually yellow but in boys' rooms it was generally blue.

Preparation

1. Choose who you are working with.
2. Decide on a topic to investigate (for example, but not necessarily, one of the above).
3. Decide on the source you will observe, e.g. children, adults, television programmes etc.
4. Plan your experiment in outline, choosing at least two levels of your IV and at least two categories for your DV, bearing in mind that you must collect nominal data.
5. Devise suitable alternative and null hypotheses for a chi-squared test
6. Think about how you will collect quantitative data. What behavioural categories will you record? How will you operationalise them?
7. Having decided on your source or 'target population' you will also need to decide on the sample size you need (for example how many TV programmes or how many minutes' viewing time?). Consider also how you will select this sample (e.g. by opportunity, randomly or in a systematic way). Will this sample generate generalisable data?
8. Think about whether your study will raise ethical issues. If you are observing children or adults decide how you will avoid or resolve them. For example, you may need to think about whether the participants will be aware that they are being observed.
9. Decide on the observational procedures you will use. Think about the way your choices will affect the credibility of your findings. Will your:
   a) observation be naturalistic or contrived? – plan your environment
   b) observers be participant or non-participant? – decide who will observe and how
   c) observations be covert or overt? – decide where the observers will be.
10. It is likely that you will have more than one observer. What can you do to raise their inter-observer reliability before they start collecting data? Can you do a pilot study? Have your observers discussed and agreed the operational definitions for the categories?
11. Carefully plan who will record what, when and where.

Evidence of practice *continued*

12. Conduct your observations and collate the data from different observers.
13. Are your categories and operational definitions valid?
14. Use descriptive statistics to summarise your data. Make sure there are titles and column and row headings on tables of totals or modes and on the axes of graphs.
15. Conduct and record the results of a chi-squared test to decide whether any differences you have found between levels of the IV are significant. Ensure that you know:
    - the degrees of freedom (number of rows × number of columns – 1)
    - the significance level ($p \leq ?$)
    - whether your alternative hypothesis was directional or non-directional.

Gender in journals

Clark (1999) investigated whether the portrayal of men and women on the cover of an academic journal was stereotyped. Using the cover artwork on 50 consecutive editions of the *Journal of the American Medical Association*, she recorded the number of men and women, what they were doing, and how they were depicted (e.g. as dominant or submissive). Mostly men were in a dominant posture, looking at the viewer and most were in authoritative roles such as doctors, clergymen, military or academic figures. Women were shown in roles such as cleaners or carers. Thirty-four of the covers depicted humans although in six of these there were either both males and females or the individual's sex was not clear.

	Number depicted	Dominant posture*	Submissive posture	Stereotypically male roles*	Stereotypically female roles	Sexual image	With child
Males	13	11	0	11	0	0	1
Females	15	0	13	0	5	6	12

* estimated

A chi-squared test on the above data for number depicted and posture (the grey section) produced an observed value of 23.98.

Critical values for the chi-squared test

	Level of significance for a two-tailed test				
	0.2	0.1	0.05	0.02	0.01
	Level of significance for a one-tailed test				
df	0.1	0.05	0.025	0.01	0.005
1	2.706	3.841	5.024	6.635	7.879
2	4.605	5.991	7.387	9.210	10.597
3	6.251	7.815	9.348	11.345	12.838
4	7.779	9.488	11.143	13.277	14.860

To be significant the observed value for chi-squared must be greater than or equal to the critical value.

1. Clark's independent variable was gender and the dependent variable was the various measures of stereotyping apparent in the pictures.
   a) Write a null hypothesis for Clark's study.
   b) Why would it be acceptable to have a directional hypothesis for this study?
2. The chi-squared test is an inferential test and is suitable for the data given in the table above.
   a) Explain why a chi-squared test would be a suitable way to analyse these data.
   b) Calculate the degrees of freedom for the data table above.
   c) Find the critical value for a directional hypothesis at $p \leq 0.05$.
   d) Is the pattern of results in the table above significant? Explain your conclusion.
3. In a commentary about Clark's study, three of the criticisms raised were that:
   - a larger sample should have been used
   - the study should have looked back (e.g. to the 1960s) to see if there were any changes in the way men and women were portrayed
   - the variables could have been more effectively defined.

   a) What size was Clark's sample?
   b) Write a hypothesis for a study investigating changing trends in the images.
   c) Operationalise **two** of the measures of the dependent variable.

Brave boys?

Urberg (1982) tested gender stereotyping in 140 children aged three to seven years by reading them stories and asking them questions. The stories illustrated gender-stereotyped traits like caring and bravery. One story read: 'Some people are brave. If a house was on fire they would go inside to rescue people.' The children were then shown four boxes, one with a picture of a male and one of a female, one with both and one with no people. They were asked, 'Who are the brave people? Are they girls (women), boys (men), both boys and girls (men and women), or nobody?' The wording depended on whether the story and pictures were of adult or child males and females.

She found that the children saw more overlap between male and female characteristics as they grew older. The children's responses were also more stereotyped when the pictures used were of children rather than adults. Girls were also found to be less sex-typed than boys.

1. Urberg tested two independent variables, age and gender.
   a) Identify and operationalise the dependent variable.
   b) Write a non-directional hypothesis for this study.
   c) What research method was used in this study?
2. The children were shown boxes with different pictures on when they were asked about the stories.
   a) This was to help them to remember the task. Why was this important in this study?
   b) How many different pictures would have been used in total in the experiment? List them.
3. The story above about bravery is very short.
   a) Write a suitable story about 'caring' or any other characteristic that might be stereotyped by children that could be used in this study.
   b) Write out in full the question you would ask the children after reading them the story you have written.
   c) There were 18 different stories when the stimulus pictures were of children and 20 when they were of adults. Explain why using so many stories would have improved validity and reliability.
4. Urberg also found that children whose mothers worked outside the home were less sex-typed than those with 'at-home' mums.
   a) Write a directional hypothesis for this part of the study.
   b) To analyse the results of this part of the study, a Mann–Whitney test could have been used. Justify why this would have been an appropriate choice.
5. During testing, two children were excluded from the sample, one three-year-old and one five-year-old. Both children were replaced to maintain the sample size.
   a) The five-year-old was eliminated because they failed to co-operate with the experimental procedure. Why was it important that the researcher did not make the child co-operate?
   b) If more children had been eliminated from the study and the sample size had been reduced, this would have affected the results. Explain why a larger sample is preferable to a smaller one.

The learning approach quick quiz

1

a) What is the difference between a participant and a non-participant observation?
b) What is extinction?
c) What is an unconditioned stimulus?
d) Define negative reinforcement.
e) Identify one study that demonstrates social learning.
f) Define punishment.
g) What did Bandura *et al.* (1961) find?
h) What is meant by a 'primary reinforcer'?
i) Identify one study that demonstrates operant conditioning.
j) Give an example of vicarious reinforcement.
k) Suggest one criticism of Bandura *et al.* (1961).
l) What is meant by shaping?
m) Give two reasons why you would use the chi-squared test.
n) Identify one study that suggests that gender stereotyped behaviour is not learned.
o) Which test did you use when you analysed the data for your study in the learning approach?
p) Describe the key issue for the learning approach.

2

a) Define positive reinforcement.
b) What is an unconditioned response?
c) What is the difference between a covert and an overt observation?
d) Name one therapy based on conditioning.
e) What is meant by spontaneous recovery?
f) Which two studies must you know in detail for the learning approach?
g) Give one example of negative reinforcement.
h) What is social learning?
i) What is meant by a 'secondary reinforcer'?
j) Which research method did Bandura *et al.* (1961) use?
k) Identify one study that demonstrates classical conditioning.
l) Name two pieces of information you need to know to look up a critical value for the chi-squared test.
m) What is vicarious reinforcement?
n) Suggest one methodological strength of Bandura *et al.* (1961).
o) Identify one study that shows that gender stereotypes are affected by learning.
p) How can you apply the issue of credibility to your study in the learning approach?

The learning approach quick quiz

Answers

1

a) What is the difference between a participant and a non-participant observation? **In participant observation the observer is integrated as part of the social group being observed**

b) What is extinction? **The cessation of a response when the conditioned stimulus is repeatedly presented without the unconditioned stimulus**

c) What is an unconditioned stimulus? **A natural trigger for a behaviour that produces a response**

d) Define negative reinforcement. **A consequence that increases the frequency of the behaviour it follows because it is nice when it stops**

e) Identify one study that demonstrates social learning. **e.g. Bandura *et al.* (1961)**

f) Define punishment. **A consequence that decreases the frequency of the behaviour it follows because it is unpleasant**

g) What did Bandura *et al.* (1961) find? **That children would imitate aggressive behaviour they had seen in an adult model**

h) What is meant by a 'primary reinforcer'? **A consequence that a person or animal naturally finds rewarding**

i) Identify one study that demonstrates operant conditioning. e.g. **Skinner (1948), Pickens & Thompson (1968)**

j) Give an example of vicarious reinforcement. **Working harder at college because you see other people working hard and getting good grades**

k) Suggest one criticism of Bandura *et al.* (1961). **The children may have thought that they were supposed to copy the adults**

l) What is meant by shaping? **Reinforcing successive approximation to a desired response**

m) Give two reasons why you would use the chi-squared test. **Experiment, independent groups, nominal data**

n) Identify one study that suggests that gender-stereotyped behaviour is not learned. **Money (1975)**

o) Which test did you use when you analysed the data for your study in the learning approach? **Chi-squared test**

p) Describe the key issue for the learning approach. **e.g. media violence/phobias**

The learning approach quick quiz

Answers *continued*

2

a) Define positive reinforcement. **A consequence that increases the frequency of the behaviour it follows because it is nice**

b) What is an unconditioned response? **A naturally occurring behaviour such as a reflex that is produced in response to an unconditioned stimulus**

c) What is the difference between a covert and an overt observation? **In a covert observation the participants are unaware that they are being watched whereas in an overt observation they are**

d) Name one therapy based on conditioning. **Aversion therapy/systematic desensitisation/token economy**

e) What is meant by spontaneous recovery? **The reappearance of a response that has undergone extinction**

f) Which two studies must you know in detail for the learning approach? **Bandura *et al.* (1961) and one of: Watson & Rayner (1920)/Skinner (1948)/Pickens & Thompson (1968)**

g) Give one example of negative reinforcement. **Taking painkillers again when they previously cured a headache**

h) What is social learning? **The acquisition of a new behaviour by observation and imitation**

i) What is meant by a 'secondary reinforcer'? **A source of reward that increases the frequency of a behaviour because it has become associated with a primary reinforcer**

j) Which research method did Bandura *et al.* (1961) use? **Laboratory experiment**

k) Identify one study that demonstrates classical conditioning. **e.g. Watson & Rayner (1920)**

l) Name two pieces of information you need to know to look up a critical value for the chi-squared test. **Significance level, degrees of freedom (*df*), whether the hypothesis was directional or non-directional (i.e. whether the test is one- or two-tailed)**

m) What is vicarious reinforcement? **The effect of increasing the frequency of a behaviour when another individual is seen being rewarded for that behaviour**

n) Suggest one methodological strength of Bandura *et al.* (1961). **e.g. the children were tested for aggressiveness beforehand and spread evenly between the groups**

o) Identify one study that shows that gender stereotypes are affected by learning. **e.g. Johnson & Ettema (1982)**

p) How can you apply the issue of credibility to your study in the learning approach? **Depends on student's own study e.g. observation of gender on TV or children's toys**

Learning approach test

Centre No.						Paper Reference							Surname	Initial(s)
Candidate No.						6	P	S	0	2	/	1	Signature	

Psychology Advanced Subsidiary

Unit 2: The Learning Approach

Time: 50 minutes

Instructions to candidates

Answer ALL the questions.

Information for candidates

The total mark for this paper is 40.

Advice to candidates

Quality of written communication will be taken into account in the marking of your response to question 11. This question is indicated with an asterisk (*). Quality of written communication includes clarity of expression, the structure and presentation of ideas, and grammar, punctuation and spelling.

Question number	Leave blank
1	
2	
3	
4	
5	
6	
7	
8	
9	
10	
11	
Total	

SECTION A

Answer ALL questions.
You are advised to spend approximately 7 minutes on this section.

Choose answer A, B, C or D, and put a cross in the box (☒). If you change your mind, put a line through the box (~~☒~~) and then put a cross in another box (☒).

1. In learning theory, extinction means:

☐ **A** all the animals fail to learn a new task because it is too difficult
☐ **B** all the animals die because they cannot learn
☐ **C** a learned behaviour stops because the learning situation is removed
☐ **D** a learned behaviour stops because it is not adaptive for the animal **(1)**

2. Classical conditioning is where a new behaviour is learned by:

☐ **A** pairing a new stimulus with an old response
☐ **B** pairing a new stimulus with a new response
☐ **C** pairing a new stimulus with an old stimulus
☐ **D** pairing an old stimulus with a new response **(1)**

3. A Mann–Whitney test is conducted when the study is:

☐ **A** an experiment with nominal data and a repeated measures design
☐ **B** an experiment with ordinal data and a repeated measures design
☐ **C** a correlation with nominal data and an independent groups design
☐ **D** an experiment with ordinal data and an independent groups design **(1)**

4. The number produced by an inferential test is called the:

☐ **A** critical value
☐ **B** observed value
☐ **C** significance level
☐ **D** degrees of freedom **(1)**

Use this situation to answer the next two questions

Peter's parents want Peter to learn to ride a bike but he isn't very keen.

5. Peter's mum says that negative reinforcement would help. Which one of the following would be negative reinforcement?

☐ **A** Peter falling off his bike and hurting himself
☐ **B** his mum laughing at Peter when he wobbles but stopping when he is balanced
☐ **C** his mum clapping every time Peter gets near the bike, sits on it or peddles the bike
☐ **D** Peter's PlayStation being taken away if he doesn't try riding his bike every day **(1)**

6. Peter's dad says that he should have someone to copy. According to social learning theory, who would be best?

☐ **A** his older sister
☐ **B** the boy next door who is about the same age
☐ **C** Peter's uncle whom he dislikes
☐ **D** anybody who can ride a bike **(1)**

(Total 6 marks)

TOTAL FOR SECTION A: 6 MARKS

SECTION B

Answer ALL questions.
You are advised to spend approximately 25 minutes on this section.

7. There are four different levels of measurement. Pair up each level of measurement with the correct definition.

Levels of measurement	Definition
	Data with equal divisions between the points and a real zero
Ratio	Data with unequal divisions between the points and a real zero
Nominal	Data on a rating scale with unequal divisions between the points
Interval	Data with equal divisions between the points and no real zero
Ordinal	Data in named groups or categories

(Total 4 marks)

8. Percy decides to train his tortoise. It usually takes no notice of Percy, even if he talks to it, whistles or stamps his feet. However, even if the tortoise is resting, it will stretch its head out of its shell if it can smell lettuce.

(a) For several weeks, every time Percy sees his tortoise he holds out some lettuce so that it stretches out its head and then Percy whistles. Eventually, the tortoise will stretch its head out when it hears Percy whistling.

Use classical conditioning to explain how Percy changed the tortoise's behaviour.

....

....

....

....

....

....

....

....

....

....

....

.... **(5)**

(b) Percy decides he wants to find out if he can condition the tortoise to stretch its head out when he stamps his feet. Explain how Percy could do this *without* using any more lettuce.

....

....

....

....

....

....

....

....

.... **(4)**

(Total 9 marks)

9. To conduct a study about toy choice in boys and girls, a researcher found a selection of children's toys. He asked five men and five women to decide which were stereotypically 'boys' toys', 'girls' toys' or were gender neutral toys. The researcher then showed a group of children all of the toys and asked them to choose their favourite one. The children's choices are shown in the graph below.

Children's choice of toy type

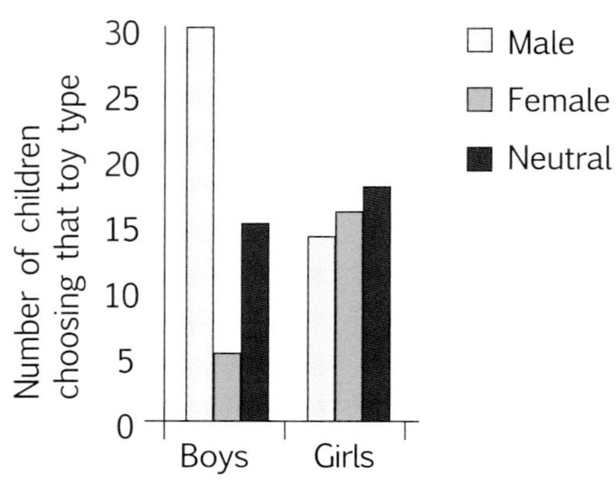

(a) Why was it important to have the group of adults rate the toys first?

....

.... **(1)**

(b) **(i)** Describe the conclusions you could draw from the graph above.

....

....

....

....

.... **(3)**

(ii) If the researchers wanted to be more sure about their conclusions, they could conduct a statistical test.

Which test should they choose and why?

....

....

....

....

....

.... **(3)**

(Total 7 marks)

TOTAL FOR SECTION B: 20 MARKS

SECTION C

Answer ALL questions.
You are advised to spend approximately 18 minutes on this section.

10. In observational studies there are several different techniques that can be used, such as participant or non-participant and covert or overt procedures.

With regard to any aspect(s) of observations, evaluate the research method in terms of validity and reliability.

....

....

....

....

....

....

....

.... **(4)**

(Total 4 marks)

***11.** One factor affecting gender development is social learning. Describe and evaluate this explanation of gender development.

....

....

....

....

....

....

....

....

....

....

.... **(10)**

(Total 10 marks)

TOTAL FOR SECTION C: 14 MARKS

TOTAL MARKS FOR PAPER: 40 MARKS

Mark scheme

SECTION A

1. **C** a learned behaviour stops because the learning situation is removed **(1)**

2. **C** pairing a new stimulus with an old stimulus **(1)**

3. **D** an experiment with ordinal data and an independent groups design **(1)**

4. **B** observed value **(1)**

5. **B** his mum laughing at Peter when he wobbles but stopping when he is balanced **(1)**

6. **B** the boy next door who is about the same age **(1)**

SECTION B

7. *There are four different levels of measurement. Pair up each level of measurement with the correct definition.* **(4)**

Level of measurement	Definition

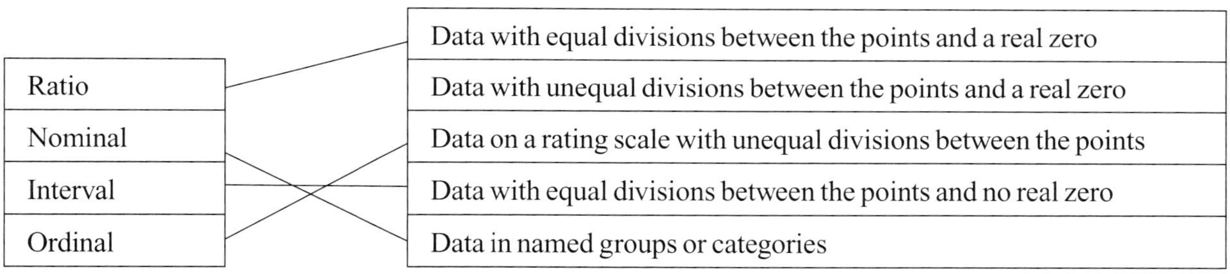

8. *Percy decides to train his tortoise. It usually takes no notice of Percy, even if he talks to it, whistles or stamps his feet. However, even if the tortoise is resting, it will stretch its head out of its shell if it can smell lettuce.*

   (a) *For several weeks, every time Percy sees his tortoise he holds out some lettuce so that it stretches out its head and then Percy whistles. Eventually, the tortoise will stretch its head out when it hears Percy whistling.*

   Use classical conditioning to explain how Percy changed the tortoise's behaviour.

   UCS = lettuce ⟶ UCR = head out;
   NS = whistle;
   NS ⟶ no response;
   UCS + NS;
   Pairing/association/repetition leads to:
   CS = whistle ⟶ CR = head out; **(5)**

(b) *Percy decides he wants to find out if he can condition the tortoise to stretch its head out when he stamps his feet. Explain how Percy could do this* without *using any more lettuce.*

CS_1 = whistle ⟶ CR_1 = head out;

CS_2 = stamp feet;

$CS_1 + CS_2$;

Pairing/association/repetition leads to:

CS_2 = stamp feet ⟶ CR_2 = head out;

This is higher order conditioning; (4)

9. *To conduct a study about toy choice in boys and girls, a researcher found a selection of children's toys. He asked five men and five women to decide which were stereotypically 'boys' toys', 'girls' toys' or were gender-neutral toys. The researcher then showed a group of children all of the toys and asked them to choose their favourite one. The children's choices are shown in the graph below.*

(a) *Why was it important to have the group of adults rate the toys first?*

Because it provided views of both males and females;

Because it provided a more varied view than just one person who might be biased; (1)

(b) (i) *Describe the conclusions you could draw from the graph above.*

Boys are more stereotyped in their choice of toys than girls;

Both genders preferred sex-typed toys over opposite-sex-typed toys;

This is much more apparent in boys than girls/girls also like boys toys whereas boys do not like girls' toys;

Girls prefer gender-neutral toys to sex-typed toys but boys do not; (3)

(ii) *If the researchers wanted to be more sure about their conclusions, they could conduct a statistical test. Which test should they choose and why?*

Chi-squared;

Because it's an experimental study;

With an independent groups/measures design;

And nominal data/data in named categories; (3)

SECTION C

10. In observational studies there are several different techniques that can be used, such as participant or non-participant and covert or overt procedures. With regard to any aspect(s) of observations, evaluate the research method in terms of validity and reliability.

Validity:

Participant observations may be more valid because the observer has greater insight into the emotions and motivation of the participants;

Non-participant observations may be more valid because the observer is less likely to become subjective as they are unlikely to become personally involved in the social situation;

Covert observations may be more valid because the observer is less likely to cause bias in the responses of the participants;

e.g. children are less likely to behave differently from normal if they are unaware that they are being observed;

Reliability:

Observations conducted by more than one person may be unreliable if they do not apply operational definitions of behavioural categories in the same way;

Although inter-observer reliability can be increased by practising together; **(4)**

***11.** *One factor affecting gender development is social learning. Describe and evaluate this explanation of gender development.* **(10)**

Level	Mark	Descriptor
		AO1: Knowledge and understanding of psychological concepts. AO2: Application of psychological concepts.
1	0	No content worth of marks.
2	1–2	A brief, simple answer with some relevance to the social learning but with little reference to gender development or evaluation. Answer lacks clarity and/or organisation. Little use of relevant terminology and poor spelling, punctuation and/or grammar.
3	3–5	An answer with simple but largely relevant description which is accurate but limited. Limited clarity and/or organisation. Some use of relevant terminology. Frequent spelling, punctuation and/or grammatical errors. At the top of the band some reference to either gender development or evaluation is present.
4	6–8	The answer contains both relevant and accurate evidence and has some effective application of ideas to gender development. Clarity of expression and organisation are competent with some use of relevant terminology. Some spelling, punctuation and/or grammatical errors are likely to be present. At the top of the band both reference to gender development and some evaluation are present.
5	9–10	The answer contains accurate evidence (from studies and/or theories) and this is effectively applied to gender development. Description and evaluation are well balanced. Clarity of expression and organisation are effective and the candidate makes good use of relevant terminology. Few spelling, punctuation or grammatical errors are present.

Indicative content:

- **Social learning theory (SIT) says that people learn by observing and imitating; (AO1)**
- **Bandura *et al.* (1961) showed that children were more likely to imitate same-sex models; (AO2)**
- **So gender development is likely to be influenced more by same-gender models leading to gender-stereotyped behaviour; (AO2)**
- **Children are also affected by vicarious reinforcements, that is, seeing other people being rewarded so are more likely to imitate these behaviours; (AO1)**
- **Society is more likely to reinforce gender-typical behaviour, so this is more likely to be vicariously reinforced; (AO2)**
- **Bandura (1977) said that for social learning to occur, the learner must be attentive, able to remember, able to reproduce the behaviour and motivated; (AO1)**
- **Since lots of media is gender stereotyped we are more likely to see this so are most likely to attend to gender-stereotyped models; (AO2)**
- **For example, Evans & Davis (2000) found that children's books were stereotyped with male characters being more aggressive and female characters being more passive so attention would be important; (AO2)**
- **Motivation may also be affected by direct reinforcement as Lytton & Romney (1991) found that parents are more likely to reinforce children's behaviour when it is gender-stereotyped; (AO2)**
- **Although they also found that the difference wasn't very big so this alone can't explain the differences between boys and girls; (AO2)**
- **Although there is a lot of evidence for gender-stereotyped behaviour in young children, this can decline with age, e.g. Cherney & London (2006) found teenagers became less sex-typed in some respects; (AO1)**
- **So even though teenagers are still exposed to stereotyped models, their behaviour changes showing that other factors must be important. (AO2)**

Resources

See PowerPoint 6-22: *Resources.*

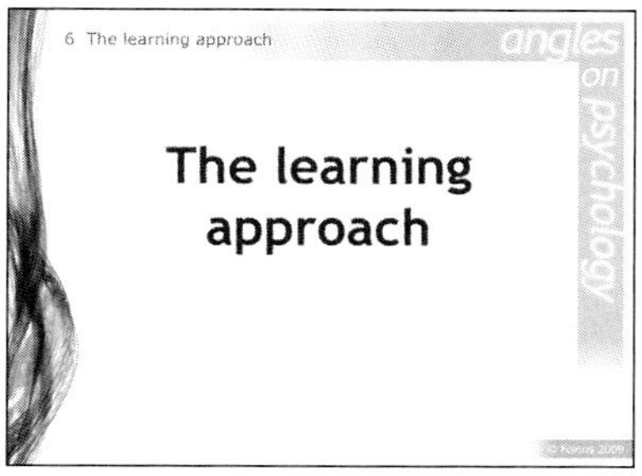

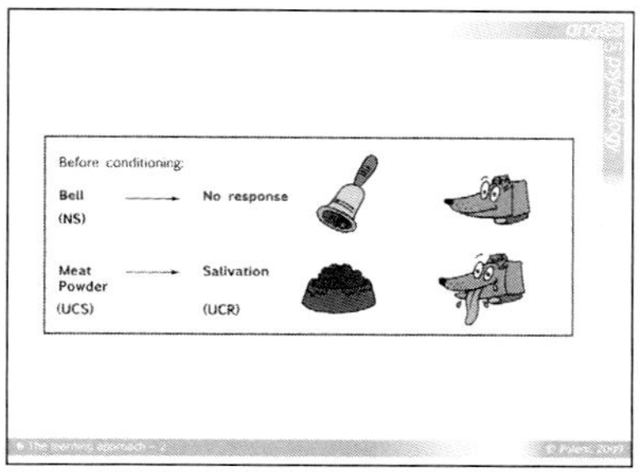

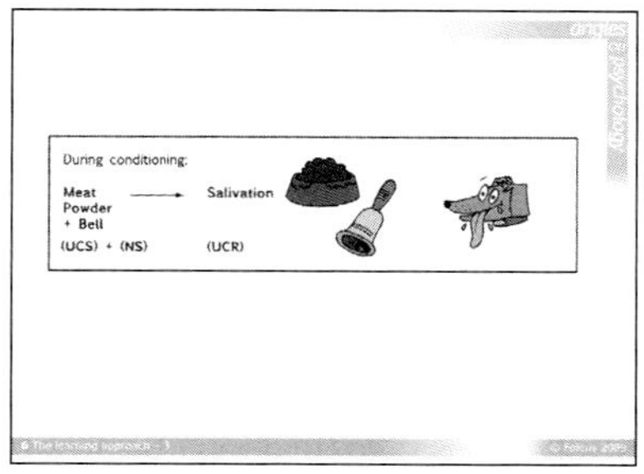

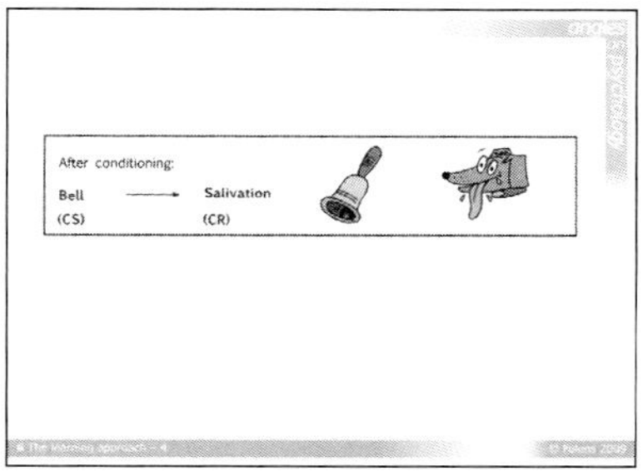

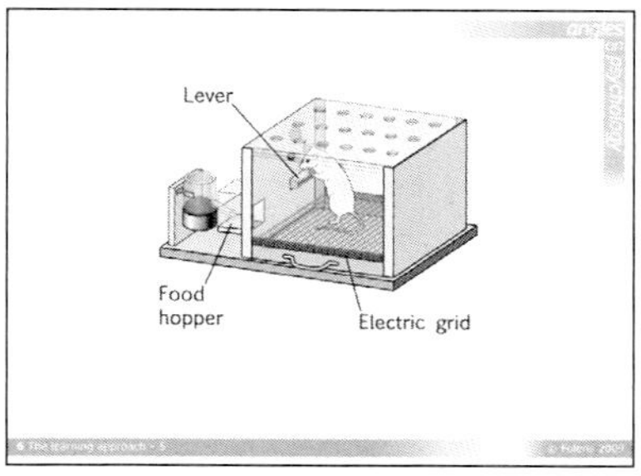

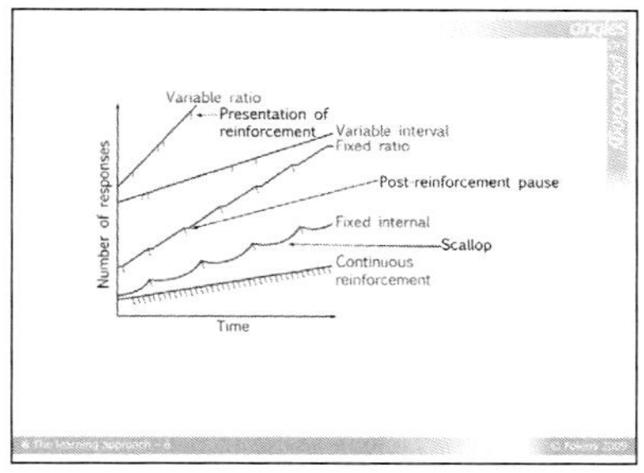

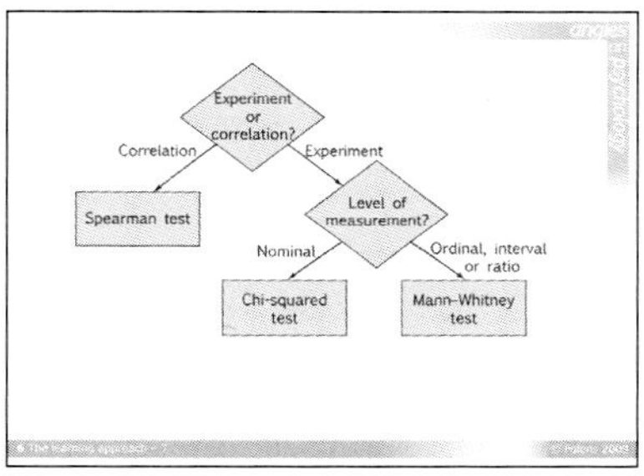

References:

Bandura, A. (1965) 'Influence of models' reinforcement contingencies on the acquisition of imitative responses'. *Journal of Personality & Social Psychology*, 5: 587–95.

Clark, J.P. (1999) 'Babes and boobs? Analysis of JAMA cover art'. *British Medical Journal*, 319(7225): 1603–5. Full text: http://www.pubmedcentral.nih.gov/articlerender.fcgi?tool=pubmed&pubmedid=10600956

Davis, D.M. (1990) 'Portrayals of women in prime time network television: some demongraphic characteristics'. *Sex Roles*, 23: 325–32.

De Loache, J., Cassidy, D.J., & Carpenter, J.C. (1987) 'Three bears are all boys: mothers' gender labeling of neutral picture book characters'. *Sex Roles*, 17: 163–78.

Pomerleau, A., Bolduc, D., Malcuit, G. & Cossette, L. (1990) 'Pink or blue: environmental gender stereotypes in the first two years of life'. *Sex Roles*, 22: 359–67.

Rogers, S. & Evans, J. (2006) 'Playing the game: exploring role play from the children's perspective'. *European Early Childhood Education Research Journal*, 14(1): 43–55.

Schooler, D. & Ward LM (2006) Average Joes: Men's relationship with media, real bodies and sexuality. *Psychology of men and masculinity*, 7(1): 27–41.

Stamp, Dawkins, M. (1985) 'The scientific basis for assessing suffering in animals'. In P. Singer (ed.), *In Defense of Animals*. New York: Basil Blackwell.

Urberg, K.A. (1982) 'The development of the concepts of masculinity and femininity in young children'. *Sex Roles*, 8(6): 659–68.

Teacher's Support Guide

Chapter 7

Mock Examinations

Centre No.						Paper Reference							Surname	Initial(s)
Candidate No.					■	6	P	S	0	1	/	1	Signature	

Psychology Advanced Subsidiary

Unit 1: Social and cognitive psychology

Time: 1 hour 20 minutes

Instructions to candidates

Answer ALL the questions.

Information for candidates

The total mark for this paper is 60.

Advice to candidates

Quality of written communication will be taken into account in the marking of your response to question 16. This question is indicated with an asterisk (*). Quality of written communication includes clarity of expression, the structure and presentation of ideas, and grammar, punctuation and spelling.

Question number	Leave blank
1	
2	
3	
4	
5	
6	
7	
8	
9	
10	
11	
12	
13	
14	
15	
16	
Total	

SECTION A

Answer ALL questions.
You are advised to spend approximately 15 minutes on this section.

Choose answer A, B, C or D, and put a cross in the box (☒). If you change your mind, put a line through the box (~~☒~~) and then put a cross in another box (☒).

1. Which is the best definition of discrimination in social psychology?

☐ **A** holding a stereotyped belief about another person or group
☐ **B** behaving in a different way to some people because of their social group
☐ **C** being violent or aggressive to people you do not like
☐ **D** being an eyewitness who can tell which person was the perpetrator of a crime in a line-up **(1)**

2. What is a repeated measures design?

☐ **A** an experimental design where all participants do all conditions
☐ **B** an experimental design where different participants do different conditions
☐ **C** a design for testing the reliability of surveys by doing them again
☐ **D** a design for testing the validity of surveys by doing them again **(1)**

3. Which of the following could **not** collect qualitative data?

☐ **A** interview
☐ **B** closed question
☐ **C** open question
☐ **D** questionnaire **(1)**

4. Mervyn has decided to use phonemic processing to help him revise. Which is the most likely way he will try to learn his work:

☐ **A** repeating it over and over again to rehearse it
☐ **B** reading his notes and looking at the colours of the text and the shape of the words
☐ **C** making up rhymes to learn lists of terms
☐ **D** answering past paper questions **(1)**

Use the information below to answer questions 5 and 6.

Charlotte and Abdul are conducting a survey about sexist attitudes. Here are some possible hypotheses they have suggested:

A men and women differ in their sexist beliefs
B there is no difference between the sexist beliefs of men and women
C women have more sexist beliefs than men
D there is a difference between gender and sexist beliefs

5. Which statement is a suitable directional hypothesis for Charlotte and Abdul's study?

☐ **A**
☐ **B**
☐ **C**
☐ **D** **(1)**

6. Which statement is a suitable non-directional hypothesis for Charlotte and Abdul's study?

☐ **A**
☐ **B**
☐ **C**
☐ **D** **(1)**

7. Sharon is doing a geography test in class but can't remember much. She likes geography and has a friendly teacher so is always relaxed in lessons. Today she is feeling stressed because her hamster isn't well. Which is the best explanation for her finding it hard to remember her work?

☐ **A** decay
☐ **B** displacement
☐ **C** context-dependent forgetting
☐ **D** state-dependent forgetting **(1)**

8. Which of the following is not an experimental method?

☐ **A** field
☐ **B** causal
☐ **C** laboratory
☐ **D** natural **(1)**

9. Gilbert and his class have been told to go on a cross-country run but Gilbert doesn't like exercise. He knows he could get the whole class in trouble but he hides in a hollow tree and waits until they run back past him, then he joins in again.

Using knowledge from the social approach, decide which statement best describes Gilbert. He is:

☐ **A** being objective
☐ **B** demonstrating social identification
☐ **C** in the autonomous state
☐ **D** in the agentic state **(1)**

Choose two answers A, B, C, D or E.

10. Which two of the following are sampling methods?

☐ **A** stratified
☐ **B** counterbalanced
☐ **C** self-selected
☐ **D** self-report
☐ **E** ordinal **(2)**

(Total 11 marks)

TOTAL FOR SECTION A: 11 MARKS

SECTION B

Answer ALL questions.
You are advised to spend approximately 40 minutes on this section.

11. In your course you will have learned about two studies on obedience, Milgram (1963) and Hofling *et al.* (1966).

(a) Describe **one** way in which these two studies are similar.

....

....

....

.... **(2)**

(b) Describe **two** ways in which these two studies are different.

....

....

....

....

....

....

.... **(4)**

(c) Evaluate the procedure used by Hofling *et al.* in terms of the methods used.

....

....

....

....

.... **(3)**

(d) Evaluate the procedure used by Milgram in terms of **one** ethical issue.

....

....

....

....

.... **(3)**

(Total 12 marks)

12. One topic in social psychology is prejudice.

(a) Define the term 'prejudice'.

....

.... **(2)**

(b) One theory that attempts to explain prejudice is Tajfel's social identity theory. Evaluate social identity theory.

....

....

....

....

....

....

....

.... **(4)**

(Total 6 marks)

13. As part of the requirements for the Biological Psychology part of your course you will have conducted a survey.

Write the aim or hypothesis of your experiment here: ....

(a) Which sampling method did you use?

.... **(1)**

(b) (i) Give an example of a question you used to gather qualitative data.

....

.... **(1)**

(ii) Give an example of a question you used to gather quantitative data.

....

.... **(1)**

(c) Explain why you chose to do either a questionnaire or an interview.

....

....

....

.... **(2)**

(Total 5 marks)

14. Social identity theory can be tested using surveys that ask about people's beliefs and behaviours.

The table below gives two participants' results from a study looking at the opinions of participants about young and old people.

	Rate the characteristic for old people on a scale of 1–5 where 5 is 'very'				**An example of individual participants' responses**
	1	2	3	4	
Participant's age	Rudeness	Happiness	Wealth	Laziness	What do you feel when you look at an old person?
Young	4	1	3	2	I feel very sorry for them and hope I don't end up like that
Old	1	3	1	4	I want to talk to them but don't want to intrude

(a) (i) What is meant by the term 'measure of dispersion'?

....

.... **(1)**

(ii) Which measure of dispersion would be appropriate for the data from questions 1–4?

....

.... **(1)**

(b) State the type of graph you would use to display the data from questions 1–4 and justify your choice.

....

....

....

.... **(2)**

(c) Briefly explain how data from question 5 could be analysed.

....

....

....

.... **(2)**

(Total 6 marks)

TOTAL FOR SECTION B: 29 MARKS

SECTION C

Answer ALL questions.
You are advised to spend approximately 25 minutes on this section.

15. Godden & Baddeley (1975) investigated cue-dependency. Their research method was a field experiment.

(a) What experimental design did they use?

.... **(1)**

(b) What were the levels of the independent variable?

....

.... **(1)**

(c) Evaluate Godden & Baddeley's study with reference to strengths, weaknesses and ethics.

....

....

....

....

....

....

....

....

....

....

....

....

....

....

....

....

....

....

.... **(8)**

(Total 10 marks)

***16.** Describe and evaluate the levels of processing model of memory.

....

....

....

....

....

....

....

....

....

....

....

....

....

....

....

....

....

....

....

....

....

....

....

....

....

....

(Total 10 marks)

TOTAL FOR SECTION C: 20 MARKS

TOTAL MARKS FOR PAPER: 60 MARKS

Mark scheme

SECTION A

1. **B** behaving in a different way to some people because of their social group **(1)**
2. **A** an experimental design where all participants do all conditions **(1)**
3. **B** closed question **(1)**
4. **C** making up rhymes to learn lists of terms **(1)**
5. **C** Women have more sexist beliefs than men **(1)**
6. **A** Men and women differ in their sexist beliefs **(1)**
7. **D** state-dependent forgetting **(1)**
8. **B** causal **(1)**
9. **C** in the autonomous state **(1)**
10. **A** stratified and **C** self-selected **(2)**

SECTION B

11. *In your course you will have learned about two studies on obedience, Milgram (1963) and Hofling* et al. *(1966).*

(a) *Describe* ***one*** *way in which these two studies are similar.*

Both aim to demonstrate obedience;

Both use an experimental method;

Participants in both were unaware of the real aim; **(2)**

(b) *Describe* ***two*** *ways in which these two studies are different.*

Hofling *et al.* was a field experiment, Milgram used a laboratory setting; 2 marks

In Hofling *et al.* the task was a realistic one – nurses do administer drugs but in Milgram's study people thought they were administering electric shocks which people don't normally do to others; 2 marks **(4)**

(c) *Evaluate the procedure used by Hofling* et al. *in terms of the methods used.*

It was good because a field experiment is more realistic as the participants are more likely to react in a normal way as the setting is familiar;

It was good because the order (of being told to administer a drug) was a realistic one as nurses do follow doctors' orders;

It was good because they checked that the nurses did actually know that they had been obedient by asking whether they had noticed the dosage on the box;

It wasn't good because nurses shouldn't follow orders given by telephone (although, in fact, they do); **(3)**

(d) *Evaluate the procedure used by Milgram in terms of **one** ethical issue.*

e.g. deception:

The participants were deceived about the aim, which was to test obedience not memory;

The participants were deceived about the shocks, which was distressing because they thought they had hurt someone;

Milgram told them as soon as the experiment was over what it was really about in order to reduce the negative effects of having been deceived;

e.g. right to withdraw:

The particpants were initially given the right to wthdraw;

The participants' didn't really have a right to withdraw because they were put under pressure to stay by the verbal prods;

Some participants did leave before they reached the maximum so it was possible for them to withdraw; **(3)**

12. *One topic in social psychology is prejudice.*

(a) *Define the term 'prejudice'.*

A judgement made about a person on the basis of their membership of a group rather than their individual characteristics; **(2)**

(b) *One theory that attempts to explain prejudice is Tajfel's social identity theory. Evaluate social identity theory.*

Strengths:

Evidence from well controlled laboratory experiments such as the minimal groups studies suggest that being part of a group, i.e. social identification, is sufficient to create prejudice;

Evidence from real groups, such as Poppe & Linssen/Levine et al. shows that people do demonstrate in-group favouritism;

Studies such as Verkooijen et al. have shown that people's behaviour conforms to the group to which they belong, supporting social identification;

Weaknesses:

Minimal groups studies don't always show in-group favouritism, e.g. Dobbs & Crano found that less prejudice is shown when participants have to justify their decisions;

Social identity theory cannot explain individual differences in prejudice which can be seen in the results of minimal groups studies;

For example in an experimental comparison, Platow et al. found that competitive people showed more in-group favouritism than co-operative people; **(4)**

13. *As part of the requirements for the Biological Psychology part of your course you will have conducted a survey. Write the aim or hypothesis of your experiment here:*

(a) *Which sampling method did you use?*

one of: opportunity/random/stratified/volunteer; **(1)**

(b) (i) *Give an example of a question you used to gather qualitative data.*

(should be an open question) **(1)**

(ii) *Give an example of a question you used to gather quantitative data.*

(should be some type of closed question, can be a likert scale, semantic differential, visual-analgue scale, etc.) **(1)**

(c) *Explain why you chose to do either a questionnaire or an interview.* **(2)**

Either response can earn full credit.

Reasons for doing a questionnaire are likely to include:

ease of distribution allows larger number of participants making the results more valid;

avoids problems of low inter-interviewer reliability when working in a group;

Reasons for doing an interview are likely to include:

allows for unstructured protocol so participants can give exact answers making the results more valid;

avoids problems of response biases if participants answer many similar questions in a questionnaire;

14. *Social identity theory can be tested using surveys that ask about people's beliefs and behaviours. The table below gives two participants' results from a study looking at the opinions of participants about young and old people.*

	Rate the characteristic for old people on a scale of 1–5 where 5 is 'very'				**An example of individual participants' responses**
	1	2	3	4	
Participant's age	Rudeness	Happiness	Wealth	Laziness	What do you feel when you look at an old person?
Young	4	1	3	2	I feel very sorry for them and hope I don't end up like that
Old	1	3	1	4	I want to talk to them but don't want to intrude

(a) (i) *What is meant by the term 'measure of dispersion'?*

An indicator of how spread out the data are; **(1)**

(ii) *Which measure of dispersion would be appropriate for the data from questions 1–4?*

Range; **(1)**

(b) *State the type of graph you would use to display the data from questions 1–4 and justify your choice.*

Bar chart;

Because the data are nominal / in named categories; **(2)**

(c) *Briefly explain how data from question 5 could be analysed.*

Using themes;

e.g. looking for positive and negative comments, so 'I feel sorry for them' would be negative; **(2)**

SECTION C

15. *Godden & Baddeley (1975) investigated cue-dependency. Their research method was a field experiment.*

(a) *What experimental design did they use?*

Repeated measures; **(1)**

(b) *What were the levels of the independent variable?*

'Same environment for learning and recall' and 'different environment for learning and recall';

accept: wet/wet and dry/dry versus wet/dry and dry/wet; **(1)**

(c) *Evaluate Godden & Baddeley's study with reference to strengths, weaknesses and ethics.*

Strengths:

They tested both possible combinations of contexts (i.e. wet to dry and vice versa);

So they showed that it wasn't the context itself that affected the divers' memory;

They conducted a second test where the dry/dry participants had to get in and out of the water between learning and recall;

This meant they could be sure that it wasn't interference that caused forgetting;

The 'dry' particpants still had their breathing gear on;

This meant they had the same noises and discomfort so it was well controlled;

The divers were weighted so that when they dived they could sit easily at the bottom;

This meant that they were sitting as easily as when they were on dry land;

They used trained divers so they were not at any more risk than they would be in their normal life;

This satisfies the ethical guideline of not putting people at risk of physical harm;

Weaknesses:

All the 'water' tests weren't done in the same location and some were in seawater and some were in freshwater;

This might have made a difference to the divers that affected their memory;

Not all the participants had 24 hours between tests;

So some might have had a greater practice or fatigue effect than others;

Even though they were trained divers there were still some risks, like one nearly being hit by an underwater truck; **(8)**

***16.** *Describe and evaluate the levels of processing model of memory.* **(10)**

Level	Mark	Descriptor
		AO1: Knowledge and understanding of psychological concepts. AO2: Application of psychological concepts.
1	0	No content worth of marks.
2	1–2	A brief, simple answer with some relevance to the social learning but with little reference to gender development or evaluation. Answer lacks clarity and/or organisation. Little use of relevant terminology and poor spelling, punctuation and/or grammar.
3	3–5	An answer with simple but largely relevant description which is accurate but limited. Limited clarity and/or organisation. Some use of relevant terminology. Frequent spelling, punctuation and/or grammatical errors. At the top of the band some reference to either gender development or evaluation is present.
4	6–8	The answer contains both relevant and accurate evidence and has some effective application of ideas to gender development. Clarity of expression and organisation are competent with some use of relevant terminology. Some spelling, punctuation and/or grammatical errors are likely to be present. At the top of the band both reference to gender development and some evaluation are present.
5	9–10	The answer contains accurate evidence (from studies and/or theories) and this is effectively applied to gender development. Description and evaluation are well balanced. Clarity of expression and organisation are effective and the candidate makes good use of relevant terminology. Few spelling, punctuation or grammatical errors are present.

Indicative content:

- **Levels of processing (LoP) suggests that memory is a by-product of processing information; (AO1)**
- **So the more deeply information is processed the better it is remembered; (AO1)**
- **There are three levels of processing, the shallowest is structural which produces the worst recall; (AO1)**
- **This would include things like looking at the shape or colour of a word; (AO1)**
- **The deepest is semantic processing which involves considering meaning and this produces the best recall; (AO1)**
- **For example deciding whether a word is the name of a type of food; (AO1)**
- **In between is phonemic processing which is about rhyme eg does 'dog' rhyme with 'frog'; (AO1)**
- **Craik & Tulving (1974) used sentences such as 'is it in capital letters' to test memory for differently processed words and found that semantic was the best, then phonemic, then structural; (AO2)**
- **Nyberg used brain scanning to show that there is more brain activity during semantic processing supporting the idea that more processing does happen in semantic tasks; (AO2)**
- **A case study by Gardiner et al. found that although practice didn't help an amnesic to remember, meaning did, supporting the idea that semantic processing is best for promoting good recall;**
- **However, Reber *et al.* found that the type of processing didn't make any difference when the words to be remembered were high in emotion;**

(Total 10 marks)

TOTAL FOR SECTION C: 20 MARKS

TOTAL MARKS FOR PAPER: 60 MARKS

Centre No.						Paper Reference							Surname	Initial(s)
Candidate No.						6	P	S	0	2	/	1	Signature	

Psychology Advanced Subsidiary

Unit 2: Understanding the individual

Time: 1 hour 40 minutes

Question number	Leave blank
1	
2	
3	
4	
5	
6	
7	
8	
9	
10	
11	
12	
13	
14	
15	
16	
17	
18	
19	
20	
Total	

Instructions to candidates

Answer ALL the questions.

Information for candidates

The total mark for this paper is 80.

Advice to candidates

Quality of written communication will be taken into account in the marking of your response to questions 19 and 20. This question is indicated with an asterisk (*). Quality of written communication includes clarity of expression, the structure and presentation of ideas, and grammar, punctuation and spelling.

SECTION A

Answer ALL questions.
You are advised to spend approximately 15 minutes on this section.

Choose answer A, B, C, D or E, and put a cross in the box (☒). If you change your mind, put a line through the box (~~☒~~) and then put a cross in another box (☒).

1. Repression is best defined as a defence mechanism that:

☐ **A** results in the patient being depressed
☐ **B** makes the patient behave as if they were a little child
☐ **C** causes the patient to forget unpleasant emotions or events
☐ **D** makes the patient adopt a strategy opposite to how they really feel **(1)**

2. In the Oedipus complex a boy finally:

☐ **A** wants to kill his father
☐ **B** wants to make love to his mother
☐ **C** identifies with his father
☐ **D** identifies with his mother **(1)**

3. A positive correlation between two variables means that:

☐ **A** there is a definite relationship between the variables
☐ **B** as one variable increases, the other one decreases
☐ **C** as one variable increases, so does the other one
☐ **D** one variable must be making the other one change **(1)**

4. The order of the stages in Freud's psychosexual theory of development is:

☐ **A** oral, anal, genital, phallic, latency
☐ **B** anal, oral, genital, phallic, latency
☐ **C** oral, anal, genital, latency, phallic
☐ **D** oral, anal, phallic, latency, genital **(1)**

5. Which **two** of the following could be found in a synapse?

☐ **A** androgen
☐ **B** receptor
☐ **C** hypothalamus
☐ **D** neurotransmitter
☐ **E** axon **(2)**

6. Spontaneous recovery means that animals:

☐ **A** get better after electric shocks in Skinner boxes
☐ **B** can learn without any obvious reinforcement
☐ **C** that have stopped responding may start again later
☐ **D** stop repeating a learned behaviour if there is no reward **(1)**

7. What sex chromosomes does a normal human male have?

☐ **A** XO
☐ **B** XX
☐ **C** XY
☐ **D** A or C above **(1)**

8. Which of the following describes interval data?

- ☐ **A** results on a rating scale
- ☐ **B** results that are totals in named categories
- ☐ **C** results on a scale with equal gaps and a real zero
- ☐ **D** results on a scale with equal gaps and no real zero **(1)**

Use the information below to answer questions 9 and 10.

Verity has taught her pet rabbit to blink when she claps her hands. She did this by blowing in the rabbit's face and clapping her hands at the same time. At first the rabbit just blinked because Verity was blowing air at its eyes but eventually it would blink just when she clapped her hands.

A the unconditioned stimulus
B the conditioned stimulus
C the unconditioned response
D the conditioned response

9. Which term refers to the puff of air Verity blew into the rabbit's eyes?

- ☐ **A**
- ☐ **B**
- ☐ **C**
- ☐ **D** **(1)**

10. Which term refers to the rabbit blinking when Verity claps her hands?

- ☐ **A**
- ☐ **B**
- ☐ **C**
- ☐ **D** **(1)**

Use the information below to answer questions 11, 12 and 13.

For each question below the same four descriptions of studies are described. For each question, choose the study that you think would use the statistical test named.

11. Which study would use a chi-squared test?

- ☐ **A** a study collecting ratio data from old and young people
- ☐ **B** a study collecting ordinal data about personality from twin pairs
- ☐ **C** a study looking in detail at the mental health of one person
- ☐ **D** a study comparing boys and girls, collecting nominal data **(1)**

12. Which study would use a Spearman test?

- ☐ **A** a study collecting ratio data from old and young people
- ☐ **B** a study collecting ordinal data about personality from twin pairs
- ☐ **C** a study looking in detail at the mental health of one person
- ☐ **D** a study comparing boys and girls, collecting nominal data **(1)**

13. Which study would use a Mann–Whitney test?

- ☐ **A** a study collecting ratio data from old and young people
- ☐ **B** a study collecting ordinal data about personality from twin pairs
- ☐ **C** a study looking in detail at the mental health of one person
- ☐ **D** a study comparing boys and girls, collecting nominal data **(1)**

(Total 14 marks)

TOTAL FOR SECTION A: 14 MARKS

SECTION B

Answer ALL questions.
You are advised to spend approximately 50 minutes on this section.

14. Brain scans and other techniques can help us to look for gender differences in brain activity.

(a) Outline how an MRI (magnetic image resonance) scan works.

....

....

....

....

....

.... **(3)**

(b) In a study on gender differences, some researchers used functional magnetic image resonance (fMRI) scans of men and women responding to words. They were particularly interested in the speed of response in the right hemisphere. The table below shows their results.

Activity level in the right hemisphere

	Time taken for fMRI to detect a response in the right hemisphere (seconds)										**Median**
Males	0.58	0.61	0.73	0.59	0.61	0.62	0.58	0.64	0.57	0.66	0.61
Females	0.67	0.56	0.73	0.71	0.69	0.72	0.77	0.78	0.77	0.76	0.725

(i) Write a null hypothesis for this study.

....

....

....

....

.... **(2)**

(ii) If the researchers had a directional hypothesis, would they use a one- or a two-tailed test?

.... **(1)**

(iii) Draw **one** conclusion from the data table.

....

....

.... **(1)**

(iv) A Mann–Whitney test on the data produced an observed value of 14.5. Use the table below to decide whether the difference between males and females is significant. Explain how you reached your conclusion.

n_a	**Critical values for the Mann–Whitney test** To be significant the observed value for Mann–Whitney must be less than or equal to the critical value.				
	n_b				
	6	7	8	9	10
8	10	13	15	18	20
9	12	15	18	21	24
10	14	17	20	24	27
11	16	19	23	27	31

....

....

....

.... **(2)**

(v) The researchers chose to use a significance level of $p \leq 0.05$. What does 'significance level' mean?

....

....

....

.... **(2)**

(c) (i) What does the term 'validity' mean?

....

.... **(1)**

(ii) Explain why this study might lack validity.

....

....

....

....

.... **(2)**

(Total 14 marks)

15. Freud (1909) conducted a case study on Little Hans.

(a) Outline the case study method in general.

....

....

....

....

....

.... **(3)**

(b) Outline **one** example of symbolism that Freud described.

....

....

....

.... **(2)**

(c) Evaluate this study.

....

....

....

....

....

.... **(3)**

(Total 8 marks)

16. As part of the course requirements for the Learning Approach you will have conducted an observation. Write the aim or hypothesis of your experiment here: ....

(a) (i) Give an operational definition for **one** of the categories or behaviours that you observed.

....

.... **(2)**

(b) How reliable do you believe your findings were? Justify your answer.

....

....

....

.... **(2)**

(c) How credible do you believe your findings were? Justify your answer.

....

....

....

....

....

.... **(2)**

(Total 6 marks)

17. (a) (i) Briefly describe an example of how genes can affect a psychological characteristic.

....

....

....

.... **(2)**

(ii) Explain how valid and/or reliable the evidence is for the genetic influence on the characteristic you have described in (a) (i).

....

....

....

....

....

....

....

....

....

....

....

....

....

....

.... **(4)**

(Total 6 marks)

18. Bandura, Ross & Ross (1961) investigated the imitation of aggression in children.

(a) Identify **two** factors that they found to affect levels of aggression in this study.

....

....

....

.... **(2)**

(b) Explain **one or more** controls that Bandura *et al.* used and explain why they were important.

....

....

....

....

....

....

....

....

....

.... **(4)**

(Total 6 marks)

TOTAL FOR SECTION B: 40 MARKS

SECTION C

Answer ALL questions.
You are advised to spend approximately 35 minutes on this section.

***19. (a)** Describe the experimental method as used in psychological research.

....

....

....

....

....

....

....

....

....

....

.... **(4)**

(b) Evaluate the **laboratory** experiment as a research method in psychology.

....

....

....

....

....

....

....

....

....

....

....

....

.... **(10)**

(Total 14 marks)

*20. As part of your study of the psychodynamic approach, you will have learned about a key issue. Imagine that you have been asked to speak on a radio programme to inform people about this issue. As preparation for this, you will need to tell the radio station all about the issue. Using your knowledge of concepts and ideas from the psychodynamic approach, provide an explanation of this issue.

....

....

....

....

....

....

....

....

....

....

....

....

....

....

....

....

....

....

....

....

....

....

....

....

....

(Total 12 marks)

TOTAL FOR SECTION C: 26 MARKS

TOTAL MARKS FOR PAPER: 80 MARKS

Mark scheme

SECTION A

1. **C** causes the patient to forget unpleasant emotions or events **(1)**
2. **C** identify with the father **(1)**
3. **C** as one variable increases, so does the other one **(1)**
4. **D** oral, anal, phallic, latency, genital **(1)**
5. **B** receptor and **D** neurotransmitter **(2)**
6. **C** that have stopped responding may start again later **(1)**
7. **C** XY **(1)**
8. **D** results on a scale with equal gaps and no real zero **(1)**
9. **A** the unconditioned stimulus **(1)**
10. **D** the conditioned response **(1)**
11. **D** a study comparing boys and girls, collecting nominal data. **(1)**
12. **B** a study collecting ordinal data about personality from twin pairs **(1)**
13. **A** a study collecting ratio data from old and young people **(1)**

SECTION B

14. *Brain scans and other techniques can help us to look for gender differences in brain activity.*

(a) *Outline how an MRI (magnetic image resonance) scan works.*

An (electro)magnetic field affects (protons in) water which move/respond like needles on a compass. When they move back to their original positions they affect the emission of radio waves, which is detected by the scanner; **(3)**

(b) *In a study on gender differences, some researchers used functional magnetic image resonance (fMRI) scans of men and women responding to words. They were particularly interested in the speed of response in the right hemisphere. The table below shows their results.*

Activity level in the right hemisphere

	Time taken for fMRI to detect a response in the right hemisphere (seconds)										Median
Males	0.58	0.61	0.73	0.59	0.61	0.62	0.58	0.64	0.57	0.66	0.61
Females	0.67	0.56	0.73	0.71	0.69	0.72	0.77	0.78	0.77	0.76	0.725

(i) *Write a null hypothesis for this study.*

Any difference between speed of the right hemisphere to respond to words by males and females is due to chance; **(2)**

(ii) *If the researchers had a directional hypothesis, would they use a one- or a two-tailed test?*
One-tailed; **(1)**

(iii) *Draw **one** conclusion from the data table.*
The right hemisphere is faster to respond to words in females than males; **(1)**

(iv) *A Mann–Whitney test on the data produced an observed value of 14.5. Use the table below to decide whether the difference between males and females is significant. Explain how you reached your conclusion.*
10 participants in each group so critical value is 27;
27 is larger that the observed value of 14.5 so the difference is significant; **(2)**

n_a	**Critical values for the Mann–Whitney test** To be significant the observed value for Mann–Whitney must be less than or equal to the critical value.				
	n_b				
	6	7	8	9	**10**
8	10	13	15	18	20
9	12	15	18	21	24
10	14	17	20	24	27
11	16	19	23	27	**31**

(v) *The researchers chose to use a significance level of $p \leq 0.05$. What does 'significance level' mean?*
The probability at which the pattern/difference found in the results could not have arisen by chance; **(2)**

(c) (i) *What does the term 'validity' mean?*
The extent to which we are testing/measuring what we set out to test/measure; **(1)**

(ii) *Explain why this study might lack validity.*
Because it is unfamiliar inside a scanner and this might have disturbed one gender more than the other so biased the results; **(2)**

15. *Freud (1909) conducted a case study on Little Hans.*

(a) Outline the case study method in general.
An in-depth study of a single individual (or unit, e.g. family);
Data is collected using different techniques, e.g. interview, observation;
This is used to build up a detailed picture of the situation/to understand complex interactions using qualitative data;
And may be used to help resolve an individual's mental health problems; **(3)**

(b) *Outline **one** example of symbolism that Freud described.*
Horses (with large penises) symbolised Hans' father;
Black nosebands on horses symbolised Hans' father's moustache; **(2)**

(c) *Evaluate this study.*
The detailed data and understanding of Hans' helped to resolve his fear of horses;
Most of the data came to Freud through Hans' father whose relationship with his son could have made him biased;
The father also knew about Freud's ideas and this could also have made him more likely to report things about Hans that fitted the idea of the Oedipus complex;
A more credible explanation of Hans' fear of horses is that he saw one die;
The idea that Hans and other children have unconscious sexual feelings like fearing castration lacks believability; **(3)**

16. *As part of the course requirements for the Learning Approach you will have conducted an observation.*

Write the aim or hypothesis of your experiment here: ....

(a) (i) *Give an operational definition for one of the categories or behaviours that you observed.*
1 mark for a category, 2 marks for operationalisation **(2)**

(b) *How reliable do you believe your findings were? Justify your answer.*

1 mark for simple justification, 2 marks for full justification **(2)**

(c) *How credible do you believe your findings were? Justify your answer.*

1 mark for simple justification, 2 marks for full justification **(2)**

17. (a) (i) *Briefly describe an example of how genes can affect a psychological characteristic.*

Genes can make us more vulnerable to mental disorders; for instance if we are in a stressful situation;

So someone with genes for schizophrenia won't necessarily have the disorder unless the environment contributes too; **(2)**

(ii) *Explain how valid and/or reliable the evidence is for the genetic influence on the characteristic you have described in (a) (i).*
Some evidence for genetic factors in schizophrenia comes from twin studies, e.g. Gottesman & Shields (1961), which are good because identical twins have the same genes so you can be sure that any difference in their mental health is due to the environment;

But even if identical twins are reared separately there may be similarities, e.g. going to the same school so these might make them more similar;

And they may have grown up together before being separated/been united before being tested, which would make them seem more similar;

When comparing MZs and DZs the belief that DZs are only more different because they don't have identical genes may be wrong because MZs look alike so tend to get treated more similarly than DZs;

Evidence also comes from adoption studies, e.g. Heston (1966) but these can also be biased as children are generally placed with adoptive families similar to their biological family; **(4)**

18. *Bandura* et al. *(1961) investigated the imitation of aggression in children.*

(a) *Identify* ***two*** *factors that they found affect levels of aggression in this study.*

Whether the adult model was aggressive or non-aggressive;

Whether the adult model was the same sex as the child or the opposite sex; **(2)**

(b) *Explain* ***one or more*** *controls that Bandura* et al. *used and explain why they were important.*
They measured the children's aggression and spread them evenly across the groups;

So that differences in aggression between groups were not due to individual differences;

The model always plays with the Tinker toys in both the non-aggressive and aggressive conditions;

This meant they had a baseline of play to see whether the children copied aggression more;

The Bobo doll was always there for the children to play with if they wanted to;

This made sure that it wasn't just a preferred play item; **(4)**

SECTION C

*19. (a) *Describe the experimental method as used in psychological research.*

Experiments have an independent variable that is manipulated by the experimenter and a dependent variable which is measured;

All other factors are controlled so that they cannot affect the DV;

This means that causal conclusions can be drawn as the IV must be causing changes in the DV;

In a laboratory experiment the IV is manipulated and the environment is fully controlled;

In a field experiment the IV is manipulated but as the setting is a 'real' one fewer controls are possible;

In a natural experiment the researcher cannot control the levels of the IV but has to use pre-existing differences for the levels of the IV;

Experiments are used to compare two or more levels of the IV, such as males and females;

Three experimental designs are possible such as independent groups in which different participants are used in each level of the IV;

Or repeated measures in which the same participants are used in each level of the IV; **(4)**

(b) *Evaluate the **laboratory** experiment as a research method in psychology.*

Because factors are well controlled in a lab compared to the field, extraneous variables cannot affect the DV;

This means that conclusions are more valid than from field or natural experiments;

The findings are also more reliable because the rigorous controls mean that the way the conditions are set up is easily replicated;

Measures of the DV are also more likely to be reliable as the participants know they are in a study so can be measured directly rather than indirectly, which may be necessary in the field;

However, a lab setting is artificial and this may make participants behave differently than they would normally, lowering the validity of the findings;

The tasks in lab experiments are often very unlike ordinary life, e.g. learning lists of digits, so they lack mundane realism;

Together this would make the ecological validity lower because the results are less likely to generalise outside the lab setting to the 'real world';

Because participants in a lab setting know they are in an experiment, they are likely to try to work out the aim and this can affect their behaviour if they respond to demand characteristics;

Although it can be overcome by using a single blind procedure in which the participant is unaware of the condition in which they are participating so they are less likely to guess the aims;

In a way it is good that the participants know they are in a study because they can be asked for their consent, which is ethical;

However, participants may need to be deceived in lab experiments in order to reduce demand characteristics and make the experiment more valid;

And this leads to ethical issues as the participants cannot give informed consent/may be distressed when they find out;

Another source of bias is the experimenter effect in which the experimenter behaves differently to participants in different levels of the IV potentially causing a source of error;

This can be overcome by a double blind procedure in which the experimenter collecting results is unaware of the level of the IV to which the participant they are testing has been allocated; **(10)**

Level	Mark	Descriptor
		AO1: Knowledge and understanding of psychological concepts. AO2: Application of psychological concepts.
1	0	No content worth of marks.
2	1–2	A brief, simple answer with some relevance to the social learning but with little reference to gender development or evaluation. Answer lacks clarity and/or organisation. Little use of relevant terminology and poor spelling, punctuation and/or grammar.
3	3–5	An answer with simple but largely relevant description which is accurate but limited. Limited clarity and/or organisation. Some use of relevant terminology. Frequent spelling, punctuation and/or grammatical errors. At the top of the band some reference to either gender development or evaluation is present.
4	6–8	The answer contains both relevant and accurate evidence and has some effective application of ideas to gender development. Clarity of expression and organisation are competent with some use of relevant terminology. Some spelling, punctuation and/or grammatical errors are likely to be present. At the top of the band both reference to gender development and some evaluation are present.
5	9–10	The answer contains accurate evidence (from studies and/or theories) and this is effectively applied to gender development. Description and evaluation are well balanced. Clarity of expression and organisation are effective and the candidate makes good use of relevant terminology. Few spelling, punctuation or grammatical errors are present.

***20.** *As part of your study of the psychodynamic approach, you will have learned about a key issue. Imagine that you have been asked to speak on a radio programme to inform people about this issue. As preparation for this, you will need to tell the radio station all about the issue. Using your knowledge of concepts and ideas from the psychodynamic approach, provide an explanation of this issue.* **(12)**

Level	Mark	Descriptor
		AO1: Knowledge and understanding of psychological concepts. AO2: Application of psychological concepts.
1	0	No content worth of marks.
2	1–3	A brief, simple answer with some relevance to the social learning but with little reference to gender development or evaluation. Answer lacks clarity and/or organisation. Little use of relevant terminology and poor spelling, punctuation and/or grammar.

3	4–6	An answer with simple but largely relevant description which is accurate but limited. Limited clarity and/or organisation. Some use of relevant terminology. Frequent spelling, punctuation and/or grammatical errors. At the top of the band some reference to either gender development or evaluation is present.
4	7–9	The answer contains both relevant and accurate evidence and has some effective application of ideas to gender development. Clarity of expression and organisation are competent with some use of relevant terminology. Some spelling, punctuation and/or grammatical errors are likely to be present. At the top of the band both reference to gender development and some evaluation are present.
5	10–12	The answer contains accurate evidence (from studies and/or theories) and this is effectively applied to gender development. Description and evaluation are well balanced. Clarity of expression and organisation are effective and the candidate makes good use of relevant terminology. Few spelling, punctuation or grammatical errors are present.

Indicative content:

e.g. is psychoanalysis effective?

- **Psychoanalysis comes in many forms, e.g. classical psychoanalysis which needs lots of sessions a week for many years; (AO1)**
- **In these sessions the therapist uses techniques such as free association in which the patient says whatever comes to mind like memories or dreams, which the therapist interprets; (AO1)**
- **The aim is to unearth things in the patient's unconscious so they can be understood and dealt with to remove symptoms; (AO1)**
- **Working safely through bad unconscious memories that have been 'found' is called catharsis and is helpful; (AO1)**
- **Axline (1947) helped Dibs using catharsis in the context of play; (AO2)**
- **Because it takes so long it is expensive so psychotherapy for adults is rarely funded on the NHS; (AO2)**
- **Another technique is transference, in which feelings from one relationship, e.g. with parents, is transferred onto another, e.g. with the therapist; (AO1)**
- **Dibs did this too, and as his relationship with the therapist grew, he developed a stronger relationship with his parents; (AO2)**
- **However, evidence such as Eysenk's (1952) review has suggested that psychoanalysis is no more effective than no treatment; (AO2)**
- **But this can be criticised because the criteria for selection and assessing the studies used as evidence was biased against pyschoanalysis; (AO2)**
- **More recent reviews have found that psychoanalysis is effective, e.g. Bachrach et al. (1991) found it helped between 60 and 90% of patients; (AO2)**
- **But this can be criticised too as some studies didn't have control groups so you can't be sure that the patients wouldn't have improved without psychoanalysis; (AO2)**
- **And some of the decisions on the success of the treatment were made by the therapists themselves and they wouldn't have necessarily been objective; (AO2)**
- **Although Leichsering & Leibing (2007) avoided these problems and still found that 23 /24 studies showed psychoanalysis to be as effective as other therapies; (AO2)**

Acknowledgements

The authors and publishers are grateful to the following for permissions to reproduce copyright material.

Teacher Support Guide

p.17, © Lucian Coman/Shutterstock; p.21, Julia Russell; p.27, © Clara/Shutterstock; p.29, © David Gilder/Shutterstock; p.30, © David Gilder/Shutterstock; p.37, © magičinfoto/Shutterstock; p.38, © Losevsky Pavel/Shutterstock; p.38, © Andrzej Fryda/Fotolia; p.50, © Martin Garnham/Fotolia; p.50, © Renee Jansoa/Fotolia; p.60, both Julia Russell; p.85, MirrorPix; p.97, www.koolaiduk.com; p.97, Julia Russell; p.100, all Julia Russell; p.102, © Bochkarev Photography/Shutterstock; p.126, © Eric Isselée /Shutterstock; p.127, © Tomasz Trojanowski /Shutterstock; p.128, © Yuri Arcurs/ Shutterstock; p.135, Julia Russell; p.137, © Lisa Eastman/Shutterstock; p.142, both Mirrorpix; p.143, © Andreas Speer/Fotolia; p.143, © 2007 Five/John Wright; p.145, all Julia Russell; p.146, Julia Russell; p.169, © Kenneth Sponsler/Shutterstock; p.169, © fred Goldstein/Shutterstock; p.169, © Kenneth Sponsler/Shutterstock; p.169, © Zdorov Kirill Vladimirovich/Shutterstock; p.182, © Sipa Press/Rex Features; p.190, © Galina Barskaya/Shutterstock; p.194, © aguirre_mar/Shutterstock; p.198, © 2009 Elsevier B.V.; p.218, © alma_sacra/Fotolia; p.242, © Lucas Allen White/Shutterstock; p.250, © sa2324/Shutterstock; p.250, © Gelpi/Shutterstock; p.251, © govicinity/Fotolia; p.251, © Ustin/Shutterstock.

PowerPoint presentation

2-1, © Oleksandr Gumerov/istockphoto; © moodboard/Corbis; © Monkey Business/Fotolia; © Yuri Arcurs/Fotolia; © Nadav/Shutterstock; Artem Efimov/Shutterstock; Mark at slapupsideyourhead; **2-9,** © prism_68/Shutterstock; Jaimie Duplass/Shutterstock; © Petr Nad/Shutterstock; © Konstantin Tavrov/Shutterstock; © ABC photos/Shutterstock; © Larry St. Pierre/Shutterstock; Alvaro Pantoja/Shutterstock; Julia Russell; © CREATISTA/Shutterstock; © Darrell J. Rohl/Shutterstock; © salamanderman/Shutterstock; © Lucian Coman/Shutterstock; © Yuri Arcurs/Shutterstock; **2-24,** © photogl/Shutterstock; **3-1,** © Yuri Arcurs/Shutterstock; © Laurence Gough/Shutterstock; **3-3,** All Julia Russell; **3-17,** © Sujit Mahapatra/Fotolia;, **4-1,** © gualtiero boffi/Shutterstock; © Vladimir Melnikov/Shutterstock; © F J Mortimer/Getty Images; © Allie van Niekerk/Shutterstock; Lajos Répási/Istock; © Kellie L. Folkerts/Shutterstock; © ajt/Shutterstock; **4-11,** Julia Russell; © kristian sekulic/Shutterstock; Julia Russell; © Losevsky Pavel/Shutterstock; Julia Russell; © Olga Solovei/ Shutterstock; © Konstantin Sutyagin/Shutterstock; © Kellie L. Folkerts/Shutterstock; Julia Russell; © KennStilger47/Shutterstock; **5-1,** Slide 1-5 Julia Russell; © Konstantin Sutyagin/Fotolia; © Tatiana Popova/Shutterstock; **5-6,** PNASnews@nas.edu; **5-22,** © weim/Fotolia; Julia Russell.

Every effort has been made to contact the holders of copyright material, but if any have been overlooked the publishers will be happy to make the appropriate arrangements at the first opportunity.